MOTHER JONES THE MINERS' ANGEL

A Portrait

By DALE FETHERLING

— SOUTHERN ILLINOIS UNIVERSITY PRESS
Carbondale and Edwardsville

Feffer & Simons, Inc.
London and Amsterdam

To the memory of G. S. F.

who aspired

Library of Congress Cataloging in Publication Data

Fetherling, Dale, 1941–
    Mother Jones the miners' angel; a portrait.

    Bibliography: p.
    1. Jones, Mary (Harris) 1830–1930. I. Title.
HD8073.J6F48   331.88′092′4 [B]   73-12444
ISBN 0-8093-0643-3

CONTENTS

v

LIST OF ILLUSTRATIONS

(between pages 128–129)

PREFACE

T H E life of Mother Jones "is an epic and it is the shame of American writers that it has never been told," George West wrote to the *Nation* in July 1922. "She is a great woman," he added, "unsung because of our tradition of cheap gentility." The truth of West's lament has endured. Despite a long and dramatic career that made her loved by millions, Mother Mary Jones today is known but to few and often for the wrong reasons. In most labor histories, she, if mentioned at all, is noted as being among the founders of the Industrial Workers of the World, a group from which she soon became estranged.

Mother Jones was a labor agitator. Her life has been ignored largely because she was not important to the labor movement in an institutional or intellectual sense. She did not shape organizations or fashion movements or create new concepts. Her skill was the invaluable but incalculable one of tending to men's spirits, of buoying them, of goading them to fight even though the battle seemed hopeless. Her sex, her advanced age, and her eccentricities not only did not hinder her, they may have accounted for much of her success in the face of violence and hardship. That she was a supernumerary cannot be denied. But that she had an extraordinary effect on many workers—and why—cannot be ignored.

Mother Jones's life defies definitiveness. Her birth, her youth, her early labor endeavors are obscured by time and by her own erratic sense of history. As a vagabond agitator, she herself left little behind. But as a larger-than-life figure, she spawned endless apocrypha to cloud and confuse. This book is an attempt to chronicle her major actions, to sketch her personality, to begin to distill her legacy. Like any research into Mother Jones's long and elusive life, it is highly eclectic. But the work seeks to present a portrait of Mother Jones of interest to the academic and general audience alike.

I am indebted to many for their cooperation. Particularly helpful were the staffs of the Wisconsin State Historical Society, the Chicago Historical Society, the Houghton County (Michigan) Historical Society, and the state library and archives in Arizona and in Tennessee. Personnel at the libraries of West Virginia University, University of Illinois, and Indiana University as well as public libraries at Denver, Minneapolis, and Memphis kindly accommodated my queries and visits.

Quotation from "Memoir of a Proud Boy," by Carl Sandburg, reprinted from his *Complete Poems* (1950), by permission of Harcourt Brace Jovanovich, Inc.

Particular acknowledgment also is due to Moreau B. C. Chambers, archivist at the Catholic University of America. Professors Fred Barkey, Bernard Brommel, and Keith Dix gave aid and suggestions. Vivian Germer, Joseph Ozanic, and Helen Camp helped secure other material, and Andrew Barth, Sharon Adams, William Lindley, and Mark Patterson gave clear testament to their friendship. And, of course, I thank my wife, Rae, who endured with grace.

Dale Fetherling

Corona del Mar, California
January 1973

ONE

I was born in revolution.

—Mother Jones[1]

THE fire, at times a 100-foot-high wall of flame, hurtled down streets, burst through buildings, and engulfed whole blocks. It bore down with heat and smoke and ash on the refugees and sightseers who jammed the city's streets and bridges. To many of those who fled, the scene may have seemed like the preacher's most spirited description of Judgment Day. Block after block was aflame. Wagons, carts, wheelbarrows, and buggies piled high with personal effects became stalled in a sea of pedestrians rained upon by blazing embers. Desperate owners and would-be looters tossed valuables from upper-story windows. Horses, dogs, and children ran through the streets in search for their masters. Bearers of makeshift stretchers jostled with the crowd in an attempt to move the sick and the injured. Toppling walls, the crackle of flames, and a strong wind competed with the screams of the frantic and the whistling of tugboats pushing sailing ships to safety. It was 1871. Chicago—"The Gem of the Prairie"—was being destroyed by the then-most-destructive fire in American history.

It had been a nervous summer for the city's 334,000 residents. Only five inches of rain had fallen between July and October, about one-fourth of normal. Lawns were parched, wells dry, and, already, trees

1

were becoming bare. By October 8, the weather had been especially warm and dry for several days, and a number of fires had broken out. In fact, four blocks on the West Side's industrial district burned just the night before. But that was only the prelude. By 8:30 P.M., Sunday, October 8, the fire that was to raze much of Chicago began in a barn near the tiny, shingled cottage of Patrick O'Leary on the West Side.²

Driven before a southwest wind and helped by a slow alarm, weary firefighters, and a spate of tactical errors, the blaze spread rapidly. It quickly consumed the wooden buildings, fences, sidewalks, and, in some cases, the pine-paved streets, all of which mirrored the town's startling growth. By early Monday, the flames had leaped the south branch of the Chicago River and had set ablaze the courthouse and the business district. Before rain doused it beginning about 11 P.M. Monday, the holocaust also consumed much of the North Side. In all, about 18,000 buildings were destroyed at a loss of some $190 million. Nearly three and one-half square miles were leveled. At least 300 Chicagoans died, and 90,000 were made homeless.³

Among the refugees was a forty-one-year-old seamstress to whom the disaster must have seemed the ultimate blow. Her home and dress-making shop on Washington Street had burned, and now she huddled with other victims in the Plymouth Congregational Church at 9th Street and Wabash Avenue. The six-year-old limestone structure, the following year to become Saint Mary's Catholic Church, was about four blocks from the fire's path.⁴ Tragedy had been the woman's shadow, and once again she looked at the loss of all for which she had striven. If in the church the years were recounted by her, as they might well have been, they took her first back to Ireland. There, Mary Harris was born May 1, 1830, in a cottage near Cork.⁵ Her early life, she once commented, was characterized perfectly by a single line from Thomas Gray's "Elegy Written in a Country Churchyard": "The short and simple annals of the poor."⁶ Her family had been simple Irish peasants for generations. But if it was a poor heritage, it also was a proud and defiant one.

In the early 1800s famine swept the overcrowded land, and tenant farmers toiled for English landlords for slight reward. Catholic freedom —religious, political, and economic—was suppressed. Cliques controlled the government. The poor went unaided, and Irish industry suffered in competition with its larger British rivals. Mass movements sprang up to throw off the Crown and were put down bloodily. On one occasion, the child Mary Harris saw British troops march through the streets with the heads of Irishmen stuck on their bayonets.[7] Her paternal grandfather was hanged in the fight for Irish freedom. His son, Mary's father, was forced to flee the country for agitating. By one account, at least, he escaped on a fishing boat. But the British broke into his home and ransacked it and even tore down the chimney in their search for him, much to the astonishment of his young daughter.[8]

Richard Harris went to the United States and established American citizenship. He worked on a canal-building crew and then on a railroad gang. By 1838, he had his wife, also named Mary, and three children join him in Toronto, Ontario, where the railroad work had taken him. The whole family then were American citizens. In Canada, Harris apparently found the freedom he sought and for which he and his ancestors had done battle, ironically enough, against Canada's colonizer.[9] Then he turned to bettering his condition and educating his family in the bustling Canadian city. By hard work, they lived without wants but without luxuries. Young Mary soon became the intellectual delight of the household.

She attended Toronto public schools and graduated from normal school at age seventeen with a new-found talent for debating. Simultaneously, she learned the skill of dressmaking. First, Mary Harris began teaching in the Canadian public schools and then came to be a school teacher as well as a private tutor in New England.[10] In August 1859 she became a secular teacher at Saint Mary Convent in Monroe, Michigan, for a salary of $8.00 a month. She left the following March, having been "paid in full . . . $36.43." More than 60 years later, she would recall the Saint Mary experience and, as was her style, she would inject a dose of drama. "They taught me in [the convent] some things they did not have in mind," she said. "Among the details of my education was a hatred of injustice and a vast inquisitiveness."[11] Afterward, she was a dressmaker in Chicago. "I preferred sewing to bossing little children," she said.[12] By one unlikely account, at least, she helped with the sewing of the inaugural gown of Mrs. Abraham Lincoln. Later, however, Mary Harris again returned to teaching and traveled to a job in Memphis, Tennessee. There she met and married George E. Jones, an iron molder, in 1861.[13]

As a daughter, Mary Harris had been studious and obedient. As a young woman, she had been ambitious and adventuresome. And as a wife, she later recalled, she shared any new bride's chagrin when her husband drank beer after a hard day's work or spent his evenings at the union hall. But, at the same time, she learned from George Jones, especially about his unionism. Even more than that, she learned something of the psychology of the workingman. Much of her later work —which must have seemed so remote during those Memphis family-raising days—would be aimed at making other women comprehend what she had learned. That is, that the wife must care for what the husband cares for if he is to remain resolute. That a few beers might be an elixir. And, that every man needs freedom, even freedom from wifely tyranny.[14] Life had been relatively good to the iron molder and the school teacher. Within six years, the couple had produced four children. Then, in 1867, the relatively prosaic life of Mary Jones took the first of the tragic turns which were to divert her so dramatically.

Memphis's 22,623 persons in 1860 made it the sixth largest city in the South. Due to Civil War activity and completion of the railroad to the port of Charleston, South Carolina, its population would double in a decade. But, as in other burgeoning cities, sanitation did not keep pace with population. Crowded clusters of shantytowns reflected the city's rapid growth. The water was poor, and filth often filled the streets. Conditions were, as one historian put it, "perhaps no better than those of the poorest medieval borough."[15] The hot summer of 1867 followed an unusually rainy spring, producing millions of disease-bearing mosquitoes. Yellow fever, whose cause and cure were yet unknown, had struck in 1828 and killed 53. In 1855, it brought death to another 220 in Memphis. Now, in the early fall of 1867, a severe attack of cholera was followed by the town's third epidemic of yellow fever.[16]

"The victims," Mary Harris Jones later wrote, "were mainly among the poor and the workers. The rich and the well-to-do fled the city."[17] The Joneses, of course, were among the workers and as such probably lived in the Pinch area, an Irish-American section particularly hard-hit by the disease. Yellow fever victims became yellow-eyed, then yellow all over. Soon, the yellow became mottled with black, and in the later stages, black vomit poured from the victim and the body exuded an awful stench. With sponges held to their noses, doctors, nurses, and priests rushed from one victim to another upon streets soaked with strong disinfectants and carbolic acid. Flaming tar barrels were set up to drive away the disease, and along with burning bedclothes, they filled the air with smoke. Lime sprinkled over damp spots gave a strange, snowlike appearance to the sweltering city.[18]

The plague claimed its first two victims the last week in September and its last three by December 1—and in between, 231, including George Jones, his son and three daughters died.[19] Within the span of a week, Mary Harris Jones had become, at age thirty-seven, a childless widow. "All about my house I could hear weeping and the cries of delirium," she wrote. "One by one, my four little children sickened and died. I washed their little bodies and got them ready for burial. My husband caught the fever and died. I sat alone through nights of grief. No one came to me. No one could. Other homes were as stricken as mine. All day long, all night long, I heard the grating of the wheels of the death cart."[20]

Her husband was buried, and Local 66, Iron Molders International Union, held a special meeting October 15 in memory of Jones, who had died "after a short but painful illness." Condolences were offered to his widow and the local's charter was ordered to be draped in mourning for 30 days in honor of the "earnest and energetic brother." Mary Jones stayed on through the epidemic to nurse other victims, about 2,500 of whom caught the disease. Then she left for Chicago to practice dressmaking again.[21] Chicago in the late 1860s and early 1870s had a thin line of homes for the wealthy along Lake Michigan. The city then stretched westward to the hovels of the poor. This dichotomy, illustrating both the price and promise of industrialization, was not lost on the widowed seamstress. "Often while sewing for the lords and barons who lived in magnificent houses on the Lake Shore Drive, I would look out of the plate glass windows and see the poor, shivering wretches, jobless and hungry, walking alongside the frozen lake front," she later recalled. "The contrast of their condition with that of the tropical comfort of the people for whom I sewed was painful to me. My employers seemed neither to notice nor to care."[22]

The Great Fire, however, played no favorites. Having stayed a night and a day on the lakefront without food, Mother Jones now huddled with a hodgepodge of Chicagoans in the basement of a church. She had no possessions but those clothes she wore. Homeless and adrift, she was again, at age forty-one, struck by disaster. To pass the time she helped with the relief effort and wandered around the still-standing blocks adjacent to the church.[23]

"Nearby in an old, tumbled down, fire scorched building," Mother Jones recalled, was a meeting of the Noble Order of the Knights of Labor.[24] Founded in 1869 as a secret society among idealistic garment workers in Philadelphia, the early Knights of Labor was not so much a union as a mass fraternal lodge, complete with elaborate ritual and grand-sounding titles. Yet, seeking as it did to encompass both the skilled and the unskilled worker, it was ahead of its time. It would become the first large labor organization also to admit women on an equal footing with men. Originally and in theory, at least, it was a sober-sided group which disdained strikes and relied instead on education and legislation. But largely due to some spectacularly successful railroad strikes in the early 1880s, its membership soared to nearly 730,000 before the end of that decade.[25]

Mary Jones began attending gatherings of the Knights every evening and on Sundays, too, when they held picnics and meetings in the woods. The speakers were "splendid," she said, and their rhetoric apparently sounded for her for the first time an undeniable call to aid the poor and oppressed. "Those were the days of sacrifice for the cause of labor. Those were the days when we had no halls, when there were no high salaried officers, no feasting with the enemies of labor," she would recall for a more affluent era. "Those were the days of the martyrs and the saints."[26] The ideals and the sense of fraternity of the early Knights of Labor days fitted Mother Jones's heritage, meshed with what she had seen in Chicago and in the South, and paralleled the fervent unionism of her husband. Coming, as it did, on top of successive personal tragedies, the experience forged an amalgam of compassion and fervor which would serve her well in industrial wars over the next half a century.

The ashes of Chicago and the agonies of Memphis left Mary Harris Jones a homeless, childless widow. But she would find a place to live in shantytowns near the mills or in tent colonies thrown up in the shadow of coal-mine tipples. Or, as she would put it when asked where she lived, "Well, wherever there is a fight."[27] In lieu of a family, she would adopt America's toilers, and they would call her "Mother."

During the half century when she was most active in the workingmen's movement, the country was undergoing a dramatic shift from an agrarian to an industrial nation. The vehicle was corporate capitalism. Small-scale shops gave way to the large. Monopoly often supplanted competition. The nature of work and of workers was altered. Waves of immigrants and displaced farmers dug the nation's coal and forged its steel. All too often, they received in return only starvation wages and nightmarish conditions. Within these men smoldered the sparks of class conflict which Mother Jones would fan for 50 years. To these workers, she would become an anchor to the past and an arrow toward a better future.

Mother Jones was born 7 years before Queen Victoria ascended to the throne and less than 50 years after the end of the American Revolution. Yet, she died on the eve of the New Deal. She was alive when Andrew Jackson was president, and she sometimes quoted from speeches she heard Lincoln make. As an adult, she knew the Civil War, the Spanish-American War, and World War I. She rode in automobiles, and she saw the railroads link the oceans. She saw and was seen in films and came to know the everyday use of the telephone, the electric light, and the radio. She watched unions grow from secret groups of hunted men to what she feared was a complacent part of the established order. She spanned an almost incredible era. It may have been a good time to live in America. But it also was a time in which one needed to fight very hard to survive. That she did.

Crusty, ubiquitous Mother Jones was a self-appointed scolder of the nation in a period when introspection was unpopular. She may have been the most spectacular woman the country has produced, and she certainly was the most loved and dramatic female in the nation's labor movement. To millions of men, women, and children, she was a profane Joan of Arc, an industrial Carrie Nation who took up their cause without question and fought without compromise. In her day, which began when most others ponder retirement, Mother Jones blazed her name onto the front pages of the nation's newspapers and into the forefront of its conscience. She was fearless, eloquent, and utterly dedicated. At the same time, she was stubborn, addicted to exaggeration, and unable to coexist even with her own kind.

Heroes tell a lot, and hers was John Brown. Clarence Darrow once wrote that, like Brown, Mother Jones "has a singleness of purpose, a personal fearlessness, and a contempt for established wrongs. Like him, the purpose was the moving force, and the means of accomplishing the end did not matter."[28] Mother Jones defied categorization. She was an outrageously irreverent Catholic, a conservative radical, a gregarious individualist, and an ascetic who eschewed the very comforts she sought for her "boys." She did men's work all her life but remained feminine. A pioneer of social change, she was nonetheless adamantly opposed to women's suffrage. She helped found several radical groups which she almost unfailingly scorned. "If Mother Jones had stayed in Ireland, she probably would have been hanged . . . or else, she would have been President of the Irish Republic," one friend commented.[29]

She had no consistent philosophy, except altruism and economic betterment. Though she weighed no more than 100 pounds, she didn't hesitate to fight violence with violence, or even to incite some on her own. She would call a federal judge a "scab" and tell a prestigious corporation president that he was "a high class burglar." She would rally thousands of cheering men and tell them they were worthless. She would hobnob with United States presidents and revolutionaries and be castigated and praised from one end of the country to the other.

Her specialty, aside from violating injunctions and going to jail, was pageants of poverty, processions of the angry and the abused. She was also adept at smuggling out "open letters," couched in the most poignant of prose, from the scene of her latest imprisonment. And she was quick to trade barbs with men whose lungs never had sucked in coal dust or whose skin had not felt the heat of a blast furnace. But beyond the publicity-seeking and the caustic retorts and the hyperbole, there were for Mother Jones countless cold nights in miners' hovels, sleeping on a bare floor with her handbag for a pillow. Or, the incredible journeys to reach such places, or the jails, in some of which she claimed she had to fight off rats with a broken beer bottle. In all, she was a benevolent fanatic, a Celtic blend of sentiment and fire, of sweetness and fight, who captured the imagination of the American worker as no other woman—perhaps no other leader—ever has.

TWO

THROUGH either nature or nurture, Mother Jones could forget
her part in one event, embellish her role in another, or disregard
them both in a third instance. Always impish and no slave to consistency,
she clothed her early years in confusion. Whole decades appear mislaid.
But from the great Chicago fire until she appeared with regularity and
prominence on the American labor scene, Mother Jones was serving her
apprenticeship in aid to the economically oppressed. It was a rare endeavor for a woman, and she would be an uncommon unionist. Physically, however, Mother Jones was no amazon. She was of medium
height, perhaps five feet, and sturdily built, but not fat. She dressed
sedately, almost always in a dark dress garnished with bits of flowers or
lace. A bonnet usually sat on her white hair, and to many, she seemed
the essence of grandmotherliness.

When she spoke, however, she became exceptional. Her fluid
phrase-making was accentuated by an unusual voice. Low and pleasant,
it had great carrying power. According to one early observer, her voice
did not become shrill when she became excited but, rather, dropped
in pitch so that "the intensity of it became something you could almost
feel physically."[2] When she rose to speak, Mother Jones "seemed to

9

explode in all directions," another noted, "and suddenly everyone sat up alert and listened. No matter what impossible ideas she brought up, she made the miners think she and they together could do anything."[3]

The years following the fire were for Mother Jones a time of hard work, sacrifice, and slight success. It was an era she often would recount to succeeding generations of labor leaders who knew not of "our fights in Chicago when we hadn't a penny, when no organizer was paid, when we had to tramp six miles to attend a meeting, and we did it cheerfully. . . . You boys have no idea of what we went through in those days. I look back over the long struggle, the dark hours, the suffering, and I know it was not in vain."[4] Imbued with a missionarylike fervor, Mother Jones became a tough-talking ascetic totally absorbed in her work. In fact she always would be scornful of women who distributed their good will only on weekday afternoons or through their social clubs. No misguided reformer, she used an approach as direct as her speech. Once at a public meeting, a college professor referred to her as a "great humanitarian." Mother Jones interrupted him, saying, "Get it right. I'm not a humanitarian. I'm a hell-raiser."[5]

Still relatively young, a well-educated woman for her day, highly mobile, and with a growing social conscience, Mother Jones apparently stayed in Chicago as a seamstress for two or three years following the fire. After that, she may have visited San Francisco. There, some say, she became acquainted with the growing socialist movement and fought to exclude the Chinese who were flooding the labor market, lowering wages and working conditions. She also may have traveled to Europe in 1873 and again in 1881 to study conditions for workers in England, Ireland, Germany, France, and Austria.[6]

In any event, she did return to Chicago and make it her base. At one Knights of Labor meeting she asked so many questions of the speaker that the two soon were engaged in a spontaneous debate. Impressed by her grasp of labor, he asked to see her at the end of the program. The official was Terence V. Powderly, who would be the Grand Master Workman of the Knights from 1879 to 1893. Mother Jones he described at this time as "a young seamstress . . . good looking, with a quick brain and an even quicker tongue."[7] Despite strong dissimilarities, the pair became lifelong friends. Either as an envoy of the Knights or as a freelance emissary, Mother Jones participated in a minor way in many of the labor convulsions which shook the nation in the years following the Panic of 1873. There is little indication, save her own assertion, that she had a sizable following or a measurable effect on the disputes in this early period. In fact, in some cases her contribution appears to be little more than a strong sense of empathy. But she was learning of grievances—and methods—firsthand.

In September 1873, amidst a wave of postwar speculation, the banking house of Jay Cooke and Company suffered losses which closed its doors. This brought on a chain reaction of failures among smaller banks. Overnight, the entire credit structure of the nation collapsed. Five thousand businesses fell by the end of the year, and the country suffered the worst depression it had known. For the next six years, unemployment rose and wages fell. Few unions could survive. Of the 30 national labor organizations in 1873, only eight or nine remained by 1877 and even those ones lost many members. Mass demonstrations of the unemployed became common.[8] Although generally in retreat, the American worker in the summer of 1877 executed one of the most militant and successful strikes up to that time. Much of the labor unrest of the 1870s centered on the railroads. The first big combines, they gained added leverage in 1869 with the completion of the transcontinental link. Furthermore, they were led by some officials such as Jay Gould, whose labor-relations philosophy was summed up succinctly in his boast: "I can hire one-half of the working class to kill the other half."[9]

Hard times followed another financial panic in 1876, and wages again were cut. Dividends for railroad stockholders, however, remained at 8 and 10 percent. The rail workers, who often lived in shanties near the tracks, worked 15 to 18 hours a day and had average weekly earnings of $5.00 to $10.00. Irregular employment could cut even that.[10] Relatively docile, the railroaders had endured earlier wage cuts, Pinkerton spies, and blacklists. But when the Pennsylvania Railroad cut wages by another 10 percent on June 1, 1877, and other rail lines followed suit, the missing spark was found. Underground unions surfaced, and strikes, slowdowns, and confrontations began at many major rail centers.[11]

In Martinsburg, West Virginia, about 55 miles northwest of Washington, some 1,200 brakemen and firemen seized the depot and halted most of the traffic on that Baltimore and Ohio line. Corruption, rate discrimination, and the use of public land by the railroads had won them few friends among any class, and so other citizens joined in the fray.

Miners near Martinsburg helped prevent the arrest of the striking railroad leaders, and crowds of strikers in West Virginia, Maryland, and Pennsylvania blocked the tracks to keep scabs from running the trains.[12] West Virginia Governor Henry M. Matthews sent state militia against the strikers, but the troops joined them in open fraternization. Matthews requested federal troops from President Rutherford Hayes, and those soldiers, arriving in Martinsburg June 19, became part of a much-employed precedent for the use of the United States military to suppress strikes in peacetime.[13]

Strike leaders were jailed, but the walkout spread to other parts of the state as well as to Ohio, Kentucky, Maryland, Pennsylvania, New York, New Jersey, Illinois, Missouri, and California. Whole railroads swiftly were closed down. Spontaneously, the Baltimore and Ohio strikers had begun what amounted to a national strike. It reached its greatest intensity in Pittsburgh where again it had the support of all classes. Copying the Martinsburg tactics, the people massed on the tracks, allowing only passenger and mail trains to pass. It was about at this point in July that Mother Jones arrived in Pittsburgh. The strikers, she wrote, "sent for me to come help them," a dubious recollection given her lack of prominence at the time.[14]

Again, the local militia refused to act as mobs took possession of railway property. The governor ordered the Philadelphia militia across the state to Pittsburgh. There on July 21, twenty civilians were killed and 29 seriously hurt when the troops fired into a crowd after boys threw stones at them. "Since last week," one commentator wrote, "the country has been at the mercy of the mob, and on the whole the mob has behaved rather better than the country."[15] But an infuriated Pittsburgh crowd of about 20,000 forced the soldiers to retreat into a Pennsylvania Railroad roundhouse. The rioters set the roundhouse ablaze, and the troops, surrounded by smoke and flame, shot their way out. One hundred and four locomotives, 2,152 other cars, and 79 buildings were said to have been destroyed in the riot. Drunken looting followed the troop retreat and caused another $5 million to $10 million damage.[16]

By August 2, the strike ended after federal troops were sent to Pittsburgh in their first decisive strikebreaking role. City after city quieted with the arrival of soldiers. The railroads adjusted some of the workers' grievances, but the violence had obscured their original complaints.

Many employees returned to work to find their wages still reduced despite the outpouring of rage. The most lasting results were the lessons learned. Although the employers had won, the conflict revealed to them labor's latent muscle. Better control of the militia, added emphasis on the open shop, and conspiracy laws against the unions clearly were called for. Labor, on the other hand, saw its trust in government shattered. United States troops had been called out during a depression to defend the interests of the railroads. But the workers also learned that organization was needed to prevent strikes from becoming mob actions which invite suppression.[17]

Mother Jones learned, too. "Then and there I learned in the early part of my career that labor must bear the cross for others' sins, must be the vicarious sufferer for the wrong that others do," she wrote. The strikers were charged with arson and rioting "although it was common knowledge that it was not they who instigated the fire; that it was started by hoodlums backed by the business men of Pittsburgh who for a long time had felt that the Railroad Company discriminated against their city in the matter of rates."[18] The intense solidarity of the strike, the first to have such nationwide impact, left its imprint on the woman, who, in the flames consuming the roundhouse, may have seen the reflection of her own inner rage.

Two other labor confrontations—one to become a labor byword and the other an obscure but violent encounter—contributed heavily to Mother Jones's early education into the plight and the power of the workingman. In neither was she a principal participant, but on her both left their marks. The first was the Haymarket Square Riot of 1886. Two years earlier, the demand for an eight-hour day began to gather force among many labor organizations, including the Knights of Labor. A depression in 1884–85 brought fewer jobs and longer hours and emphasized the need to reverse both trends. A nationwide general strike for shorter hours was set for May 1, 1886, and Chicago, home of several powerful unions as well as a band of German anarchists, was the movement's vanguard.[19]

Mother Jones apparently was among the strong supporters of the eight-hour campaign. She also attended the anarchists' meetings, although she claimed never to have embraced their philosophy. On Christmas Day, 1885, they had staged a parade of about 400 gaunt and grim workers along fashionable Prairie Avenue. Carrying the red flag of revolt and the black flag of anarchy, the anarchists halted in front of wealthy homes where they uttered catcalls and epithets. "I thought the parade was an insane move on the part of the anarchists," Mother Jones said, "as it only served to make feeling more bitter. [It] served to increase the employers' fear, to make the police more savage, and the public less sympathetic to the real distress of the workers."[20]

As May 1 approached, uneasiness grew, and the employers were not reluctant to lend credence to the idea that the eight-hour movement was tantamount to revolution. The anarchists did their part by prodding the workers toward violence. On the appointed day, 38,000 workers left their jobs and another 20,000 soon joined them in the peaceful strike in Chicago. Some employers, such as the packinghouses, began granting the eight-hour day. But two days later when a scuffle over strikebreakers developed at a three-month-old, unrelated strike at the McCormick Reaper Works, police opened fire on a crowd. Four were killed and 20 wounded, and the anarchists found the incident they had been seeking.[21]

They called a protest meeting for the next night, May 4, and about 1,200 persons gathered in Haymarket Square in the center of the city's lumber and packinghouse area. It was a peaceful meeting, and a drizzle sent about three-fourths of the crowd home before a 180-man police contingent arrived. As the police ordered the remaining spectators to disperse, a dynamite bomb was thrown into their ranks. The police began firing through smoke and flames, and the workers fired back. In the fusillade of perhaps 75 to 100 shots, seven policemen were killed or fatally wounded, and four workers died. Many on both sides were wounded.[22]

There followed great public hysteria and a questionable trial against eight known anarchists. The identity of the bomb-tosser never was learned. But seven of the eight anarchists were sentenced to death, and another one given a 15-year prison term. Four eventually were hanged, one committed suicide, and two had their sentences commuted to life in prison after winning executive clemency.[23] Like all of her bent and her class, Mother Jones was struck forcefully by what she considered the reign of terror perpetrated upon the workingman. "The workers' cry for justice was drowned in the shriek for revenge," she wrote. Mother Jones would speak of the martyred in revered tones and forever praise the courageous intervention six years later of Governor John P.

Altgeld, who, at great political cost, freed those anarchists who had been given prison terms.[24]

Identification of the anarchists with the eight-hour campaign, even though they were but one segment of its base, killed the concept. All of labor was put on the defensive. Workers returned to their jobs at their previous hours, and concessions earlier granted were withdrawn speedily. Only about 15,000 of the nation's 190,000 May Day strikers gained or retained the eight-hour day.[25] It was the Knights of Labor which suffered most. Terence Powderly refused to join in a mercy plea for the Haymarket defendants, saying it was "better that seven times seven men hang than to hang the millstone of odium around the standard of this Order in affiliating in any way with this element of destruction."[26] Officially, the Knights had not even been in support of the May 1 general strike. But try as he might, Powderly could not disassociate his group from the general fear of anarchy which Haymarket had produced. Within two years, membership in the Knights dropped from 700,000 to 200,000, and the union lost every major strike it began after 1886.[27]

The episode influenced the direction of American trade unionism. The newly-organized American Federation of Labor (AFL), devoid of political abstractions, was seeking short-term improvements, not the dreamy political and educational goals which increasingly separated the Knights' leaders from their members. In the post-Haymarket tumult, the AFL further encroached on the strength of the Knights, and in that development was born the thread of twentieth-century labor.

The other early happening shaping Mother Jones's career was the Virden Massacre of 1898. Some south central Illinois coal operators felt unable to operate under wage rates established in a joint labor-management conference earlier that year. After their appeal for exemption failed, some companies began a lockout and started importing Negro strikebreakers under armed guard from Alabama. At Virden, on the Chicago and Alton Railroad south of Springfield, a stockade was built around the mine, and private detectives were hired to ensure the safe arrivals of the blacks by train. By September 24, angry, displaced miners filled the town's streets. On October 12, when a trainload of 180 black strikebreakers destined for the Chicago-Virden Coal Company steamed past the depot, there was an exchange of gunfire and a few casualties. But the real battle ensued at the stockade. Shots were fired by Winchester-bearing guards inside the fortress, those on the train, and the miners armed with shotguns and hunting rifles. In the onslaught which wounded 40 miners and killed seven, the train's engineer was wounded and refused to unload the strikebreakers. Five guards were killed and four wounded in the battle.[28] Afterward, the union miners attacked the company store and nearly trampled to death the proprietor. The governor ordered the national guard to the scene to prevent unloading of a second trainload of strikebreakers. Although the governor was strongly criticized, his action is believed to be the first time troops were used to defend labor's interests.[29]

After about six months, the Chicago-Virden firm capitulated. It hired back the union miners, dismissed the most obstreperous of its supervisors, and in so doing, made "Remember Virden" a union rallying cry to protect hard-won organization. Such devotion and outright rejection of compromise by the miners struck a responsive chord with Mother Jones. Although she had not been at Virden during the violence, she knew the area well and had worked as an organizer in southern Illinois only shortly before. In fact, she would ask to be buried with four of the Virden martyrs who were from Mt. Olive, Illinois. Though hallowed in Mother Jones's mind, those Mt. Olive dead were denied burial in the established cemeteries. This prompted their comrades to buy an acre of their own and create a union miners' cemetery. There, decades later, Mother Jones would, as she wished, "sleep under the clay with those brave boys."[30]

Mother Jones's endeavors before the turn of the century range from the most obscure encounters to at least peripheral participation in some of the era's most turbulent labor struggles. Apparently, her first coal strike—later to be her specialty—was in Norton, Virginia, in 1891. As if to indicate what was to follow, Mother Jones in Norton found meeting halls and churches barred to her by company officials. She was arrested, she was forced to use the public highway as a meeting ground, and she exchanged verbal barbs with the mine superintendent. All of these would become familiar tactics. Violence, too, was to be often at hand. In her autobiography, Mother Jones stated that during the Norton strike, she learned that mine owners and police conspired to burn her and another organizer in the coke ovens at night and then claim the next day that the pair had been freed and had left. "Whether they really would have carried out their plans I do not know. But I do know there

are no limits," she wrote, "to which the power of privilege will not go
to keep the workers in slavery."[31]

The Knights of Labor, which had some locals in the mining regions,
arranged, after some false starts, a merger of its miners with those of
the National Progressive Union in 1890. The result was the United Mine
Workers of America (UMW)—the union which more than any other
would receive Mother Jones's erratic allegiance. The new union emerged
from its Columbus, Ohio, founding convention with 20,000 members
out of some 255,000 miners and mine laborers in the nation. Although
it would function as an AFL affiliate, the UMW had provision at first
for allowing its two benefactors to retain some of their essential features
and administration. This overlap may help explain the facility with
which Mother Jones made the transition from the Knights to the fledgling mine union.[32]

In fact, Mother Jones was involved in a coal strike in Alabama in
1894 when she got involved on the fringes, at least, of what came to
be known as the "Debs Rebellion," or the Pullman strike. A radical
break with tradition, the American Railway Union, founded by Eugene
V. Debs the year before, encompassed all railroad employees in a single
union. It met tremendous early success in April 1894 when it led 9,000
men in a strike against James J. Hill's Great Northern Railway after
a third cut in wages. Eighteen days after the walkout closed down the
transcontinental rail line, the company capitulated, not having been able
to set one brotherhood against the other as in the past. The peaceful strike
brought the workers nearly all their demands and set the stage for a
second test.[33]

After the Great Northern victory, the railway union found new
members joining at a rate of 2,000 per day. A year after its founding,
it was the nation's largest union with 425 locals and 150,000 members.
About 4,000 of them were employed by George Pullman, inventor of
the railway sleeping car and one of the nation's most powerful industri-
alists. He also was the sole employer and landlord in Pullman, Illinois,
a small tract near Chicago and one which was widely advertised as a
model community. But the average daily wage was $.90 while rent was
from $11.00 to $12.00 a month. The employees were subject to blacklisting and favoritism, saw saloons and unions and the eight-hour day
banned, and had their wages—but not their costs—cut. One employee
framed his weekly paycheck which, after deductions, totaled $.02. In

May 1894 the workers chose a grievance committee to demand a reduction in rent, a return to former wage levels, and improvement of shop
conditions.[34]

When three of the grievance committee members were fired, about
2,000 Pullman workers struck on May 11. Debs arrived and found the
walkout justified. At the American Railway Union's first convention in
June, it was decided to boycott the Pullman shops in St. Louis and in
Ludlow, Kentucky, and to pull the union's members off Pullman cars.
Within a few days of its June 26 beginning, the boycott spread over
the central and western United States as sleeping cars were cut from
the trains and sidetracked. The boycott soon became a strike as the
railroads tried to discharge the Pullman boycotters. Never before had
there been such a strike. More than 150,000 workers were off the job.
Fifteen railroads were tied up. Thirty persons were killed and twice as
many injured during riots, and 700 were arrested. Federal courts handed
down omnibus injunctions, and President Grover Cleveland sent federal
troops to Chicago.[35]

When the strike began, Mother Jones was in Birmingham where
about 8,000 UMW coal miners had struck in April against wage cuts
and poor living and working conditions. The walkout soon turned violent, and the state militia was called in. Scabs kept the mines running,
and the union was losing the struggle when the American Railway
Union shut down the railroads. The two groups of strikers then joined
together and closed all the railroads there, depriving the mines of their
markets. But the success was short-lived. The militia again was called
to keep the trains running, crowds were dispersed from railway property
at bayonet point, and within a week, the Birmingham rail strike was
broken.[36]

"I was forbidden to leave town without permit, forbidden to hold
meetings," recalled Mother Jones, who worked with both the miners
and the railway union leaders. "Nevertheless I slipped through the ranks
of the soldiers without their knowing who I was—just an old woman
going to a missionary meeting to knit mittens for the heathens of Af-
rica!"[37] The Alabama miners' strike dragged on for four months. Over-
whelming opposition by the operators plus a hostile state government
and adverse public sentiment doomed the effort, although a few gains
were won. Nationally, too, the rail strike was hobbled by the jailing
of American Railway Union leaders, misleading newspaper reports

about a back-to-work movement, sweeping injunctions, and a lack of support by the AFL's Samuel Gompers for a general strike. On August 2, the walkout ended, although most workers had returned to work even before then. The defeat of Debs was another victory for the AFL and for craft unionism.[38]

Apparently months later, after Debs was released from an Illinois jail where he had been sentenced for violating an injunction, he came to Birmingham. City officials were not going to allow him to speak, Mother Jones said. But she forced them to change their mind after she organized a show of force which saw Debs carried through the streets on the shoulders of miners. The opera house was jammed, she said, for Debs's address. "The aisles, the window sills, every nook and corner. The churches were empty that night, and that night the crowd heard a real sermon by a preacher whose message was one of human brotherhood."[39]

Debs, twenty-five years younger than Mother Jones, would become a five-time presidential candidate. Self-educated, he had been an official of the Brotherhood of Locomotive Firemen before forming the American Railway Union. Like Mother Jones, he was neither an intellectual nor a skillful politician. But, again like her, he won a fond following because of his strength of conviction, compassion, and integrity. While in prison following the Pullman strike, Debs became interested in socialism and converted in 1897, about the same time his friend Mother Jones was showing her first such inclinations. The Pullman strike made Debs a national figure. But the American Railway Union never recovered. When it held its 1897 convention, only 24 delegates attended, contrasted with the 400 who had come three years earlier. In the strike, which again had shown labor the crushing force of government, many workers saw the need for solidarity. At the same time, the AFL and the railroad brotherhoods saw the justification of their more narrow craft unionism.[40]

After the strike, Mother Jones stayed in Alabama. She went to Cottondale, between Birmingham and Tuscaloosa, to work in the cotton mills. "I wanted to see for myself," she later wrote, "if the grewsome stories of little children working in the mills were true."[41] The miners and the railroaders had told her what to expect.. "While I imagined that these [mills] must be something of a modern Siberia, I concluded that the boys were overdrawing the picture and made up my mind to see for myself the conditions described. Accordingly I got a job and mingled with the workers in the mill and in their homes."[42]

In 1900, about 30 percent of the southern cotton mill workers were under sixteen years of age. None of the Southern states important in textile manufacturing had any age limits, literacy, or education requirements, or restrictions on night work for children. Not until 1910 or later would most southern states enter the field of child labor legislation and even then, enforcement would not make the rules a reality until after World War I.[43]

The Cottondale mill manager told Mother Jones she could not have a job unless she also had a family to work. She lied, telling him they —including her six children—would be coming later. So enthusiastic was he that he helped her find a house to rent. Actually, it was "a sort of two-story plank shanty. The windows were broken and the door sagged open." But she took it and promised to produce her farm-bound family by month's end. Then she went to work. What she found was child labor and virtual adult slavery because of a severe company store policy.

Sometimes, she said, she had an urge to flee "the most heart-rending spectacle in all life" and go to the coal fields "where the laoor fight is at least fought by grown men."[44] Children six and seven years old "were dragged out of bed at half past four in the morning when the task-master's whistle blew. They eat their scanty meals of black coffee and corn bread mixed with cottonseed oil in place of butter, and then off trots the whole army of serfs, big and little." Work began at 5:30 A.M. and continued until a half-hour break at noon and then back to the job again until 7:00 P.M. "Then a dreary march home, where we swallowed our scanty supper," Mother Jones recalled, "talked for a few minutes of our misery and then dropped down upon a pallet of straw, to lie until the whistle should once more awaken us, summoning babes and all alike to another round of toil and misery." She said she saw the machinery-tending children's "helpless limbs torn off, and then when they are disabled and of no more use to their master, thrown out to die."[45]

"But they [the children] had Sundays, for the mill owners and the mill folks themselves were pious. To Sunday School went the babies of the mills, there to hear how God had inspired the mill owner to come down and build the mill, so as to give His little ones work that they might develop into industrious, patriotic citizens and earn money to give to the missionaries to convert the poor unfortunate heathen Chinese," Mother Jones said.[46]

When her six children didn't arrive, the manager became suspicious and Mother Jones left Cottondale. Next she went to a Tuscaloosa rope factory. "The superintendent, not knowing my mission, gave me the entire freedom of the factory and I made good use of it." What she found were two little girls, nine and ten, working alongside their father 12 hours each day and earning $.10 daily. The father got $.40. The children, Mother Jones recounted, were "half-fed, half-clothed, half-housed, they toil on, while the poodle dogs of their masters are petted and coddled and sleep on pillows of down, and the capitalistic judges jail the agitators that would dare to help these helpless ones to better their condition."[47]

She visited other towns in Alabama, Georgia, and South Carolina. At one spot, she found a worker who, after deductions for company-store food, got an annual wage of $1.00. At another, she said, the mill owners started a bank for their employees. When it was discovered the mill workers were saving 10 percent of their wages, the owners cut the wages by that amount and prompted a strike.[48] In Selma, the eleven-year-old daughter of the woman with whom Mother Jones boarded was killed when her hair became caught in the mill machinery and her scalp was torn off. In another unnamed town, Mother Jones helped one family "escape from a condition as intolerable as any Negro slavery which had ever existed in the same Southern states." They had run up a $36.00 debt while the father was ill and dying. In their town, the system was to "dole out food and clothing in the smallest possible quantities" while "charging rent at the largest figure, being careful to see to it that interest, food, clothing, and rent always aggregated just a little more each month than the total of the wages earned," Mother Jones said. "The thralldom was complete. There was no hope of escape from it. Fourteen hours a day, 7 days a week, for every member of that family, year in and year out, would never clear that debt away."[49] So she "abducted" them. Greasing the axles of a borrowed wagon to keep the noise down and then securing the aid of railroad workers to make an unscheduled pickup, Mother Jones said she drove the family from the mill town while "almost listening for the baying of the bloodhounds." When they furtively boarded the train, "my charges all broke down then, quite hysterically," she said. "The strain had been so great."[50]

"From the South, burdened with the terrible things I had seen, I came to New York and held several meetings to make known conditions as I had found them. I met the opposition of the press and of capital," Mother Jones later wrote. "For a long time after my southern experience, I could scarcely eat. Not alone my clothes, but my food, too, at times seemed bought with the price of the toil of children."[51] Hatred of child labor as well as chagrin at the plight of workers' children in general would be a recurrent theme with Mother Jones. Among textile workers and among miners, the childless woman would seek to ease the suffering of the young, sometimes quietly and sometimes dramatically.

After the South, Mother Jones went to Pittsburgh and later to Omaha, Nebraska, to sell subscriptions to *Appeal to Reason,* a new socialist newspaper.[52] If nothing else, the Pullman strike had shown Mother Jones that workers needed more education if a new social order was to be forged. Unencumbered at this point with any social philosophy beyond that of trade unionism, Mother Jones went from here to develop her ideas about socialism. They would vary from a fleeting fondness to total, if erratic, embrace.

The southern mill experience and the meeting with Debs started her thinking and writing about anticapitalism. In an article about the mills for *International Socialist Review,* she concluded: "I can see no way out save in a complete overthrow of the capitalistic system, and to me the father who casts a vote for the continuance of that system is as much of a murderer as if he took a pistol and shot his own children."[53] Although she often let loose with such strong rhetoric, she just as often contradicted it. Her philosophy of collectivism was a desultory one—to be swept up in during a speech or a strike, or to share in comradeship with her more consistently committed friends. All her life, Mother Jones was a doer, not a philosopher. She was a political chameleon whose catechism reddened in relation to her mood and to the moment.

In her travels, Mother Jones had encountered Julius A. Wayland, a native of rural Indiana who had made a modest fortune in printing and real estate in Colorado. Edward Bellamy's socialism had supplanted Republicanism in Wayland's mind and led him to establish a socialist magazine, *The Coming Nation,* in Greensburg, Indiana, in 1893. Within half a year, it had 14,000 subscribers, and its success prompted Wayland to buy 1,000 acres and start a cooperative village near Tennessee City, Tennessee. He asked Mother Jones to join. She refused, claiming

that more was to be gained by uniting in economic struggle than in iso-
lating oneself from it. A year later, about 1895, she would visit there
and come away "glad I had not joined the colony but had stayed out
in the thick of the fight."[54]

Wayland left, too, after about a year, and the colony dissolved in
1899, although some of its settlers persisted and joined another cooperative in Georgia which, in turn, lasted until 1901. Meanwhile, Wayland
moved to Kansas City where on August 31, 1895, the first issue of *Appeal to Reason* appeared. It sold 5,000 copies in Kansas City alone.[55]
Published once a week, the *Appeal* railed against monopoly and the
moneyed interests and stood for socialism and such measures as direct
legislation under which all laws would be passed upon by the citizenry.

It catered to a purely American strain of radicalism and antimonop-
oly feeling, and it came to have a strong influence, especially in the
Midwest and the South.[56] It spoke the language of the common
man—oblivious to theory, suspicious of the powerful, and demanding
of action. Condemning the trusts and advocating cheap money and government ownership, the *Appeal*—like Mother Jones—did not burden
itself with tedious economic analysis. It preferred bright, if unsophisti-
cated answers to the problems of the times. Epigrams and anecdotes
were epidemic. "No oppression in America, if you please. We are free.
We are the great people. The American eagle soars—wonder if it isn't
sore." Or, "If Congress would put a tariff on bribery, and rigidly enforce
it, it would raise enough revenue from the District of Columbia to run
the government."

The *Appeal* really didn't give a great deal of news but filled its columns with polemics, excerpts from other papers ("by a recent law Colorado women are eligible to become members of the state militia"), and
the inevitable cartoons of silk-hatted factory owners swiping money
from the workers' pockets. But it nearly always contained also a list
of books "laboring people should read," and thus reflected Mother
Jones's terse political and educational philosophy. Like her, the paper
was nondoctrinaire but militant, ubiquitous but not always heeded in
the highest councils. She occasionally wrote for the *Appeal,* and it followed her exploits with front-page fervor. The paper suffered during
the William Jennings Bryan craze in 1896, and publication halted. But
in 1897, it began again, this time in Girard in southeastern Kansas.

From the paper's beginning, Mother Jones was with the *Appeal,* selling it as early as 1895, she said, to troops stationed in Omaha and to people at city hall there. Circulation generally climbed, and by 1899 it was the country's most popular socialist journal. Debs, a contributing editor, said the paper was "literally honey-combing capitalism. Wherever the *Appeal* is at work, and that seems everywhere, socialism has at least a nucleus and the light is spreading."[57] The relationship between Mother Jones and the *Appeal* would be one of her more lasting ones.

During the winter and early spring of 1898–99, Mother Jones was the guest of Wayland in Girard. It was then, Wayland later said, that he "learned to love her great heart and gray hair."[58] From Girard, she would go to a fierce struggle in eastern Pennsylvania. But first, after her early work with the *Appeal,* Mother Jones came east to work closely with the UMW. In 1897, she joined with other organizers in an attempt to unionize West Virginia, a state in which she would find both fame and frustration.

THREE

I F anyplace was home to Mother Jones, it was West Virginia. In five
major strikes there, she wove herself into the social fabric of a state
greatly blessed by nature and debased by man. The 40-year struggle to
unionize its coal fields was marked by bloodletting, legal ruses, and
illicit tactics honed to a merciless efficiency. Drumhead justice and
blanket injunctions, armored trains and gun-toting detectives, aerial
bombings and militarylike marches were among the innovations which
Mother Jones saw, reacted to, and perhaps, in part, caused. For 30 years
she tramped over those mountains. She slept and ate with miners'
families, taunted gunmen, made her most incendiary speeches, and
languished in jail. She had no possessions and no life of her own, save
that spoken by her harbingers: "Mother Jones is up in the hills raisin'
hell." Both as a paid organizer and a freelance agitator, she preached
the panacea of "Join the union, boys." But from the first, unionizing was
tough and treacherous.

Unusually thick seams—six to ten feet—of high-quality coal lie beneath about six million acres of West Virginia hillside. Much of it could
be mined by digging into the side of hills rather than mining with long,
narrow shafts, and this gave the operator an advantage over his Pennsyl-

vania or midwestern competitor. West Virginia's output would rise almost 100-fold between 1870 and 1911. But because only about 10 percent of it was consumed within the state, wages had to be kept down to compete in distant, out-of-state markets. The average annual wage of the West Virginia miner in 1897 was $275.00, the nation's lowest, except for the Pittsburgh area where immigrant labor predominated.[2]

In 1894, the UMW had struck in West Virginia but without much success. Concurrent with its first efforts, immigrants and Negroes began to be brought into the state in large numbers, often as strikebreakers. Cutthroat competition among operators reduced prices and wages, and this led to further strikes. State coal prices plummeted 28 percent between 1891 and 1897, while Illinois prices, for example, fell only 11 percent. The unorganized fields of West Virginia endangered—as they would for the next 35 years—both the UMW's power base and the markets of the other operators. But having only six locals and 206 members out of some 23,000 in the state, the union faced no small task.[3]

On July 27, 1897, the "greatest number of prominent labor leaders ever to assemble on West Virginia soil" met in the Trades Assembly Hall in Wheeling. AFL President Samuel Gompers was chairman of the delegation which included UMW President M. D. Ratchford; James Sovereign, grand master workman of the Knights of Labor; Eugene Debs; Mother Jones; and spokesmen for the printers, bicycle workers, railway trainmen, tailors, cigar workers, and other trades. Before crowds of up to 17,000, the labor leaders pledged to help the UMW "undertake the perfection of a systematic agitation and placing of organizers throughout the West Virginia field." The delegates also condemned as "unjustified, unwarranted and unprecedented" the recent issuance of broad, antilabor injunctions by West Virginia judges.[4]

As part of a nationwide strike against wage cuts, a walkout in West Virginia already had begun about July 4, and John Mitchell, a UMW vice-president, soon was sent to the state for the crucial organizing task. He reportedly found Mother Jones in jail. But she was soon freed, and along with Eugene Debs, she concentrated in the northern, or Fairmont field and held "great meetings" at Monongah, Flemington, and other towns.[5] Resistance, however, was strong. In this strike, operators for the first time made extensive use of special police, mine guards, and detectives to intimidate organizers and to escort strikebreakers. Mitchell, for example, was said to have cut short his stay when hostile police forced him to swim an icy mountain stream to save himself. Further impeding success were the raising of wages and the paying of bonuses for those who stayed on the job, evictions from company-owned homes, and the willingness of the courts to come to the employers' aid.[6]

The 1897 strike ended in September, about 12 weeks after it began as a desperate effort in the wake of a depression. In what was to be a boon for the UMW, the coal operators in Illinois, Indiana, Ohio, and western Pennsylvania agreed to a joint bargaining conference with the union. For the owners, this would help stabilize costs and curtail the overproduction which long had racked the industry. For the UMW, the plan promised recognition as well as regular benefits from the conferences which began early the next year. UMW membership nationally would spurt from 10,000 in 1898 to 115,500 in 1900 as John Mitchell became president.[7] But the failure to organize West Virginia would remain a serious shortcoming. The rates of pay there remained less than elsewhere, the hours longer, and often the costs higher because of the ubiquitous company store. UMW membership in the state, however, did increase during the 1897 strike from 206 to more than 3,600 and the number of locals from 6 to 40.[8]

Topography, institutions, and traditions all argued against the success of the organizing effort in West Virginia. Because the coal properties rarely were near established towns, mining companies built whole communities from the ground up. In return, they often exercised nearly complete dominion. As historian Herbert Harris described the company-controlled town:

Since it owned the streets, it could forbid freedom of speech and assembly. Since it often owned even the highways leading to and from the mining center, it could prevent union organizers from entering its domain. For all practical purposes, the company also owned the mayor, the village or town council, the judge, the jury, the court crier and whatever press existed. . . . Boys were brought into the world by the company doctor, attended the company schools, listened to the sermons by the company preacher, grew into manhood and worked in the company breaker or washery, and finally were buried by the company undertaker.[9]

Such conditions led Mother Jones to believe she was fighting a slavery every bit as wretched as that of the antebellum South. "The Negro slave possessed advantages that the white laboring man of today has not. When the slave was ill his master cured him; when he was hungry he was fed; when he was naked he was clothed. Who does this for the laboring man of the twentieth century?" she asked.[10]

As part of its 1898 agreement with the operators of the central competitive field, the UMW had pledged to unionize West Virginia, which each year was underselling its competitors and pushing further into midwestern markets. By late 1900, the UMW organizing campaign there was renewed with intensity.[11] Supervision of the task in the southern part of the state was in the hands of Mother Jones. Despite her seventy years, she led the other organizers on a rugged schedule. From her headquarters in Montgomery, she sent frequent status reports to John Mitchell, now UMW president, and asked him for stronger organizers, especially those from Illinois for whom she had a special liking.[12]

Her presence in the southern fields apparently was a catalyst. An organizer named George Scott reported that the meetings were very tame until "we were blessed with the presence of a new force." Mother Jones, he said, "is attracting great attention and her meetings every night are increasing. . . . Too much can not be said of her perseverance and determination" as she travels over the mountains. With "a tenacity worthy of emulation she moves on step by step without a complaint. No mountain seems too high, or path too rugged as long as she can find a receptive audience."[13] Her brand of organizing was a highly personal—and successful—one. The miners did not just accept her economic views which often were opaque. Nor did they merely succumb to the mechanics of her organizing, which were rough at best. Instead, throughout her long career, they seemed to respond by a sort of psychological purchase of her personality. She spoke earnestly and colorfully and in terms and anecdotes which they understood.

She was an old, sweet-faced Irishwoman in a risky business. She had a lively sense of the dramatic, but she also had the subject matter of drama—the deprivations of the miners which she knew and not from afar. A mildly profane but biting eloquence mated with her tiny size, white hair, handsome face, piercing blue eyes, and matronly dress made her a compelling figure. She was not at the bargaining table in some remote, pine-paneled room. But rather, despite the obvious incongruities, she was in the field. There the workingman, especially the fatalistic miner, could feel her shrill exhortations stir his blood and pierce his apathy.

"Has anyone ever told you, my children, about the lives you are living here, so that you may understand how it is you pass your days on earth?" she asked one group of about 700 West Virginia miners in a typical scenario. "Let us consider this together, for I am one of you, and I know what it is to suffer."[14] She went on to paint the picture of the life of a miner from his boyhood to his old age. She spoke of his introduction to the work in dismal caves beneath the earth, dripping with moisture and so low that he must crawl in, lie on his back to dig, and allow the sulphur water to eat through his shoes and raise sores on the flesh. She recounted for him how his hands became cracked and gnarled and his nails broken off, how the scraps in his lunch pail failed to satisfy, and how the thought of his barefoot children and their broken mother haunted him even in the bowels of the earth. He had to scrub the coal dust from his tired body every night and listen to his wife tell of what the children need but could never have, Mother Jones reminded. He could never own a home or make his wife happy or educate his children, she said. He must rise again tomorrow and do it all over again —unless, of course, the fall of rock gets him, or rheumatism cripples him, or unless the job itself is there no longer. Her voice rising, Mother Jones asked him why others, no more sons of God than he, took from the toiler all the wealth he produced, leaving him only enough to subsist so that he might labor further to their advantage. "You pity yourselves," she said, "but you do not pity your brothers, or you would stand together to help one another." She called for them to wake up so they might live another, better life.

As Mother Jones paused, a man pushed through the teary-eyed crowd and cried: "You, John Walker [a UMW organizer from Illinois], don't you go to tell us that 'ere's Mother Jones. That's Jesus Christ come down on earth again, and playing he's an old woman so he can come here and talk to us poor devils. God, God—nobody else knows what the poor suffer that away." As he was quieted and led away, Mother Jones broke out with the climax of her message—an impassioned appeal for organization. Hers was a simple socialistic sermon which indicted capitalism and castigated the miners for not uniting. She promised the dawning of a new day and a new deal for every worker willing to stand up for the union. "Her earnestness would carry conviction to a steel magnet itself," said the *Washington Post*. "When she predicted hope of improvement for the great mass of American toilers in the years to come—and not so many years, either, she declared—her face glowed with the light of a benevolent fanaticism."[15] Had she not been so determined, she would not have lasted in the West Virginia organizing task. It was physically demanding in the extreme.

John Walker later noted that he and Mother Jones traipsed from 5 to 20 miles to attend organizing meetings. Mother Jones endured the hardships good-naturedly, he said, even when they included almost being bitten by a poisonous copperhead snake or becoming lost and having to walk miles out of her way.[16] But snakes and mountains may have been benign problems compared to operator resistance. In Mt. Carbon, for example, Mother Jones said she spoke in defiance of local mine officials. "They notified the hotel not to take any of us in or give us anything to eat," she recalled. "Thereupon a miner and his wife gave me shelter for the night. The next morning they were notified to leave their miserable little shack which belonged to the company."[17]

In one West Virginia town where she spent an Easter prior to the 1902 strike, Mother Jones stayed with a family where the father often on paydays brought home no more than a bill from the company store. Ten tons of coal, Mother Jones said, went for house rent, two for the company doctor, two for the blacksmith for tool sharpening, two for water, two for powder and oil, and so on. If the miner protested, she said, he was blacklisted. He worked 10 to 12 hours a day "amid the poisonous gases. Then a crowd of temperance parasites will come along and warn the miners against wasting their money for drink."[18]

Such was the pathos and frustration Mother Jones met during this early West Virginia struggle. "Not only the school rooms, but every church or public hall is locked against us," she said, while the operators freely use the facilities. But persevering, she helped the UMW gain ground in the southern field, and she sent glowing reports to John Mitchell. "I am having glorious meeting [sic]. The boys are responding to the high call," she wrote from Montgomery. "I think we will give you this River [the Kanawha] organized by the first of May."[19]

In northern West Virginia, however, the story was not the same. The fewer coal companies there had more of a monopolylike control, and little organizing progress was being made. In October 1901 the union issued an invitation for the operators to meet with it. There was no response, and in March 1902 the UMW proposed a scale of wages it thought the operators should be paying. It also sought especially to receive recognition as the miners' bargaining agent. But still there was no response. In May, then, the union issued a June 7 strike call for the entire state.[20] Sixteen thousand miners in 15 counties left their jobs in West Virginia, swelling the UMW strike ranks which already included the anthracite diggers in Pennsylvania and other miners in Alabama and Michigan. The West Virginia operators answered with unqualified opposition. With railroad transportation developed, production soaring, and the lack of unions giving them a competitive advantage, they clung steadfastly to the principle of the open shop.

Not long before the strike began Mitchell switched Mother Jones from the southern to the northern field. She could do the most good there, he said, "as the coal companies up there have evidently scared our boys, and of course, with good reason, as they have brutally beaten some of them. I dislike to ask you always to take the dangerous fields, but I know that you are willing," he wrote.[21] Second in command there, behind Thomas Haggerty from western Pennsylvania, Mother Jones specifically was in charge of managing food supplies for the strikers. On June 8, 1902, she rode in a buggy in the miners' procession from the unionized base of Flemington to Willow Tree School near Monongah where the strike camp was to be. Fairmont Coal Company, the target of their exhortations, won an injunction the following day against their activities. Haggerty was arrested, and Mother Jones assumed command on Mitchell's orders.

Although she continued the demonstrations and even succeeded in temporarily closing down one mine, little progress was made in convincing the Italians, a big part of the work force, to quit. Company guards and unsympathetic local officials made the task doubly difficult. On one occasion, three organizers were attacked at night on a public road. Mother Jones heard their cries and deceived the assailants into thinking that help was on the way. Then she bandaged one of the victims with strips torn from her petticoat.[22] But violence proved less effective than injunctions. "In West Virginia," Mother Jones observed, "you can't step on a piece of ground without you step on an injunction."[23] When she addressed 300 persons at the Willow Tree Schoolhouse on June 15, she was served with a writ from United States District Court Judge John J. Jackson. An appointee of President Abraham Lincoln, Judge Jackson granted an injunction banning all meetings and demonstrations by the strikers, even on premises leased by them. The ruling was to stir anger and controversy but, meanwhile, deputy marshals were sent to enforce it.[24]

The strikers nonetheless planned another rally. Thousands of handbills advertised Mother Jones's June 20 speech near Clarksburg. As she delivered the 30-minute address, the federal marshal began arresting organizers in the crowd and sent word to her that she, too, was under arrest.[25] But she refused to stop talking until she had her say. She accused Judge Jackson as well as the railroads and the newspapers of being in league with the coal operators, and she ended in a dramatic farewell. As Mother Jones later recalled it, she told the crowd: "Goodbye, boys; I'm under arrest. I may have to go to jail. I may not see you for a long time. . . . Pay no attention to the injunction machine at Parkersburg. The Federal judge is a scab anyhow. While you starve he plays golf. While you serve humanity, he serves injunctions for the money powers."[26]

On the train trip to the Parkersburg jail with 11 other organizers, Mother Jones amused herself by attempting to indoctrinate her captors with her views. Once there, she refused the offer of a hotel room and was lodged in the Wood County jail, although the jailer and his wife treated her more as a guest than as an inmate. To a reporter who enterprisingly managed to interview her in confinement, she protested that the organizers had been arrested on ground which they had rented. But she pledged that others would take her place and that the strike would continue.[27] John Mitchell, meanwhile, proclaimed that the union would appeal the contempt citation and, if defeated, would seek a presidential pardon for Mother Jones, who he said was an "earnest and conscientious worker who believes in an era of greater happiness for the toilers of the world."[28] Actually, however, the union effort in West Virginia was faltering as its principal organizers were being silenced by the courts.

Released on bail, Mother Jones went to UMW national headquarters in Indianapolis where the West Virginia movement was about to be hobbled further. Mitchell already had made what was to be the crucial decision of his career: to give priority to the organizing of 140,000 anthracite miners in eastern Pennsylvania. Although both regions had a history of union failures, it was the growing output and low wages of West Virginia's miners which threatened the UMW's midwestern contracts. But Mitchell lacked the funds to wage two large-scale strikes simultaneously. He apparently felt the large railroads which dominated the anthracite field would respond better to his conciliatory approach than would the newer, more aggressive West Virginia operators. Now, in July 1902, Mitchell was sticking with this decision and was opposing a general strike of the bituminous miners. He postponed the special Indianapolis convention until he could collect enough votes to defeat the sympathy strike. The question then became how best to allocate the union's money. West Virginia still might be the scene of a partial victory if strike advocates there, such as Mother Jones, got full backing. She spoke for about 45 minutes at the meeting and gave what the minutes indicate was "a somewhat detailed account of the work being done in West Virginia." Though she was given a unanimous "vote of thanks and confidence," Mitchell's leadership prevailed. The UMW committed itself to all-out financial support only of the anthracite strikers.[29]

Back in Parkersburg on July 24, Judge Jackson studied the contempt cases before him, those of the union organizers "who are vampires that live and fatten on the honest labor of coal miners of the country, and who are busybodies creating dissatisfaction amongst a class of people who are quite well-disposed, and who do not want to be disturbed by the unceasing agitation of this class of people." Holding that freedom to work needs as much protection as an agitator's freedom of speech, the judge said the June 20 meeting violated both his court order and the bounds of free speech.[30] He continued:

I cannot forbear to express my great surprise that a woman of the apparent intelligence of Mrs. Jones should permit herself to be used as an instrument by designing and reckless agitators . . . in accomplishing an object which is entirely unworthy of a good woman. It seems to me that it would have been better far for her to follow the lines and paths which the Allwise Being intended her sex to pursue. There are many charities in life which are open to her in which she could contribute largely to mankind in distress, as well as avocations and pursuits that she could engage in of a lawful character that would be more in keeping with what we have been taught and what experience has shown to be the true sphere of womanhood.[31]

When offered a chance to defend herself, Mother Jones is said to have called the judge a "scab" once more, causing no small furor in the courtroom. (She claimed later to have apologized in private after seeing evidence that the jurist did not, as she had been told, "scab" on his father by accepting the judicial appointment meant for the elder Jackson.) However, she told the judge she had seen her duty, had done it, and would do it again. In a rejoinder that won courtroom applause, she added that they both were aged but she hoped they could become good friends and meet in heaven.[32] Six of the strike leaders got 60-day sentences, and Haggerty received 90 days. While also finding Mother Jones in contempt, Judge Jackson suspended sentencing rather than allow her to don the martyr's cloak and "force her way into jail." He pledged to hold the conviction over her and over four foreign-speaking organizers as well. But if they violated his order again, he would sentence them heavily.[33]

Mother Jones, who had in the meantime been superseded as strike leader, soon prepared to leave the northern field. Taking her place was Thomas L. Lewis, a UMW vice-president who had been cool to the strike there originally and who would permit no further demonstrations, the specialty of Mother Jones.[34] Her ongoing dialogue with Judge Jackson, who became the butt of jokes nationwide and even the target of some impeachment talk, added to the growing Jonesian legend. Repeatedly, in her long career, she would escape with her life, make spectacular forays, and say frank—and sometimes utterly false—things for which men in identical situations would have been killed, stymied, or silenced. Her age and her sex were both armor and sword.

Mother Jones left the northern field to join in the anthracite conflict. But within a few months, she resumed her arduous pace of organizing and encouraging strikers in the New River and Kanawha River fields of West Virginia. Standard UMW procedure was to "agitate and educate" first, unionize later. Making speeches, handing out leaflets, and seeding the germ of unionism until ripe for organization probably was wise in an area where union members met eviction, blacklisting, or worse. But Mother Jones liked to see early results. She would meet with the miners, often under cover of night, and then make her pitch and set up a UMW local. If the men could not produce the $15.00 needed for a charter, she paid it herself.[35]

Again, resistance to the organizing was stiff. Men who joined the union were blacklisted, Mother Jones said. "Men were shot. They were beaten. Numbers disappeared and no trace of them found. Store keepers were ordered not to sell to union men or their families. Meetings had to be held in the woods at night, in abandoned mines, in barns." Not infrequently, she reported, organizers spent the nights on the river bank where "we would hear bullets whizz past us as we sat huddled between boulders, our black clothes making us invisible in the blackness of the night."[36]

When Mother Jones arrived at a coal camp near Stanaford Mountain in Raleigh County, she found that a group of miners had been accused of violating another federal district court injunction against marching or holding meetings within sight of the mines. A deputy marshal sent to arrest them was driven away. Mother Jones chided the miners about this, claiming that even if they were not guilty, they should not defy arrest. She and a lawyer persuaded the men to go to court the next day, and apparently satisfied, Mother Jones left.[37]

But the next morning, hearing of further trouble there, she returned and said she sensed that the homes seemed to cling together as if in consolation. Reaching the first miner's cabin, "I pushed open the door. On a mattress wet with blood, lay a miner. His brains had been blown out while he slept. His shack was riddled with bullets. In five other shacks men lay dead." Apparently, the deputy marshal, perhaps not knowing of the intended surrender, gathered an 80-man posse and swept down on the homes at 4:00 A.M. In the ensuing melee, seven miners were killed and about 20 wounded. The crime went unpunished, and Mother Jones stayed for a time, consoling the widows and children.[38]

A series of letters from a mine superintendent in Ansted to his New York boss depict the tension and violence pervading the New River area during Mother Jones's activities there. He wrote repeatedly of the difficulty in keeping men on the job "as the fear of being bushwhacked or blown up is universal among the workers." "Last week a miner was bushwhacked," an August letter stated, ". . . and on the following day two miners were shot at . . . as they were going up the incline to work. The shots were fired at long range from the cliffs across the New River, smokeless powder and steel jacketed bullets being employed. One man was shot through the hips and the other through both legs."

The Ansted mine apparently was one of the few large ones on either the New or Kanawha Rivers which didn't curtail operations during the 1902 strike. On September 23, the superintendent wrote: "The strike drags on with little change, and though we have had Mother Jones with us for the last week making her usual anarchistic speechs, she has little effect upon our men."[39] Again, in late November: "Mother Jones is here, made a speech last night, and every effort is being brought to bear upon our men to induce them to join the Union. . . . On last Thursday

night, I called all of my men together in the Armory and they agreed
unanimously that if I would allow them a ten percent advance from
Oct. 1st, they would sign individual contracts binding themselves to
work at this rate until January 1st 1904 and agreeing not to affiliate
with any strikes or organizations." The superintendent added that he
got a rebate from the railroad, which needed coal, to cover the raise.[40]

The violence continued. But the all-encompassing injunctions, evictions, use of armed guards, strikebreakers, and such timely raises and
yellow-dog contracts triumphed. Furthermore, the UMW emphasis on
the anthracite strike—which did become a qualified victory—lent to the
West Virginia failure. In October 1902 the union won an agreement
in the Kanawha Valley covering some 7,000 miners. Recognition was
granted along with a nine-hour day, dues checkoff, semimonthly paydays, the right to trade where the miner pleased, and other concessions.
It was not a small success, and it was one attributable in large measure
to Mother Jones's organizing efforts there. But in the rest of the state,
the UMW not only failed to win the recognition it sought, but lost most
of its previous organization.[41] The 1902 strike, the most ambitious one
in West Virginia up to this point, largely failed. Further, it spurred the
operators to join forces. They saw the potency of their collective
strength when mated with that of the law. Elsewhere, as in the midwestern mining states, the miners had become a countervailing force
with management. But in West Virginia, the two sides just were beginning to line up in a yet uneven contest.[42]

Unionization in West Virginia had been stalled, and the problems
remained. Rates of pay still were less, hours longer, and costs of living
higher. In 1903, the average pay per ton of coal mined in West Virginia
was 49.5 cents. It was 64.4 cents in Illinois, 88 in Indiana, 76.1 in
Ohio, and 59.3 in western Pennsylvania.[43] Within the decade, the largely
nonunion mines of West Virginia would produce more than 20 percent
of the coal marketed in the Great Lakes region. This would threaten
even further the welfare of the organized coal diggers of the Midwest
and increase the pressure to unionize West Virginia.[44] But despite the
strenuous effort of Mother Jones and other organizers, the 1902 West
Virginia strike was in the long run a pulled punch. After 1903, holding
tactics were employed, and it would be 10 years before a major strike
again occurred there—and Mother Jones once more would play a vital
part.

FOUR

I am not afraid of the pen, the sword or the scaffold. I will tell the truth . . . wherever I please.

—Mother Jones[1]

HUNDREDS of eastern Pennsylvania hard-coal miners walked
more than five miles from Arnot south to Blossburg on a cold
and snowy February night in 1900. They came to the opera house to con-
gratulate a gray-haired wisp of a woman who, according to a national
UMW official, had "snatched victory out of the very jaws of defeat." A
nine-month strike in the Arnot area had ended in a union celebration,
and the miners and their families arranged a farewell and victory party
for Mother Jones. The strike had been a small-scale replay of the Civil
War clash between the forces of freedom and those of slavery, according
to Mother Jones. She urged the jubilant miners to be peaceful, forgiving,
and politically cautious.[2]

Anthracite coal, the principal domestic fuel in the eastern United
States, lies beneath seven counties in northeastern Pennsylvania. The
mines, controlled principally by the coal-carrying railroads, bred many
of the classic grievances of the coal-diggers. In fact, the UMW could
trace its antecedents to the region, including anthracite man John Siney,
founder of the early Miners and Laborers Benevolent Association in
1868. As early as 1895, the fledgling UMW began to organize there.
Although well established in the state's central and western fields by

the turn of the century, the union had little or no organization in the eastern field which had seen the crushing 25 years earlier of the Molly Maguires, a secret workers' organization accused of sabotage and murder.

Actually, conditions had not improved much since then. Wages averaged $1.50 per day. But in some areas they were pegged to the price of coal, which generally meant downward in this era of economic instability. Other miners were paid on the basis of weight produced or the number of cars filled. In either case, the miners claimed they were cheated by the common use of "tons" weighing up to 3,360 pounds and by cars of ever-growing dimensions. The workers also had to buy their own blasting powder which may have reduced their spendable income by 6 or 7 percent, and they felt robbed by the docking system under which the amount of impurities in the coal was figured.

Further, sporadic employment, the rule of the company store, poor health care, and damp, dusty conditions in the mines caused discontent. The anthracite mines were among "the world's most dangerous"—killing 7,346 men in the 21-year period ending in 1897. Among the 140,000 anthracite workers, there were about 20 nationalities and almost as many languages, and this added to the difficulty of unionizing.[3] In 1897, however, despite a national membership of less than 10,000 and a large indebtedness, the UMW launched another organizing effort in the hard-coal field. A confrontation between marching miners and the Luzerne County sheriff on September 10 ended with the deputies firing into the crowd, killing 24 unarmed miners. The tragedy gave impetus to some organizing gains. But the campaign did not resume in earnest until 1899 when the new UMW President John Mitchell made a speaking tour of the area. He then dispatched a large force of organizers in August to gird for an expected strike.[4]

In the northern area, in and around Arnot, a walkout soon developed. But when local union bickering and a solid front by the coal operators threatened the strike, the UMW called in Mother Jones in late September. Her techniques of rallying the dejected were becoming well known. On September 30, the Arnot miners voted 130 to 19 to return to work. Arriving the next day, the seventy-year-old agitator held a meeting, brought her not-so-subtle rhetorical pressures to bear, and got the vote reversed. Then, using a technique which would become something of a trademark, Mother Jones proceeded to organize the wives of the strikers. Arming them with mops and brooms, pots and pans, she laughed when the ragtag brigade frightened away the mules which hauled the coal cars and their scab drivers from the mines.[5]

For five months she went from camp to camp and city to city urging the strikers to stand together. She also went around the countryside in a mule-drawn wagon to counter the companies' urging of farmers not to aid the strikers. Sometimes, she recalled, it was after midnight and several degrees below zero when she would return. "The winds whistled down the mountains and drove the snow and sleet in our faces," she later wrote. "My hands and feet were often numb. We were all living on dry bread and black coffee. I slept in a room that never had a fire in it, and I often woke up in the morning to find snow covering the outside covers of the bed."[6]

John Brophy, then only a fifteen-year-old coal miner but later a UMW and Congress of Industrial Organizations (CIO) leader, first met Mother Jones during this period. He wrote:

She came into the mine one day and talked to us in the vernacular of the mines. How she got in I don't know; probably just walked in and defied anyone to stop her. . . . She would take a drink with the boys and spoke their idiom, including some pretty rough language when talking about the bosses. This might have been considered a little fast in ordinary women, but the miners knew and respected her. They might think her a little queer, perhaps—it *was* an odd kind of work for a woman in those days—but they knew she was a good soul. . . . She had a lively sense of humor—she could tell wonderful stories, usually at the expense of some boss, for she couldn't resist the temptation to agitate, even in a joke.[7]

At strike's end, Mother Jones left for Elkton, Fròstburg, and Lonaconing, Maryland, to agitate.[8] But within a few months she again received news of difficulty in eastern Pennsylvania. Mitchell had been pleased at the "almost phenomenal" growth in the UMW's anthracite membership. By early 1900, there were 92 locals and 8,993 members there. But the kind of agreement reached in the Arnot strike was not being readily accepted by the operators elsewhere, and by July, pressure was building among the new members for a strike. In August, a convention at Hazleton authorized a regionwide walkout the following month. About 112,000 miners left their jobs on September 17. Within two weeks, under pressure from bands of marching strikers, more workers joined the walkout and brought a full 90 percent of the anthracite industry to a halt. Some 120,000 men were on strike for demands which included a 10-percent wage increase, a fixed ton, reduction in the price of powder, abolition of the company store, and elimination of the sliding wage-price scale.[9]

Mitchell asked Mother Jones to return to the area to reinforce union loyalty. She did and immediately began holding meetings at dozens of towns and mineheads, encouraging strikers to remain resolute and scolding those who continued to work. Along with Mitchell and Samuel Gompers, she canvassed a wide area in seeking converts to the union cause. Earlier local strikes had failed, Mother Jones told the miners. But this one "will be a revelation to some people," she said.[10] Although she met some short-run failures in her attempts to recruit additional strikers, Mother Jones contributed to a generally successful campaign by leading marches. Meanwhile, the Reverend Edward S. Phillips, a Catholic priest from Hazleton, was urging an end to the walkout through individual arbitrations with the companies. Particularly, he urged the men at the G. B. Markle and Company mines to stay on the job because of a long-standing agreement there to arbitrate grievances. The union, which wanted to meet the operators collectively in a joint conference, feared that company-by-company arbitration would weaken the strikers' solidarity.[11] Mother Jones, with an aversion to both the church and to arbitration, was incensed at Father Phillips. At one point she was holding a meeting in a field next to a church where a priest, presumably Father Phillips, was speaking. He "told the men to go back and obey their masters and their reward would be in Heaven," she recalled. "Boys," she told her group, "this strike is called in order that you and your wives and your little ones may get a bit of Heaven before you die." Mother Jones was triumphant a short time later when Father Phillips, after a talk with John Mitchell, changed his mind and spoke of "a fight to the finish between organized labor and organized capital."[12]

Mother Jones continued to organize series of marches and to put on shows of force at the collieries which still were working. The operators, in turn, maintained that it was the "acme of unfairness" that miners without complaint would lay down their tools at the insistence of "foreigners" like Mother Jones. "These people get near to the mines; they appeal to the men daily and hourly in language they understand, and they arouse passions in women and men that already have brought on one fatal collision and produce daily slight encounters," the *New York Times* reported from the anthracite field.[13] On September 25, Mother Jones met at 10:00 P.M. with 5,000 miners at McAdoo, near Hazleton. She got their women to "put on their kitchen clothes and bring their mops and brooms with them and a couple of tin pans. We marched over the mountains fifteen miles, beating on the tin pans as if they were cymbals."[14] The all-night march, complete with newspaper reporters, wagons, and American flags, was to elicit support of workers in ten collieries in the Panther Creek valley which had not joined the strike. The marchers planned to arrive just as the miners were going to work and thus most susceptible to dissuasion.

At dawn, the marchers arrived at the entrance to the Panther Creek mining area. "Just as the sun came up over the hills the procession set out," the UMW *Journal* reported. "There was a band, two flags, a detachment of men, a body of women carrying brooms, a large company of men, more women, and 'Mother' Jones dressed in mourning."[15] There was also the militia with fixed bayonets. The troop commander told Mother Jones to turn back. "I told him that the American workingman never goes backward; we go forward, and we did not go out to go back, and he said he would charge bayonets" but did not, Mother Jones recalled. The McAdoo women continued on, she said, and not only convinced all the miners to join the strike but also got the streetcar men to promise to haul no scabs for the coal companies. "As there were no other groups to organize, we marched over the mountains home, beating on our pans and singing patriotic songs."[16] The march, with anywhere from 2,000 to 5,000 participants, was one of the largest of its kind. But Mother Jones's description of it also may qualify as phenomenal. Frank J. Warne, a newspaperman and coal historian who was along on the march, reported that "just as the sun was gilding the heavens with the glory of the morning, and within sight of the collieries the marchers had come all the distance to close, the front ranks of the strikers were met by the bayonets of the Pennsylvania National Guard. The weary miners turned back without accomplishing the purpose of its [sic] midnight march."[17]

In any case, 20,000 miners rallied October 2, 1900, at Wilkes-Barre. Arriving early, Mother Jones was met by a huge crowd at the depot. After a parade through town, she and Mitchell and two other organizers urged a united front. But despite appearances, her raids had come to irritate not only company and law-enforcement officials but the UMW hierarchy as well. The UMW *Journal* noted without elaboration that "leaders of the strike have discouraged parades to the mines because of the danger of conflicts with deputies." Despite repeated operator warnings that further incursions onto private property would not be tolerated, Mother Jones persisted in a tactic she considered basic to her organizing.[18]

Described as "a Chicago virago," Mother Jones was said to be "out among the miners, urging disorder in a language that made the women hysterical and got the men to marching at daybreak in masses of 600 to 1,000 to 'persuade' miners who had persisted in working." Added the *New York Times* correspondent: "The presence of this woman is generally reprobated."[19] On October 7, nearly 2,000 strikers, accompanied by Mother Jones, a fife and drum corps, and 50 women in wagons, journeyed to Lattimer. There they marched and countermarched along the roads and did manage to shut down a mine. But a few days later, the marching took a tragic turn. A special policeman was killed and other policemen and strikers were wounded in a clash between 50 officers and 500 stone-throwing miners, including a contingent of women, near Oneida.[20]

Mother Jones's conflict with John Mitchell, to spring to full bloom and lifelong dislike a few years later, had not yet shown itself. When she later wrote about her treks through the Pennsylvania mountains in 1900, she pictured Mitchell relaxing in nearby hotels, oblivious to the struggle and undeserving of its successes. Naturally, he was in charge of the strike. But he did not know about Mother Jones's pots-and-pans raids, according to her, until a reporter told him that "Mother Jones was raising hell up in the mountains with a bunch of wild women!" More likely, Mitchell did not take cognizance of the raids "officially" until October when he halted them after police told him that force would be used, if needed, to stop the practice.[21]

This strike was one of Mother Jones's most frenetic and perhaps successful actions. Her effectiveness was shown, for example, by the statements of John Markle, a key independent operator, who claimed that in September he had convinced his men not to strike. But because of threats and because of the marches led by Mother Jones, Markle's workers soon walked out along with others in the hard-coal region.[22]

Appeal to Reason was ecstatic over Mother Jones's work in Pennsylvania. Calling her "the most successful organizer and sustainer of strikes in the country," it stated:

> There is only one Mother Jones. Clara Barton has her work of mercy, Susan Anthony her equal suffrage, Mother Jones has her "boys"—the great patient army that sweats and strives and suffers wherever there is work to be done. . . . This is the time of Mother Jones. She has been called the stormy petrel of industry. Her appearance is a signal for those who grow rich by grinding the faces of the poor to "go slow," and if they disregard the warning so much the worse for them and the better for organized labor.[23]

Through unprecedented unity and luck, the anthracite miners in six weeks won—sort of. Concessions were, John Mitchell said, "flung at them rather than granted." His appeal to the operators' reason had not averted the strike. But the prospect of the walkout continuing through election time and thus lending thrust to the presidential campaign of William Jennings Bryan was enough to bring pressure from Republican politicians and financiers. At their urging, the operators unilaterally agreed to a 10-percent wage increase for the miners until 1902. Although some miners wanted to hold out for other concessions as well, a UMW convention led by Mitchell's conservative element won approval of the increase and called off the strike on October 24, 1900.[24]

But the seeds had been sown for a bitter harvest. The operators resented making concessions under political pressure. They began building stockades, establishing depots for coal storage, and making other preparations for the next battle. The UMW, however, emerged strong from the 1900 strike. Beginning the conflict with some 8,000 members in the anthracite field, it ended the strike with more than 100,000 there. Still, the union lacked a contract and union recognition, even if the strike was, as Mitchell said, "the only great contest in which the workers came out entirely and absolutely victorious."[25] The strike, for once, had been remarkably short and free of violence. Mitchell's belated reining in of Mother Jones may have helped minimize the bloodshed. But certainly her bold and wide-ranging actions contributed heavily to the unity of the miners. Mother Jones lingered in eastern Pennsylvania for a while after the settlement and before starting on an organizing jaunt back to West Virginia. She continued to report to Mitchell on the reliability of local UMW officers. "You know you need news," she wrote to him in late November. "Send any request to me. I am ever ready to help out poor helpless people. Just say the word and I am off. Suffering humanity needs out best efforts and we should not spare ourselves. The slaves of the caves need to be saved."[26]

For most of the following year, 1901, Mother Jones remained in Pennsylvania and West Virginia, save for short trips to Ohio, Missouri, and Illinois. She continued to have a special rapport—however short-lived—with Mitchell. The UMW *Journal,* quick to take the president's lead, ran favorable publicity on her. On one occasion, the *Journal* printed a flattering, front-page picture of "the grand old woman, who is revered at home, honored abroad, whose life is without reproach, whose name is a 'tower of strength,' the sheet-anchor of the miners, and one who is as 'terrible as an army with banners' to his oppressor."[27] The upcoming Anthracite Strike of 1902, however, was to kill this cameraderie by a surfeit of what Mother Jones considered to be weak-kneed compromise. Delegates from the three anthracite districts of the UMW met in March 1902, and, for the second time in three months, they asked the operators for a joint conference. Again they were turned down. On May 12, a "temporary suspension" of work was ordered by district officials, and two days later another convention at Hazleton voted by a 57 percent majority to continue the work stoppage. The miners sought a 20-percent wage increase, reduction in hours, a fixed ton, and wages and grievance procedures embodied in a contract, thus recognizing the UMW as the miners' bargaining agent.[28]

Two months after the anthracite strike began, a broad-based movement started within the union to get all bituminous miners to walk out in sympathy with the Pennsylvanians. But Mitchell, by dissuading proponents of the plan, boosted his and the UMW's image in the public mind. Further winning over the press and the public viewpoint was the companies' refusal to arbitrate. Scorn also was directed at the operators as a result of a letter written by George F. Baer, a spokesman for the companies. "The rights and interests of the laboring man will be protected and cared for—not by the labor agitators—but by the Christian men to whom God in His infinite wisdom has given control of the property interests of the country, and upon the successful management of which so much depends," Baer wrote.[29]

Mitchell's conciliatory approach, especially when contrasted to management's stubborness, continued to win accolades. Even President Theodore Roosevelt blamed the operators for "obstinancy utterly silly from their own standpoint and well nigh criminal from the standpoint of the people at large."[30] Through the summer the strike drew little fanfare, but as autumn approached, the nation became more apprehensive. Mother Jones, arriving not long after her confrontation with Judge Jackson in West Virginia, held a series of meetings in the Wilkes-Barre and Hazleton areas in late July and early August. She reported that the strikers seemed more determined than when the strike began and were unshaken in their vision of the coming victory.[31] If the miners were becoming more sanguine, so was she. In September, she stated that there "will probably be a settlement before long. I cannot say when that will be. Public sentiment is growing. . . . The public has never before realized what a big factor the miner is in civilization."[32]

Meanwhile, politicians, sociologists, and others tried their hand at mediating the dispute which was causing a shortage of hard coal. By late September, the price of anthracite, usually $5.00 to $6.00 a ton, was as high as $15.00 to $20.00, and widespread suffering was forecast for the approaching winter. Calling this threat "not merely calamity, but the direst disaster," Roosevelt began to worry about its effect on the 1902 Congressional election as well as on his own race two years hence. In an historic action, the president called for both sides to meet with him. The October 3 conference, however, did not produce agreement but yielded further public praise for Mitchell in the face of the operators' invective. With no movement apparent, Roosevelt was considering having troops take over the mines as a last resort.[33]

But a behind-the-scenes agreement was reached between a Roosevelt emissary and financier J. P. Morgan, and Roosevelt named a commission to settle the strike. This was approved by the operators and (lamentably, said Mother Jones) by the UMW at an October 20 convention. By October 23, the strikers returned to work after being off the job more than five months. The next day the commission began its inquiry into the dispute which had caused economic losses totaling $100 million. Presided over by Judge George Gray of Wilmington, Delaware, the hearings lasted nearly as long as the strike. The commission heard 558 witnesses and collected 10,000 pages of testimony, including the union's position as enunciated by attorney Clarence Darrow.[34]

Although the public considered the March 18, 1903, award as a union victory, the results were not clearcut. There was a 10 percent—instead of 20 percent—increase in wage rates tied to the rising price of coal. There was generally a 9-hour day instead of the previous 10. Checkweighmen, who tallied the amount of coal produced by each miner, were to be elected; disputes were to be submitted to a six-man conciliation board; and coal cars were to be uniform-sized. But, on the other hand, there was no fixed number of pounds per ton, no written contract, and no union recognition. This caused Mother Jones, who opposed the third-party induced settlement, to comment that "Labor walked into the House of Victory through the backdoor."[35] She urged rejection of the award because the union had won in the field and could insist upon recognition. But Mitchell felt he had no honorable alternative because he had earlier agreed to arbitration. Like Mother Jones, Mitchell knew that victory was in sight on the weight of the strike alone. Unlike her, he measured against that his own strict sense of fairness and the pendulum of public opinion which had, for once, swung to the union's side.[36]

The strike was significant because for the first time a union had tied up a strategic industry without being condemned as a revolutionary threat. In fact, Roosevelt had been able to avoid Grover Cleveland's precedent in dispatching troops eight years earlier to quell the Pullman strike. Of further import was Mitchell's decision, although hard-pressed, not to call out the soft-coal miners in support of their anthracite comrades and in violation of their own contracts. Mitchell thus promoted the principle that once a bargain is struck, all adhere to it. At the same time, Mitchell's decision to press the strike in Pennsylvania undercut the West Virginia effort and thus weakened the joint conferences in the Midwest, the UMW's stronghold. Soon, wage reductions would have to be accepted there.[37]

Valid through 1906, the anthracite settlement represented a peaceful adjustment of the union's most protracted and successful strike to date. It also was an unequaled show of mine-worker unity. Mitchell, for his moderation and discipline, emerged as the foremost American labor figure. For the same reasons, he incurred the eternal wrath of Mother Jones. By temperament, she was not given to compromise, especially with presidents and businessmen. Weakness for whatever end was anathema, and the 1902 settlement produced a dislike for the thirty-three-year-old Mitchell which outlived them both. Almost a quarter of a century later, long after Mitchell had died, Mother Jones saved her most severe rancor for him when she wrote her autobiography. " 'It would never do to refuse the president,' " she quoted Mitchell as saying obsequiously when she sought to have him reject Roosevelt's arbitration board.[38]

She wrote:

Flattery and homage did its work with John Mitchell. The strike was won. Absolutely no anthracite coal was being dug. The operators could have been made to deal with the unions if Mr. Mitchell had stood firm. A moral victory would have been won for the principle of unionism. This to my mind was more important than the material gains which the miners received through the later decision of the President's board. Mr. Mitchell died a rich man, distrusted by the working people whom he once served.[39]

The way the strike was settled was a wound on the principled psyche of Mother Jones, and it never wholly healed. She had worked tirelessly in the 1900 Pennsylvania dispute and had basked in that effort's salient success. But she was bitter at seeing her work and that of others supposedly squandered two years later at the suggestion of Roosevelt, who, in her mind, was no friend of labor. Part of her anger may have been the glory draped around Mitchell, who was not even half her age. In any event, the affair left her with a sullen opinion of "establishment" labor leaders, a species to which she would never belong or aspire.

FIVE

We ask you Mr. President, if our commercial greatness has not cost us too much by being built upon
the quivering hearts of helpless children.
                                    —Mother Jones[1]

NOT long after the anthracite strike, Mother Jones tried a new
tack. Instead of marching at the head of a band of angry women,
she formed a pathetic procession of children with lint-clogged lungs and
gnarled hands, of men weary of long hours and low pay in the textile
mills of Philadelphia. It was one of her most spectacular publicity gambits
as she led them on a 22-day hike through parts of three states to see
President Roosevelt. Predictably, perhaps, he would not be home to
them. But the nation would see and hear.

On May 29, 1903, 100,000 workers—including 16,000 children
under age sixteen—left their jobs at 600 mills in the Philadelphia area.
They demanded a reduction in the work week from 60 to 55 hours
even if this meant a decrease in wages which ranged from $2.00 a week
for children to $13.00 a week for adults.[2] Mother Jones arrived about
mid-June to help stir up sentiment for the strikers in the Kensington
district. She found that "every day little children came into Union Headquarters, some with their hands off, some with the thumb missing, some
with their fingers off at the knuckle. They were stooped little things,
round shouldered and skinny." Many of them were not over ten years
of age, although state law prohibited children working before they were
13.[3]

Considering child labor the worst of industrial sins and disappointed at the lack of newspaper space given to the plight of the children, Mother Jones began to seek publicity. On June 17, she paraded a number of the children to city hall.

"I put the little boys with their fingers off and hands crushed and maimed on a platform. I held up their mutilated hands and showed them to the crowd and made the statement that Philadelphia's mansions were built on the broken bones, the quivering hearts and drooping heads of these children. . . .

"I called upon the millionaire manufacturers to cease their moral murders, and I cried to the officials in the open windows opposite, 'Some day the workers will take possession of your city hall, and when we do, no child will be sacrificed on the altar of profit.' "

But, Mother Jones recalled, "The officials quickly closed the windows, just as they had closed their eyes and hearts."[4]

The textile industry was the country's largest user of child labor, employing 80,000 children and most of them being little girls. In cotton, 13.1 percent of all workers in the United States were under age sixteen in the year 1900. In the South, where the figure ran as high as 30 percent, parents often would not be hired unless they brought along their children, as Mother Jones had learned a few years earlier.[5] In Pennsylvania and other northern states, only the parents' oath was required to certify a child's age. Thus, poorly paid parents of large families, faced with starvation or perjury, often chose the latter as a way to bolster family income. Children between the ages of eight and thirteen were found in nearly 100 different kinds of work in Philadelphia alone, according to one study.[6]

John Spargo was a socialist intellectual who assisted the Kensington strikers and joined Mother Jones's march for the first few days. He recalled one little girl who was not quite eleven telling him with pride "that she had 'worked two years and never missed a day.' "[7] Mother Jones's early efforts in Philadelphia, however, brought little press coverage or money into the union's coffers. So, drawing inspiration from a tour of the historic Liberty Bell, she and the textile union leaders next seized upon the idea of marching the mill children to Roosevelt's home at Oyster Bay on Long Island, some 125 miles away.

After convincing some hesitant parents that the pace would not be too arduous for their young daughters, Mother Jones led the 300 men, women, and children out of Kensington on July 7. To the accompaniment of fifes and drums, the group—with its four wagons, flags and banners, placards, and Mother Jones in her familiar lace-fringed black dress—reached Torresdale Park in northeastern Philadelphia by the end of the first day. Already a roll call showed the ranks reduced to 218 because many of the young women were sent home for lack of accommodations. The next day, as the temperature reached 91 degrees, the remainder of the girls—who had numbered almost a third of the original marchers—were sent home as were a number of the boys. But the group, now apparently less than 100 strong, made it to Bristol, Pennsylvania, that evening where policemen halted them. After emphasizing their peaceful intent, the marchers entered the town where that night Mother Jones addressed a crowd of more than 2,000.[8]

Hot weather and meager rations accelerated the attrition. One striker, disgruntled at Mother Jones's leadership, tried to depose her on the third day. When he failed, he returned with several others to Philadelphia. The rest of the "children's crusade" bivouacked on the shore of the Delaware River, across from Trenton, New Jersey.[9] Here, as at the other stops along the way, Mother Jones and the union leaders spoke to various sympathetic groups and garnered contributions for the strikers. In many cases, Mother Jones traveled ahead of her brood and attempted to secure them free lodging, meeting halls, and food as well as to herald their coming.[10]

Reports of the aims of the march varied as widely as the number and composition of those said to be marching. A principal goal was the winning of federal child-labor legislation and the whipping up of public support for that cause. But to raise money and support for the Kensington strikers also was given high priority. Costumes and jewelry were brought along to stage "tableaus" on the class struggle in major cities, and Mother Jones also mentioned visiting financier J. Pierpont Morgan.

The pronouncements of Mother Jones didn't lessen the confusion. On July 10, she told the *New York Tribune* that she did not really intend to visit Roosevelt or Morgan. "That's only a joke!" she said. "Sometimes it takes extraordinary means to attract ordinary interest. Morgan and Roosevelt are names that attract attention at once, and I guess that is why I used them in talking to some reporters. Don't you think they could be put to worse use than to get people interested in opposing child labor." The same day, however, the *New York World* reported her saying: "We will march right up Sagamore Hill and dine with 'Teddy.' " She also said the strikers would parade up and down Wall Street in hopes of receiving a sizeable contribution from Morgan.[11]

The reports of desertions were "all wrong," Mother Jones added. Some marchers only intended to go as far as the outer limits of Philadelphia. "That was the programme," she said. "We never intended that the whole four hundred should go all the way to New York, or even to Trenton."[12] In any case, after paying under protest a toll of two cents for each of the now 52 marchers to cross the Delaware River Bridge, Mother Jones led the "army" into Trenton on July 10. Before a crowd of up to 5,000 in the city's Monument Park, she asked: "What is the use of bringing children into the world to make more money for plutocrats while their little lives are being ground out in the mill and workshop? The army I am leading on to New York is composed of intelligent workmen . . . our cause is a just one and we propose to show the New York millionaires our grievances."[13]

After having enjoyed the hospitality of a union carpenter the previous night, Mother Jones endured great heat and a fierce rainstorm to arrive the next day at the home of former President Grover Cleveland near Princeton. The Clevelands were on vacation at Buzzards Bay, and the caretaker invited "the boys and girls" to come in. Mother Jones enthusiastically accepted the use of the barn as a makeshift dormitory, and while in Princeton she took more than a few swipes at Princeton College. "What are your young men at Princeton but a lot of bums who think they know more than the President of the United States? They are wasting money on education which will do no good. The money ought to go to organized labor," she said.[14] Asked by a professor to speak to his class, Mother Jones paraded before the undergraduates a stooped, ten-year-old boy and said: "Here's a text book on economics. He gets three dollars a week and his sister who is fourteen gets six dollars. They work in a carpet factory ten hours a day while the children of the rich are getting their higher education."[15]

Pushing on to New Brunswick, Mother Jones gave yet more speeches while the drum and fife corps performed impromptu concerts on street corners and passed the hat. Two nights, July 11 and 12, the group—now down to about 41 members—camped in Highland Park, across the Raritan River from New Brunswick in a grove belonging to a brewery.[16] "They looked tired and disgusted with the whole thing," a *New York Times* report stated. "When the rain soaked the tents of the party last night more of the men deserted toward the railroad tracks. When the rain had finished, mosquitoes made a raid upon the camp, and there were more deserters." One of the men told the *Times:* "It's all right for Mother Jones. She sleeps in a hotel. I would rather work 60 hours a day than endure this torture. We seem to be in a sort of side show to help her get some notoriety about the country."[17]

On Monday, the 13th, the column marched another five miles to Metuchen where they dried out and regrouped before marching into Rahway the next afternoon. There Mother Jones addressed a crowd of 2,000 and promised to travel around the country until an aroused public would "result in a blessing not only to the children but to the whole nation."[18] The Socialist Party of Elizabeth, New Jersey, was among the hosts of the marchers at the next stop. At least one marcher blamed lack of beer for the attrition. So the Elizabeth saloonkeepers gave free drinks to the strikers. Mother Jones lent her consent to the beer-drinking but ruled out hard liquor.[19]

After another mass meeting, Mother Jones wrote the first of two letters to President Roosevelt, asking to see him. The Kensington strike could have been averted, she told him, by passage of a federal eight-hour law. She also explained to him the hardships of the mill children. "We who know of these sufferings have taken up their cause and are now marching toward you in the hope that your tender heart will counsel with us to abolish this crime," she wrote.[20] Spending an extra day in Elizabeth, Mother Jones's "army" received extraordinary hospitality. Two businessmen even took Mother Jones on her first automobile ride, and later at a union banquet, some sizable contributions were made to the strikers.

The group pushed on to Newark and then up to Paterson as rumors persisted that the Secret Service, anxious to head off a confrontation with the president, was attempting to dissuade individual marchers from continuing. After addressing silk weavers on Sunday morning, the 20th, Mother Jones made a side trip to the annual picnic of the New York City Social Democratic Party. Having to wait several minutes for the cheers of about 4,000 to subside, she promised to arrive with her group in New York by Thursday.[21] "I am going to complete the journey to Oyster Bay with my army to see the President. The newspapers say he will not see me. I am going to find out if he is the President of the capitalists only or whether he is the president of the workingmen, too. If he is the President of the capitalists only," Mother Jones said, "he will be wiped out at the next election."[22] She strolled among the picnickers, admiring their energy in contests like the sledgehammer test of strength and the children's games. She also acidly remarked that the beer drinkers at the celebration would do better to put their money into strike funds.[23]

Via Passaic and West Hoboken, the group inched closer to New York City. According to one story, a hotel proprietor at about this point gave the marchers free berths. But as the group ate at the hotel, a waitress complained to Mother Jones about the poor working conditions. Mother Jones organized a strike for that evening and in return, of course, got kicked out of the hotel. "I'm a bit of a devil, I guess," she later said. "But the stuff he was giving those poor girls to eat and the filthy places they had to sleep in, well, he deserved it and I have no regrets."[24] Mother Jones, incensed because Secret Service agents reportedly had been spying on her, said she felt Roosevelt had not seen her letter at all. Rather, he had been told an "agitator named Mother Jones wanted to come out and make a scene and plague him." This, she promised, would not be the case.[25]

After the New York City police commissioner refused to issue a parade permit because the marchers weren't city residents, Mother Jones went to Mayor Seth Low. She hammered away at the paradox of excluding them but earlier entertaining Prince Henry of Germany ("a piece of rotten royalty") as well as a Chinese dignitary. The mayor finally agreed, and the strikers were allowed to march from Social Democratic headquarters at 64 East Fourth Street to a meeting place a block from Madison Square, near Twenty-seventh. With 600 policemen overseeing the march, the group proceeded by torchlight through the East Side on July 23.[26] "A great crowd of young sightseers followed the army," the *Times* said, and the "noise they made was equal to the combined effort of a whole regular regiment." "55 hours or nothing," "Give us more schools", "Prosperity: where is our share?" were among the signs carried by the marchers.[27]

Nearly 30,000 spectators crowded around the meeting site where Benjamin Hanford, a former Socialist candidate for governor, castigated the mayor, the police commissioner, J. P. Morgan, and John D. Rockefeller. The New York police are "the finest in the world and had the distinction of being the first to club women," Hanford said. Mother Jones later indicated she did not approve of his speech, which dwelt at length on the fact that policemen have guns but workers are not supposed to.[28] With her arms draped around the shoulders of two young Kensington strikers, Mother Jones followed Hanford to the platform. "We are quietly marching toward the President's home," she told the crowd. "I believe he can do something for these children, although the press declares he cannot. Congress last year passed a bill giving $45,000 to fill the stomach of an old prince, and he indorsed that, and if he could do that he surely could tell Congress to pass a bill that would take the children out of the God-accursed mills and put them into the schools." Mother Jones blamed the people for allowing the "unspeakable crime of child labor" to continue.[29]

The marchers stayed in New York a second day, swimming in the East River and relaxing at Socialist headquarters. Secret Service agents reportedly visited Mother Jones and asked her to give up her plan to march to Sagamore Hill. Naturally, she refused. Police forbade a second night's meeting at Madison Square and insisted on a move to Fourth Avenue and Twenty-fourth Street. Mother Jones not only cooperated, but in her speech that night, she also praised the policemen and promised to ask Roosevelt if he could arrange shorter hours for them, too.[30]

The next day, Frank Bostock, an animal-show owner, invited the marchers on an outing to Coney Island where "Mme. Morelli and her cage full of snapping, snarling leopards" did not "excite half the interest there was in Mother Jones and her army," the newspapers said. Before a backdrop simulating the Roman Colosseum with two emperors giving the thumbs-down signal, Mother Jones spoke while some of the children were put into empty animal cages. The scenery was typical, she said, of the employers with their thumbs down to the children imprisoned in the mills while the public sits idly by.[31]

Interrupted throughout her speech by the roar of lions, Mother Jones again affirmed her intent to urge Roosevelt to seek passage of a national child labor statute. "We want him to hear the wail of the children who never have a chance to go to school but work from 10 to 12 hours a day in the textile mills of Philadelphia, weaving the carpets he and you walk on." She said that "fifty years ago there was a cry against slavery and the men of the North gave up their lives to stop the selling of black children on the block. Today the white child is sold for $2 a week. . . . he might die at his tasks and the manufacturer with the automobile and the yacht and the daughter who talks French to a poodle dog" should be made to stop such industrial peonage.[32] Mother Jones said she saw Congress pass three railroad bills in one hour during the previous winter. But "when labor cries for the little ones they turn their back and will not listen to her. I asked a man in prison once how he happened to get there. He had stolen a pair of shoes. I told him if he had stolen a railroad he could be a United States Senator."[33]

The marchers spent two days at Coney Island, sleeping in a loft. Early Monday, July 27, the group, equipped with an elephant loaned to them by the animal show, set out to persuade United States Senator Thomas C. Platt to arrange an audience with the president. Reaching the Oriental Hotel in Manhattan Beach, Mother Jones strode toward Platt's office. But the senator already was on an interurban car preparing to leave. He soon did, despite a brief interruption when the elephant sat on the railroad tracks. Although Mother Jones did not get to see Platt, she took revenge by ordering breakfast for the marchers and charging it to the senator's bill.[34] Afterward, about half of the remaining marchers were given carfare back to Philadelphia. Mother Jones retained three boys, the band, some union men, and their wives. Throughout the march, the press had reported that the president's aides were nervous about the "invasion." Mother Jones would be courteously received, they said, through regular channels, but a demonstration would not be appreciated.[35]

On Wednesday, July 29, a party of six—including the three youngsters from the mills—arrived at Oyster Bay. The Secret Service would not allow them through the gates. Roosevelt's secretary told them that the president had no authority to act on child-labor matters and suggested that Mother Jones submit her comments to the president in writing. The group then returned quickly to New York City. Collared by the press, the disappointed Mother Jones first tried to conceal her identity. Then she said she would write to Roosevelt again, "but I do not care to say just now whether or not I will go to Oyster Bay again." She also reportedly pledged to keep "my army" in the area until "by its very numbers" it would force the president to act.[36] Her voice surely must have lacked its usual sense of confidence.

The marchers, apparently numbering not many more than 20 by now, did stay in New York for a few more days. Mother Jones received an answer to her second letter. That reply, from the president's secretary, said that while Roosevelt sympathized with her cause, neither he nor Congress could help. The states alone, he said, had that power. The marchers then returned to Philadelphia by train.[37] Of the bellicose Roosevelt, Mother Jones would reminisce: "He is a brave guy when he wants to take a gun out and fight other grown people, but when those children went to him he could not see them." Her dislike for him, which had begun with the anthracite strike, would grow and endure.[38]

Mother Jones did not, as she had threatened, march to Washington and continue to protest there until federal action was forthcoming. Her proposed "congress" of 2,000 "child slaves" never assembled in the capital for parades and the presenting of petitions. Mother Jones, who was said to have "aged perceptibly" during the march, soon would be distracted from any further child-labor extravaganzas even if she desired them, which is doubtful.[39] The Philadelphia textile strike, too, was lost. But the "children's crusade" did, if often in a sporadic and contradictory manner, achieve the renown it sought. As the mine workers' *Journal* noted, "The New York press, and indeed the press of the whole country, has given the child labor problem columns where they would not otherwise have devoted lines to this [s]ubject." Editorial comment, too, was largely favorable, and huge crowds along the route underscored the popularity, or infamy, of the "army's" commander-in-chief.[40]

Mother Jones uncommon patience and persistence may have diluted the wrath usually reserved for those who march to protest their condition. Indeed, it was rare for her to cooperate with police who challenged her right to speak at a given location. She kept the march nonviolent and thus made official fears seem overdrawn. The incendiary utterances for which she was most known were notably absent on this trip. She refused to accept nonstrikers into the ranks. And she retreated in dignity when it became clear the march had not accomplished its announced aims. All of this was not the Mother Jones of legend and often of fact. But her remarkable restraint did contribute to the limited success of the march by not alienating the public.

No federal panacea was born of the march. There would be a White House Conference on Children and Youth in 1909 and other executive actions which, at least, signified a growing awareness of the problem.

But an effective federal child-labor law would not be passed and declared constitutional until 1941. However, a number of states—including Pennsylvania, New York, and New Jersey—did enact stricter laws within a few years after the march. The pressures for reform came from the AFL, the Progressives, and perhaps in smaller part from the march of the mill children. The march also is said to have "unquestionably" assisted settlement-house workers who advocated welfare measures to keep families together.[41] But it also seemed clear that better pay and working conditions were needed if parents were not to be forced to prostitute their children. This was the call to which Mother Jones soon returned.

SIX

COLORADO and West Virginia came to be Mother Jones's two
stepdaughters of misery. A half continent apart and despite
obvious dissimilarities, they shared the commonality of coal and greed,
of toil and despair. The techniques of violence, too, would prove to be
exportable. Soon after the textile march Mother Jones visited Eugene
Debs's home in Terre Haute, Indiana. Then she was back in West Virginia for a time before heading to a miners' memorial service for the
Virden martyrs in Mt. Olive, Illinois. Enroute, she stopped by the UMW
national headquarters in Indianapolis where she found a new task
awaiting her. President John Mitchell sent the seventy-three-year-old
national organizer to reconnoiter Colorado where a recent unionizing
campaign had given birth—perhaps prematurely, Mitchell thought—to
talk of a strike.[2]

With about 11,000 miners then in the state and roughly 15 percent
of them organized, the UMW had begun a renewed organizing effort
in the spring of 1903. Most of the union's members were in the northern
field, largely Boulder County, while Huerfano and Las Animas Counties, in the more productive southern field, were almost devoid of unionism and conditions there smacked of feudal West Virginia.[3] The griev-

58

ances of the miners over pay, hours, and working conditions further were inflamed by the state's stance on an eight-hour-day law. In 1899, the Colorado legislature passed such a bill, copied almost verbatim from a Utah statute which that state's highest court and the United States Supreme Court had upheld. But the Colorado Supreme Court ruled the act unconstitutional.

Having worked with the metalliferous Western Federation of Miners (WFM) on the issue since 1894, the UMW helped whip up enough public support in 1902 to pass a referendum which required the legislature to amend the constitution and then enact an eight-hour law. But the following year, when the lawmakers convened to do just that, an intensive lobbying effort by industry got the mandate stalled, then abandoned.[4] "Rarely, indeed, has there been in this country a more brazen, conscienceless defeat of the will of the people, plainly expressed, not only at the ballot box, but by the pledges of both parties," muckraker Ray Stannard Baker wrote. "And the great corporations of Colorado continued smugly with their nine, ten, and twelve hour days—earning a little more profit."[5]

Colorado, plagued by 13 mining strikes in the years 1880 to 1904, would reel most under the strikes of metal and coal miners in 1903 and 1904. In August 1903 a "manifesto" to the governor and the public spelled out the coal miners' grievances, which were aggravated, especially in the southern field, by the refusal of the mine operators to meet with the union. In September, UMW District 15 in Colorado called a convention to formulate demands and consider strike action.[6] The latter suggestion worried John Mitchell. Essentially a conciliatory man, his ideas ran counter to those of the much more militant, but far smaller WFM, which also had—over Mitchell's objections—some coal miners. Jurisdictional problems had sprung up between the WFM and the UMW. There also was conflict over the transfer of men from one union to the other.

Formed in 1893, the WFM made spectacular early gains, such as winning the eight-hour day for its gold miners and mill workers within a year. But the thrust of the Socialist-dominated WFM was contrary to the UMW's capitalist orientation and to Mitchell's whole idea of conservative advance. This rivalry was not masked. WFM President Charles Moyer, promising "a complete revolution of the present system of industrial slavery," remarked in 1903 that "John Mitchell need not be surprised should his membership turn their faces to the West, seeking affiliation with organizations which have sent out their message to the world, that as labor produces all the wealth, such wealth belongs to the producer thereof."[7]

Back in February 1903 some 75 WFM smelters had left their jobs in Colorado City in a dispute over pay and the firing of union activists. Pickets were thrown up at other mills, and, despite few acts of violence, the national guard was brought in. There were some temporary truces, but, in August, the WFM called out all its miners in the Teller County area to drive the strike on to a successful conclusion. It soon would develop into one of the state's bloodiest, most disgraceful disputes. UMW's leadership, meanwhile, was cautious about appearing to be in concert with the metal miners.[8]

It was into such a maelstrom of motives that Mother Jones entered in late October 1903, her temperament making her a dubious candidate for the mantle of impartiality. She arrived "unannounced and unattended" in Trinidad in southern Colorado on October 26. She registered at the Coronado Hotel as "M. Jones, Chicago." Then she went into semiseclusion, despite great curiosity which sent swarms of people—including mine owners and deputies—to the hotel to look at the guest register.

After first having talked to WFM strike leaders, Mother Jones disguised herself as a peddler to gain unheralded access to the homes of the miners. Observing and listening, she deduced, not surprisingly, that they "were in practical slavery to the company." In fact, she said, conditions were worse than in Pennsylvania. Although the Coloradans earned more, their net earnings were less. There were discharges for not buying at the company store, she found, plus wage deductions for medical and other services. Even the saloons had to pay a "royalty" to the coal company to operate. Company houses were subject to search, and company guards were cruel. Deciding the "time was ripe for revolt against such brutal conditions," Mother Jones returned to Indianapolis with a recommendation for a strike.[9]

As sometimes was the case, her opinion was not what the national UMW office wanted to hear. Leaders there questioned if the district organization was fully prepared for a strike. A committee from headquarters was said to have investigated the Colorado situation earlier and found little sympathy with either organizing or a strike, and District 15 may have encouraged Mother Jones's militant conclusions. In any event, Mitchell asked the operators for a meeting.[10] After being told by the companies that the UMW did not represent their employees, the national executive board acceded to the prostrike fervor. The walkout was set to begin November 9, 1903. Thus, six months after the first WFM workers left their jobs, the state's mining industry—metal and coal—was strikebound.[11]

The situation soon shifted. By November 21, northern Colorado's coal miners were gathering at the town of Louisville to consider an early offer which largely met their demands. A week earlier they had turned down an offer of a 15-percent wage increase and an eight-hour day conditioned upon a similar concession in the south. But now, the northern operators waived the condition, and the northern miners were expected to approve an agreement.[12] But Mother Jones feared the settlement would weaken the southern strike. She and William Howells, president of District 15, arrived at the Louisville meeting to recommend against what they considered betrayal of the southern miners. This flew in the face of national UMW leaders who urged acceptance of the northern offer. Rejection of the offer would sour public opinion against the miners, they said, and a coal famine would work its worst hardship on the poor. Furthermore, an influx of strikebreakers already meant that the southern strike was in some jeopardy, Mitchell's representatives reasoned.[13] After Howells spoke against a settlement, there were loud calls for Mother Jones. She "was not slow coming to the front of the stage," the *Denver Post* reported, and she "had victory in her deep, black eyes and there was a vigor about her step which boded no good for the friends of an acceptance of the operators' terms." Her speech began calmly and with humor, but soon became an exhortation of "fervid eloquence."[14]

Although Mitchell sent a telegram to the meeting endorsing a settlement, Mother Jones told the men that a "general cannot give orders unless he is in the field; unless he is at the battleground." Then she turned to the miners themselves.

Are you brave men? Can you fight as well as you can work? I had rather fall fighting than working. If you go back to work here and your brothers fall in the south, you will be responsible for their defeat. . . .

I don't know what you will do, but I know very well what I would do if I were in one of your places. I would stand or fall with this question of eight hours for every worker in every mine in Colorado. I would say we will all go to glory together or we will die and go down together. We must stand together; if we don't there will be no victory for any of us.[15]

"The effect she produced upon the men was instantaneously electrical, and her voice seemed talismanic," the press reported. Mother Jones also announced she was leaving to aid the strikers of the rival WFM in the Cripple Creek area. "I am not afraid to be classed as a friend of [that] organization, and all criticism of me on that account falls flat upon my ears," she said.[16] Prolonged applause greeted the conclusion of her remarks, and many of the miners rose to honor her. Although John F. Ream, Mitchell's representative, tried to counter Mother Jones's speech, her fervent address had struck the mark. The northern miners voted 228 to 165 to defy John Mitchell and stay on strike.[17] Mother Jones's passion was contagious but its fever was short-lived. The rejection of the attractive offer angered and stunned many northern miners. Soon there was a motion to reconsider, and on November 28, the miners, by a vote of 483 to 130, accepted the operators' terms, vindicated their national leaders, and agreed to return to work on November 30.[18]

Mother Jones was furious at the acceptance of the settlement which she said "created practical peonage" for those still on strike. Roughly a year later, the southern strike would be lost at great expense, and for ending the northern walkout early, Mother Jones never forgave Mitchell. The southern miners "went out on the bleak mountain sides, lived in tents through a horrible winter with eighteen inches of snow on the ground," she later wrote. "They tied their feet in gunny sacks and lived lean and lank and hungry as timber wolves. They received sixty-three cents a week strike benefit while John Mitchell went traveling through Europe, staying at fashionable hotels, studying the labor movement."[19]

Self-indulgence was abhorred by Mother Jones. A conservative acquaintance once took her to a Madison Square Garden horse show. As he escorted her through the box-seat area, she stared with amazement and disgust at the women in gold dresses and the men decked out in top hats and cutaway coats. When told that the necklace on one woman was worth $150,000, Mother Jones retorted that with such a sum she could buy warm coats and decent shoes for all the miners' wives in West Virginia and Pennsylvania. Not being able to stand such display for long, she walked out. Two blocks away, she watched with interest where poor children queued up at a bakery to receive stale loaves of bread.[20]

Union leaders, she believed, should try to live as do those they seek to help. Her sense of sacrifice, however, was rarely matched. Her relationship with Mitchell was not helped when, a year or so earlier, she reportedly tore up a rank-and-file petition which would have assessed the miners to buy Mitchell a $10,000 house.[21] The schism with Mitchell probably was for Mother Jones more the rule than the exception in her stormy relationship with organizations. She was dubious of all institutions and skeptical of good will unaccompanied by swift action. Hers was a mind radically different from that of the typical leader who rose through the ranks by diplomacy and calculated caution.

Mitchell was conservative in attitude. He was more willing to accept arbitration and more scornful of radicalism and violence than was Mother Jones. Also unlike her, he possessed an almost diffident manner. His strengths were his patience, conciliatory attitude, and inclination to compromise on all but what he felt were the critical issues.[22] Mother Jones, on the other hand, acted as if she felt workers were entitled to natural rights, not just concessions from management. Her temperament was that of the mob leader. Her identification was with the oppressed. Her weapons were physical courage, endurance, and an awesome eloquence. She would rather have starved than supped on half a loaf. Mitchell was more tolerant of her than she was of him. Mother Jones had shown open disfavor with his policies before, especially in the way he ended the anthracite strike a year earlier. While not always agreeing with her methods, Mitchell "recognized her influence and ability as an agitator," his biographer wrote, "and kept her in the field. He had a capacity for appreciating people who were unlike him, enjoying the hearty Falstaffian mirth . . . admiring daredevils like Mother Jones."[23]

Even Mother Jones was an erratic grudge-carrier. A correspondent of Mitchell's wrote him that Mother Jones, when speaking at a Socialist gathering in Kansas, called the UMW president "a traitor, a coward, and a seller out" and became enraged at any who challenged this description.[24] But in a letter that same year to John Walker, she said of Mitchell: *"I want to say right here,* I may never see him again, but one thing one thing [*sic*] certain I will fight to death for him against any false assertion. I know the labor movement; I know the philosophy of the *monster capitalism.* Sometimes a man or women [*sic*] are to be

carried away by the glitter of the tinsel. I *for one shall be his defender."*
She added that not Mitchell but other national officers were the targets
of her rancor in Colorado. "John Mitchell can always depend on me,"
she wrote, "I know whatever mistakes he has made, he is right at
heart."[25] Walker and Mitchell were close friends. But the lessons of the
northern Colorado experience were not lost on Mother Jones, either.
"From the day I opposed John Mitchell's authority, the guns were
turned on me," she would later write. "Slander and persecution followed
me like black shadows." At times she believed Mitchell conspired with
Colorado Governor James H. Peabody to drive her from the state.[26]

Soon after the northern miners had settled, the level of violence rose
in the south. The two largest coal operators there, Colorado Fuel and
Iron Company and the Victor Fuel Company, were controlled by the
Rockefeller and Gould interests. In addition to the problems posed by
such large opponents, the union also had to contend with the fact that
many of the southern miners, unlike those in northern Colorado and
West Virginia, were Slavs, Austrians, and Italians.[27] In December 1903
John Mitchell, traveled to Denver to consult, without satisfaction, with
Governor Peabody. Meanwhile, Mother Jones returned to the southern
strike area and also visited the increasingly violent WFM battle in the
Cripple Creek area of Teller County. But her peripatetic campaign was
proving debilitating. By the end of January 1904 she was in a Trinidad
hospital, having narrowly escaped "the fatal pneumonia." Bertha Mailly,
wife of the national secretary of the Socialist Party, wrote from Trinidad
glowing accounts of Mother Jones's work. But, she noted: "These days
men in Trinidad are asking on every hand, 'How is Mother Jones?' or
from the poor Italian, 'Mr. Mudder Jones, she well?' "[28]

Well again she soon was. She addressed the striking UMW miners
in Trinidad on March 24, the day after the national guard arrived there.
The next night she was gotten out of bed by a military messenger and
taken to militia headquarters. There she was told she was to be deported, and on March 26, Mother Jones and three other organizers and
sympathizers were put on a Santa Fe train for La Junta, Colorado,
about 65 miles northeast of Trinidad. The deportees were told never
to return.[29] Still holding a note banning her from the state, Mother Jones
enlisted the help of a friendly railroad conductor in La Junta who put
her aboard a northbound train for Denver. Arriving there she got a
hotel room and wrote a letter to the governor. "I wish to notify you,

governor, that you don't own the state. . . . I am right here in the capital, after being out nine or ten hours, four or five blocks from your office. I want to ask you, governor, what in Hell are you going to do about it?"[30]

The governor apparently did nothing at this time, and in early April, Mother Jones went down the western slope of the Rocky Mountains and held a series of meetings. "I have been on the go ever since I was driven out of Trinidad, the history of which you know," she wrote to John Mitchell on April 16. "The next thing the [illegible] cannibals will do will be to kill me. That's all they have left undone."[31] About mid-April, she arrived in Helper in northeastern Utah where she lived with an Italian miner's family. Since the mayor forbade her to speak in the Carbon County town, she addressed evicted coal miners in a no-man's-land where a tent colony had sprung up. She urged them to be peaceful but to persist in their strike. "This nation was founded on a strike. . . . Washington struck against King George, and we will strike against King Gould," she said.[32]

The next day Mother Jones was notified that she had been exposed to smallpox. Placed under quarantine, she was forbidden to hold meetings and was confined to "a frame shack." But it burned down "somehow that night," and Mother Jones went to live with another miner's family. Their house, too, was placed under quarantine. Soon a force of mine guards raided the tent colony, arresting some 120 persons for breaking quarantine. Some of the striking UMW members fled to the hills with their rifles. Others were caught, "packed in a box car and run down to Price, the county seat, and put in jail," Mother Jones recalled. "Not one law had these miners broken. The pitiful screams of the women and children would have penetrated Heaven."[33] Mother Jones was kept under virtual house arrest. One night a company detective broke into her room and demanded $3,000, backing up the demand with a gun. "He pressed the gun into my throat," Mother Jones said, "and I thought my time had come." But, finally, she convinced him that she was not the custodian of the strike fund.[34]

An attempt at a resistance meeting on April 27 failed, and the following day, Mother Jones was called to Indianapolis by John Mitchell. Although she claimed to have been held captive under the guise of quarantine for 26 days in Helper, it appears she was not in Utah for that length of time. It is not clear if she did make it to Indianapolis, but she at least reached Salt Lake City and then appeared later in Trinidad.[35] Meanwhile, Mitchell was trying to persuade President Theodore Roosevelt to intervene in southern Colorado. The president did send a team of investigators to the area, but they reported no justification for federation intervention. "Roosevelt went out to hunt four-legged bears," Mother Jones would comment, "but when the two-legged bears were driving men, women and children from their homes, he had nothing to say."[36]

After backing the embattled northern miners for seven months, the national UMW declared that after July 1 no further funds would be available from Indianapolis. "Close inquiry satisfied us," one national board member said, "that the mines were being operated with reasonable success and there was no possibility of winning the strike."[37] The walkout ended, as it had begun, in bitterness. Some 8,000 miners had struck, but only 2,500 were still on strike in April. Others had left the area or gone back to the mines. UMW's national leaders, who had expended $437,000 on the Colorado strikes, blamed the southerners for not realizing earlier that they were being defeated. District 15 claimed it had not been given full support.[38] Although Mitchell had saved the northerners from hardship, the union still was not officially recognized there. In the larger southern field, the company policies which had fomented the unrest remained largely unchanged. This was a festering situation which would, within a decade, explode with dreadful violence. Until October 1904 District 15 continued the southern strike, then surrendered that area less organized than before.

The Cripple Creek strike of the WFM's metal miners, with whom Mother Jones shared her time and certainly her allegiance, ended in abject defeat. Many of the miners never had been strongly sympathetic to the walkout, and desertions had begun quickly. Dynamiting and shootings led to the death of at least 33 persons and bred antiunion mobs which, protected by the militia, attacked WFM's leaders and property. Hundreds had to flee or face deportation, and the national guard made a mockery of civil law. WFM saw eight locals destroyed in the Cripple Creek area, and with them went the WFM's power in Colorado.[39]

In August, Mother Jones was in New York City promoting *Unionism or Socialism,* a pamphlet by Eugene Debs which urged unions to become revolutionary and align with the Socialist Party. During one successful sales pitch to the Central Federated Union, Mother Jones said "there is a danger line" and when the oppressors exceed it, "the French Revolution will be repeated." In Colorado, she said, President Roosevelt "was called on twice to interfere, but the poor fellow said in a helpless way that he could do nothing." But "when the mine operators began to disobey the law and got into a conflict with the miners he soon sent troops against the miners." She also bragged that it took six militiamen "to get me, a woman of 65, and put me on a train to get out of the country."[40]

She was, of course, seventy-four years of age by her own manner of reckoning and, in addition, federal troops were not sent into the Colorado strike. Mother Jones's aversion to ages, dates, full names, and sometimes facts never left her. Twenty years later in writing her autobiography, she would misplace events by as much as 10 or 15 years, omit unfavorable episodes, and slant others. She was then, as throughout her whole career, a woman with abilities more akin to histrionics than history, more inclined to view the past as a passion than as a photograph. But if her memory was erratic, she rarely failed to recall what she said was Mitchell's culpability for the 1903 failure. "You ask why the miners did not win. First the generals in charge of the field of battle were not accustomed to deal with great industrial conflicts. Their mental ability was not trained in that line," Mother Jones wrote in a retrospective on the strike. "Some of them could tell you about benevolent feudalism, all about Herbert Spencer, but they had no grasp of the weak points of the enemy," she claimed. "In fact, they remained in their rooms and were not out in the field watching the pirates. . . . I felt then, and have not yet changed my mind, those who were instrumental in settling the strike in the Northern fields were responsible for the defeat of the miners in the Southern fields."[41]

Mother Jones and John Mitchell never again would have a friendship such as that they enjoyed prior to the 1902 anthracite strike. After the Colorado strike, Mother Jones resigned from the UMW for a time to work for the Socialist Party. Simultaneously, she moved closer, through the Colorado experience, to the WFM and to the soon-to-be-heard Industrial Workers of the World. Although estranged from the UMW, she pledged to "fight the cause of the miners anyway, whether I am directly in their service or not." She was leaving, she wrote to a friend, with her eyes wide open. "You know the Socialist Party has never in its history given me five cents. I am going out for the cause to wake the people up," she wrote, "and I can be more independent as I am. There is no man in the world that I will I will [*sic*] approach for a job." Besides, she added, "The boys of the W.F. of Miners will see that I am not hungry, if the time ever comes; and what if it does?"[42]

Something of a wild card in the continuing rivalry between the two miners' unions, Mother Jones would find her name invoked by each side. At the 1905 UMW convention, for example, her conflict with John Mitchell was resurrected. Robert Randell, a Wyoming miner from District 15's northern area, exhumed the charges that Mitchell forced the northern miners back to work against the wishes of the rank-and-file. Randell suggested that Mitchell succumbed to pressure from the coal companies and from the Denver Citizens Alliance, an antiunion businessmen's group, to call off the northern strike despite prospects of imminent victory. Mitchell, whom Randell called "the little tin labor god of the capitalist class" and "a traitor," also was said to have persecuted and driven Mother Jones from the union because she refused to betray the southern miners.[43]

"Mother Jones' dear, white head will soon be laid at rest; her voice will soon be hushed," Randell said. "Her heart, that beat so warmly for suffering humanity will be still in death. When she is laid in the grave no one can say she ever played false to the toiling and suffering masses."[44] Randell's eulogy was highly premature. And his facts, Mitchell and other national officers rebutted, were inaccurate. Strikebreakers and ineptitude at the district level contributed to the southern defeat, despite generous financial aid and encouragement from the national office. Furthermore, said Mitchell, "Mother Jones and I worked hand in hand through some of the most stirring strikes this country has ever seen. For several years Mother Jones has been paid a salary by this organization. It is true that when Mother Jones went to Northern Colorado she disregarded the advice given her, and it is true that I said she should not do it again, and that if she expected to be employed by us she must carry out the orders of the National Board and the national convention."[45]

But, Mitchell stressed, she was not fired or forced out of the UMW. In fact, despite her insubordination, he had appointed her again as a national organizer in April 1904, and she "would be in the employ of the organization now if she wanted to be."[46] Randell, who admitted also to working for the WFM, was given a chance by the convention to publicly retract his statement or be expelled from the convention and from the union. He did not retract his remarks, and he was expelled.[47] By that time, though, Mother Jones was meeting with leaders of a different breed, who, however briefly, would provide an outlet for her more radical nature.

SEVEN

O N the second day of January 1905, 34 radicals secretly gathered
in Chicago for an "Industrial Union Congress" which, for a time,
would change the face of American labor and politics. The conferees,
summoned by six socialists, radical labor leaders and journalists, included only one woman—Mother Jones. The invitations had asserted
"our confidence in the ability of the working class, if correctly organized
on both political and industrial lines, to take possession of and operate
successfully . . . the industries of our country."[2] For three days the
delegates met and drew up a manifesto—later circulated in several
languages—which criticized the AFL and claimed that because of the
"irrepressible conflict between the capitalist class and the working class,"
the need was for "one great industrial union embracing all industries—
providing for craft autonomy locally, industrial autonomy nationally,
and working class unity generally."[3]

By the start of the twentieth century, the AFL had given up any
attempt to restructure society. Under the leadership of Samuel Gompers,
its founder and longtime president, the federation merged its short- and
long-term aims into a single objective—"more." What the socialists,
anarchists, syndicalists, and trade unionists were seeking to do at the

70

Chicago meeting was in large part propelled by the AFL's abdication of the left. And what the radicals would do in the next decade and a half would make them the object of countless folk songs, not to mention epithets and lynchings.

At the January cabal, it was decided to meet again in Chicago in June with a broader group of representatives for what would come to be the constitutional convention of the Industrial Workers of the World (IWW). So it was that on June 27 that 186 delegates gathered in Brand's Hall, a rendezvous of the Chicago anarchists back in the Haymarket era. The delegates heard William ("Big Bill") Haywood thump a piece of wood on the lectern and address them as "Fellow Workers," shunning the "brother" salutation of the trade unionists and the "comrade" of the socialists. The "Continental Congress of the working class" had begun.[4]

On the speakers' platform near the huge, one-eyed Haywood was Mother Jones. Like Eugene Debs and unlike Haywood, who was WFM secretary-treasurer, Mother Jones was an individual delegate with only her own vote. It was assumed that the unattached delegates would become the cutting edge of the IWW.[5] In this, Mother Jones again would demonstrate her independence. Disparaging Gompers and the "American Separation of Labor," the convention delegates called for a radical departure from the racism and narrow craft unionism which they said discriminated against the unwhite and the unskilled. Amid "many tall glasses of beer, sent up from the saloon below," the delegates fought over credentials and made majestic pronouncements. But the IWW's slogan—"An Injury To One An Injury to All"—expressed its drive toward a single union to which every workingman could belong and which would match the leverage of the oligopolies.[6]

Such a colorful, forceful group of radicals probably has not met before or since. In addition to Debs, there was Socialist Labor Party leader Daniel DeLeon, a devastating orator and pamphleteer; Lucy Parsons, anarchist wife of Haymarket martyr Albert Parsons; and A. M. Simons, fiery editor of the *International Socialist Review*. Simons called the meeting "the beginning of the greatest battle in history. The proletariat of America stands ready," he said, "to grasp any weapon, the ballot, the strike, the boycott, and the bullet, if necessary."[7] Then there was Thomas Haggerty, big, bearded socialist ex-priest and proponent of industrial unionism; William Trautmann, a radical leader of the United

Brewery Workers; Mother Jones; and Haywood. Once described as "a bundle of primitive instincts," Haywood was a former cowboy who also had been a miner and homesteader. A western activist by temperament, he was, like his friend Mother Jones, a passionate orator with a fondness for direct action.

The delegates represented not only stable unions like the 27,000-member WFM but also largely "paper" organizations like the American Labor Union, formed by the WFM to bring the West's workers together in a single industrial union. Also represented at the meeting were such diverse groups as the Punch Press Operators union with 168 members and the UMW's Illinois district with is 50,000 members.[8]

In the shadow of the strong-willed, politically-adept organizers, Mother Jones took only a minor part in the 12-day-long course of business. She did vote for final adoption of the group's constitution, but her role and apparently her commitment ended there.[9] In her autobiography, her speeches, interviews, and letters, she did not mention her IWW link, and it appears she never had any connection with the "Wobblies," as they came to be called, after the two founding meetings. In fact, the IWW's biggest strikes—at Lawrence, Massachusetts, in 1912; Paterson, New Jersey, in 1914; and Minnesota's Mesabi Iron Range in 1916—saw Mother Jones elsewhere or, at the very most, in no more than a cameo role. It was as if she erased from memory her participation in one of American labor's most unusual and telling events—the founding of the IWW.

Until the end of World War I, during which the Wobblies were the object of almost incredible repression, the IWW reached out to the downtrodden and the unrepresented. It flourished despite hysteria-spawned reaction by business and resentment by craft unions. Supplanting of capitalism was its dream, and direct action became its method. IWW came to represent especially the migratory worker in the lumber camps, construction sites, and farms of the West and the unorganized, often foreign-speaking, factory workers of the East. Organizing hundreds of thousands of workers and leading many successful strikes, the IWW in a short and stormy history brought a new, antinationalistic, anticapitalistic fervor to the labor movement. Unlike the AFL, it was revolutionary and sought to be a mass movement. Also unlike the AFL, it was centralized—similar to the later CIO—and aimed at having all workers in an industry belonging to the same union. Although its philosophy had great appeal, especially in the West, it never really developed into a major rival of the AFL, and its membership never exceeded 250,000. After the war—which crippled its leadership and dispersed its members—the IWW grew, but it was not the same militant organization. But the IWW did show that the unskilled could be welded into a fighting organization.[10]

It is curious but perhaps predictable that Mother Jones sidestepped the thrust of the IWW. Certainly she did so not out of fear. As events would have it, the years between the IWW's founding and America's entry into World War I would be her most perilous ones. She would face dungeons, bayonets, incensed governors, disease, and gunmen unflinchingly. Rather, her second thoughts about the IWW probably were two. For one thing, despite the illusion of an united front shown by IWW's diverse founders at the 1905 convention, they soon returned to hating one another. They had been disputants for years. Much in the tradition of American radicalism, they fought each other as much as they did the capitalist foe. The WFM would drop out in 1907, and cliques favoring political over economic action developed. Not until 1908–9 did the IWW overcome this friction and begin to win strikes and a substantial membership.[11] Mother Jones was forever faction-wary, and it was natural that IWW's early infighting would hold little lure for her.

Furthermore, she was not as radical as many of the Wobblies. She came to see them as spasmodic, often fanatic in their zeal, adjectives also applied to her by the more conservative. She recoiled from IWW extremism such as what she said was talk of wiping embattled Paterson off the map. "Strikes," she said, "can not be won without funds. To bring in a strike and go back licked by hunger is not progress for labor."[12] Mother Jones was an individualist. She had chafed under John Mitchell's guidance, and she would prove to be a notably nondoctrinaire socialist. Her strength of personality combined with a mind more given to theater than to theory made her, throughout her long career, an ideological butterfly. Despite the fact that she almost continually, especially after the Great War, chided the growing conservatism of labor leaders, she was herself a revolutionary only on impulse and not upon reflection.

But if the Wobbly conferences left no other imprint upon Mother Jones, they did strengthen her bonds with the WFM leaders. Haywood and WFM President Charles Moyer were in the IWW vanguard, and the union for a time became the mining arm of the Wobblies. As fate would have it, Haywood and Moyer soon were to be in the thoughts of union advocates everywhere, especially Mother Jones. In 1893, the WFM had been formed as a result of a bitter struggle in the Coeur d'Alene district of Idaho where gold discoveries had brought in hordes of fortune seekers a decade earlier. Vast deposits of lead and silver added to the area's importance as a mining center. After the first Coeur d'Alene battle, some operators abrogated contracts, reduced wages, and in general threatened the union, which in 1899 led another bloody strike in the lead mines after 17 union members were fired.

For a while the strike was peaceful. Then a ton and a half of dynamite reduced the huge smelting mill at the Bunker Hill and Sullivan Company to rubble, killing two men and causing some $250,000 damage. Governor Frank Steunenberg, a Populist elected largely by miners' votes, openly sided with the operators. He declared martial law and brought in troops who guarded strikebreakers, established "bullpens" for prisoners, and cracked down hard on the strikers. For two years the troops remained. Sniping, sieges, and starvation became common tactics. Nearly the whole male population of the district was imprisoned at some time during the strike and often subjected to indignities and atrocities. The strike eventually died out, but its legacy was bitter hatred and one of the century's most intriguing criminal trials.[13]

When in December 1905 a bomb exploded and killed Steunenberg as he opened the gate to his home in Caldwell, Idaho, the WFM naturally was suspect. On February 17, 1906, Haywood, Moyer, and George Pettibone, a blacklisted miner who had become a Denver businessman, were seized and taken secretly to Idaho on a special train. Their arrest and "kidnapping" kicked up a flurry of protest around the nation. After the prisoners arrived in Idaho, it was revealed that a man named Harry Orchard had confessed to the crime as well as to the murder of 17 other men, all on orders, he said, from the "inner circle" of the WFM. The confession was extracted by James McParlan, a Pinkerton agent whose fame had faded since his cracking of the Molly Maguires conspiracy in Pennsylvania in 1877.[14]

The year and a half from the arrest of the three WFM suspects until their acquittal saw rare unity among American labor, socialists, and radicals. Virtually every labor and leftist group in the country defended the trio and believed that Orchard had been promised freedom, or at least life in prison, if he implicated the metal miners' union. Money for a defense fund was solicited both by the WFM and the IWW and by Mother Jones, who began a vigorous cross-country tour and who was a premiere attraction in the fund-raising effort. From July to October 1906 she campaigned as well for Socialist office-seekers in Arkansas, Texas, and other western states. As the election neared, she also traveled to the 11th Congressional District of Pennsylvania where William B. Wilson, a friend and national secretary-treasurer of the UMW, was running.[15] Wilson, who had worked with Mother Jones in the Arnot area strike back in 1899, was elected and eventually became United States secretary of labor.

By the time the trial for conspiracy to murder Governor Steunenberg began on May 3, 1907, Mother Jones and others had contributed sufficiently so that Clarence Darrow, the nation's foremost trial lawyer and liberal, accepted the case in Boise. He had won labor's praise earlier for his defense of Debs in the Pullman strike case of 1894. Unionists generally believed the defendants were being tried in revenge for their Coeur d'Alene successes. Debs compared Haywood and Moyer to the Haymarket defendants, and he promised to seek a physical uprising, if necessary, to prevent their execution. "If they attempt to murder Moyer, Haywood and their brothers," Debs wrote, "a million revolutionists at least will meet them with guns."[16]

President Theodore Roosevelt won particular ignominy by labeling Haywood, Moyer, and Pettibone, as well as Debs and others as "undesirable citizens" in a private letter. Mother Jones, writing to Terence Powderly a few weeks after the trial began, thanked him for the "manly and fearless steps you have taken in defense of our brave boys in Idaho.

"It is needless for me to say to you, that capitalism has no soul, nor no love for humanity or its sufferings, and those who take up the battle for the oppressed, must bear the penalty.

"How the spectacular performer in Washington has put his foot in it. The word 'undesirable citizen' will go down in history. He and his crew of pirates would no doubt give a great deal to undo that," Mother Jones wrote.[17]

Although she flitted to the copper mines of southern Arizona at one point, Mother Jones was a spectator at much of the Haywood trial.[18] The state, which included Senator William Borah among the prosecution attorneys, relied solely on Orchard's testimony and circumstantial evidence. But Darrow hammered away at the ridiculousness of convicting anyone upon the testimony of a confessed murderer of 18 men. He also claimed that Orchard had a personal grievance against Steunenberg because the governor's policies during the Coeur d'Alene strife forced Orchard to flee, thus losing his one-sixteenth interest in a mine later found to contain a rich ore vein.

After an eloquent 11-hour summation by Darrow, the jury deliberated 20 hours and found Haywood innocent. Pettibone soon was acquitted summarily, Moyer was never brought to trial, and Orchard received life imprisonment.[19] The freeing of the WFM suspects was a triumph for the workingman. But the trial also was a reminder of the proportions of the class struggle and its dangers. For Mother Jones, the period marked something of a high point in her affinity with the Socialists.

Between 1904 and 1911, she came the closest to being a Socialist functionary in the absence of any major, drawnout strike such as those in which she participated—to the virtual exclusion of politics—just before and following this era. It was during this period that she spoke most frequently of the irrepressibility of the class struggle and the need for an alternative to capitalism. Yet, she had earlier Socialist roots. In fact, she had been an active participant in the founding of the Social Democratic Party, a forerunner of the Socialist Party of America.

In June 1897 Debs's American Railway Union, broke and defeated, closed its affairs and launched the Social Democracy of America. Its platform included government ownership of all transportation and communication as well as mines and minerals. It also sought a shortening of hours, relief for the unemployed, and proportional representation. Among the delegates in Uhlich Hall in Chicago were Mother Jones and Lucy Parsons. But the unity of that convention, which adjourned with the singing of the "Marseillaise," was to be shattered over an issue on which Mother Jones had some insight—the cooperative colony.

When the delegates—again including Mother Jones—reconvened in 1898, they split over a scheme whereby the members would settle gradually in one of the sparsely populated western states and then capture political control. The colonizationists won a platform fight, and the other Socialists, including Debs and Mother Jones, bolted the convention. Meeting nearby in the same room where the Haymarket jury reached its verdict, the rump session of about 30 delegates, who favored political action instead of the cooperative effort, formed the Social Democratic Party.[20] In the next few years, the party saw a gain in membership and even the election of some local officers in Milwaukee and in Haverhill, Massachusetts. It began to outstrip the Socialist Labor Party, and, in 1901, uniting with several splinter groups, it formed the Socialist Party of America.[21]

Mother Jones courted socialist ideas all her life, and the Socialists welcomed her. But, save for brief periods, she shunned formal association with the Socialist Party, much as she remained aloof from the IWW after having helped found it. In essence, she was a socialist, but not a Socialist. She was an individual believer in collectivism. Mother Jones wrote several articles for the early issues of the *International Socialist Review,* which was founded along with the Socialist Party about the turn of the century and which featured pieces by Carl Sandburg, Jack London, Big Bill Haywood, and others. Mother Jones made many speeches before Socialist groups, and she distributed a great deal of Socialist literature. She usually aligned herself more on the Socialist side of issues than with middle-of-the road labor. And her pronouncements on the class struggle won for her from Debs the sobriquet of the "unique old agitator" whose "very name expresses the Spirit of the Revolution."[22]

Yet she sometimes went to great lengths to deride the Socialists. In her public statements, she rarely mentioned her many Socialist friends or her fleeting leftist affiliations. Often in interviews she referred to the Socialists as weeping sentimentalists shielded from "the screams and groans and heartaches of women and children" by their own doctrinal squabbles.[23] This did not deter Mother Jones, of course, from urging Congressional investigators to nationalize the mines and the transportation industry. It did not stop her from extolling at length some collectivist experiments or writing for leftist publications. Her public stance, furthermore, did not diminish her fondness for the Socialist-led WFM or from working most closely with the UMW's Illinois district, its largest and most radical.

This disparity between her private acts and public image in politics is one of Mother Jones's most enduring paradoxes. But it may not have been motivated as much by deceit as by her own gut inclination toward socialism combined with a realization of her own failings as a theorist. As a rule, the Socialist miners tended to be bright, self-educated immigrants with whom she readily identified. To her the uplifting aspects of socialism, its moral tone, may have appealed to her more than did the fine points of its economics. "I have always advised men to read. All my life I have told them to study the works of those great authors who have been interested in making this world a happier place for those who do its drudgery," Mother Jones explained. Her own favorite books were Voltaire's *Candide* and those by Victor Hugo and Thomas Paine.[24]

In selling the socialist book, *Merrie England* by Robert Blatchford, she would implore: "Instead of going to the pool and gambling rooms, go up to the mountain and read this book. Sit under the trees, listen to the birds and take a lesson from those little feathered creatures who do not exploit one another, nor betray one another, nor put their little ones to work digging worms before their time. You will hear them sing while they work. The best you can do is swear and smoke."[25] That is pure Jonesian: a vague utopian blend of natural law, original sin, and the work ethic. Not for her the thicket of unearned income or whether to recognize postrevolutionary Russia. Not for her the intraparty power struggles, the necessary tedium of organizational details, or the obligatory support of endorsed candidates. While simultaneously embracing and rejecting Socialism, Mother Jones's actions never deviated. She was a trade unionist. Her concerns, thus, were directly with the workers' problems: the hours of his toil, the tyranny of the company store, the dearth of pleasure, and the stark imperatives of housing and of hunger.

"I live in the United States," Mother Jones enjoyed telling Congressional investigators. "But I do not know exactly where. . . . My address is like my shoes: it travels with me."[26] From 1905 to 1911, she was at her peripatetic best, zigzagging across the nation in pursuit of frays to join. She found many, ranging from minor strikes to ill-fated fund-raisers to disputes of international scope. In all of them, her reputation preceded her and sometimes blossomed in her wake.

In April 1905 after her work in Colorado and between the IWW meetings, Mother Jones ventured into a territory new to her—Upper Michigan's copper country. Copper production began there in 1845, and the WFM's organizing campaign got under way in 1904. But the union had not yet gotten a foothold, and Mother Jones's influence, it was hoped, would give impetus to the unionizing drive as well as to a strike by employees of the Houghton County Street Railway Company. In fact, after one of her addresses to a band of strikers at Larium, three streetcars were stoned.[27]

At Lake Linden, on April 16, Mother Jones ridiculed the "poor, contemptible lap dogs, miserable curs" of men who work 13 hours a day without complaining. A speech to the miners two days later at Red Jacket was described by the nearby Calumet press as "pyrotechnic, enthusiastic, spectacular." But the paper then added that the talk "was not appealing and contained nothing that would make one wish to see the conditions changed that have prevailed in Michigan copper country for half a century."[28]

The seventy-five-year-old agitator in her Red Jacket address paid tribute to the WFM and to the women of the copper miners. But again she saved the sharpest scorn for the men themselves. "How a woman can degrade herself by marrying a measly man who does not dare to join a union is beyond my comprehension," she declared. "You say you cannot join the union because you would lose your job. Poor, dreamy wretch. You never owned a job for those who own the machinery own the job and you have got to get permission to earn your bread and butter.

"You can change masters, it is true," she said, "but you have to hunt your master for that job you call yours."[29]

Two weeks of Mother Jones's cajoling to the contrary, unionism did not gain strength in the copper country until 1908.[30] By 1913, the polyglot miners would rebel against their conditions, Mother Jones would return, and the nation's conscience would be stung.

Bitter strikes and startling antiunion repression brought Mother Jones to the Arizona copper mines several times in the decade just prior to World War I. In May 1907, during the Haywood trial, she first journeyed to southern Arizona, and, as she wrote Terence Powderly from Bisbee, she was "fighting the common enemy as best I know how."[31] But her work in the Arizona Territory also led to her involvement in the insurgency against entrenched Mexican President Porfirio Díaz, who had ruled since 1884. While Mother Jones was speaking to smelter workers June 30 on the streets of Douglas, Arizona, a few blocks away occurred what one historian came to call the "most notable case of refugee kidnapping on record."[32]

Manuel Sarabia, a leader of the Organizing Junta of the Liberal Party, was arrested by American authorities in Douglas. Then he was taken to the border where Mexican police led him on a five-day mule-back journey to the Hermosillo, Sonora, jail.[33] But Sarabia, who had been working incognito as a printer in Douglas before a Mexican consul spotted him, managed to yell out his name as he was forced into a car. Mother Jones and others became enraged at what she called the "idea of any bloodthristy pirate on a throne reaching across these lines and crushing under his feet the Constitution which our forefathers fought and bled for."[34] Her anger spurred several years of efforts on behalf of Díaz opponents and won for her wide acclaim in postrevolutionary Mexico.

In the case of Sarabia, she engineered telegrams of protest to state and federal officials. "We got Teddy out of bed that night, I can tell you," she later recalled.[35] Then with the help of a friendly local news-paper, she set up a rally for the next day. "I told the audience that the kidnapping of Manuel Sarabia by Mexican police with the con-nivance of American authorities was an incident in the struggle for liberty. I put it strong," she said.[36] Mother Jones contended that large American corporations were behind the kidnapping, presumably to prevent the expropriation which might result if the Liberals got into power. As it turned out, the protests apparently had their effect. Eight days later, the young revolutionist was returned, although Mother Jones and others believed he would have been killed had his kidnapping gone undetected.[37]

The Liberal Junta, formed in 1900, had assumed a revolutionary character by 1906 under the leadership of Ricardo Flores Magón, an anarchist and charter member of the party. Magón and a small group of followers came to the United States in early 1904. But they met con-tinual harassment because General Díaz was popular for having ap-peared to have brought order to chaotic Mexico. The Liberals, failing in a beleaguered attempt to put out a newspaper, fled to Canada for a while and then in October 1906 launched an armed rebellion against Díaz. The effort was unsuccessful, and the insurgents, after eluding their would-be captors, regrouped in the Los Angeles area.[38]

Early in August 1907, however, their hiding place was found. Al-though there apparently were plans to kidnap Magón and his two prin-cipal comrades, Librado Rivera and Antonio Villarreal, they managed, like Sarabia, to kick up a commotion at the time of their arrest. They were taken to jail after receiving beatings from the Los Angeles police.

The charges against them eventually included resisting officers, murder, robbery, criminal libel, and conspiracy to violate neutrality laws.[39] The jailings, allegedly at the request of Díaz, led Gompers to intercede with the United States government to prevent the extradition of the Liberals. A defense movement of national scope sprung up among American labor unions.[40] When Mother Jones learned of the jailings, she felt the prisoners "were just like Kosciuszko, Carl Schurz, Kossuth, and Garibaldi, and men of that kind who received protection in our country from the tyrannical governments which they fled." Although she was "not in very good health," Mother Jones joined strenuously in the fund-raising effort.[41]

She was not optimistic that the revolutionaries would be freed. "But I still felt that probably through the efforts we were making, and the publicity we were giving it, they would not be turned over to be murdered."[42] After nearly two years in county jails, the trio was found guilty of conspiring to violate the neutrality laws. They were sentenced to 18 months in the prison at Florence, Arizona.[43] Through their long ordeal, Magón and his lieutenants had followed the efforts of Mother Jones and others to aid them. In November 1909 they wrote her from Florence. "You are setting a noble example and teaching a lesson humanity should not forget," they said. "You, an old woman, are fighting with indomitable courage; you, an American, are devoting your life to free Mexican slaves. And they will be freed in the near future, and they will learn to call you Mother."[44]

Mother Jones appealed on behalf of the Mexicans to the 1909 UMW convention. "We have got to get those boys out of jail," she implored. "We have got to let them live in this land; we have got to let them fight Mexico from here." The convention voted to donate $1,000 for the Mexicans' defense fund, and Mother Jones also raised $3,000 from other miners' groups.[45] In addition to receiving praise from the Mexicans, Mother Jones also claimed to have been offered "a beautiful piece of land in Mexico" in return for acting as an advocate for Antonio Villarreal, who sought a pardon in connection with a later arrest. He was pardoned, but Mother Jones turned down the reward, saying "I cannot accept compensation for doing a humane act for my fellow man."[46]

The persecution of the Liberals continued until June 1910, when Congressman William B. Wilson won a fight for a five-day hearing by the House Rules Committee. Mother Jones and John Kenneth Turner, author of the classic indictment of the Díaz regime, *Barbarous Mexico,* were among those who testified about American implication in the political kidnappings. After their release in the summer of 1910, Magón and his followers participated that fall in the revolution which had begun against Díaz. Although aligned with Francisco Madero's democratic upheaval, the Liberals had their own aims, which included capture of Baja California. They succeeded in taking Mexicali and Tijuana.[47] Madero assumed control when Díaz fled to Europe in mid-1911, and he headed off the Liberals' plans for Baja. However, Mother Jones's efforts against Díaz won her admiration in postrevolutionary Mexico among both factions.

Soon after his triumph, Madero granted wage-earners the right to organize, and in October 1911 Mother Jones went to Mexico City along with UMW Vice-President Frank Hayes and a WFM official. The three organizers were sent to consult on the question of the influx of Mexican miners into the American West. They met with President-elect Madero, who pledged to help them organize the Mexican miners.[48] Mother Jones, obviously impressed, wrote in *Appeal to Reason* that the opportunity was specifically afforded her. "This is the first time that any one has ever been granted that privilege in the history of the Mexican nation. . . . I am the first person who has been permitted to carry the banner of industrial freedom to the long suffering peons of this nation," she stated.[49]

But the offer perished with Madero's assassination and the turmoil which followed. Although Mother Jones was only one of a number of American who aided the young revolutionists and celebrated the insurgents' victory, she won amazing adulation. As at home, her age, her fervor, and her compassion won her a fond following, including a friendship with Pancho Villa. He would later seek to aid her when the tables were turned, and she would praise him, saying she wished "to God that we had two or three Villas in this country."[50] The call to organize the Mexican workers probably would not have worked out. Mother Jones knew not a word of Spanish, and soon she would have her energies taxed to the utmost in violent encounters in the United States. But she could reasonably claim that her actions did help call attention to questionable American acts in arresting Mexican refugees. Furthermore, her

Mexican ties would rebound to her delight and advantage a decade later.

After the Sarabia incident, Mother Jones left Arizona to work briefly on the Mesabi Range of Minnesota. One of the world's great ore-producing areas, the 70-mile crescent in northern Minnesota saw mining begin in 1892. More than 10,000 iron miners—many of them Finns—struck in July 1907 after a two-year organizing effort by the WFM.[51] Mother Jones, said to be representing the Socialist Party at this time, was among the principal agitators. As usual, she addressed fund-raising meetings and sought to bolster striker morale. But the effort in this first widespread Mesabi strike proved futile. Whole trainloads of southern and eastern European immigrants were brought in as strikebreakers. By mid-August, most of the mines were working again, despite a holdout by the socialist Finns.[52] Nine years later, a larger and more violent strike on the Mesabi would stir the nation. But, led as it was by the IWW, it would do without Mother Jones's presence.

Mother Jones helped organize women bottlers in the Milwaukee breweries in 1910 and made speeches to striking shirtwaist makers in New York and Philadelphia.[53] She shared labor's shock at the arrest and irregular extradition of John J. McNamara in connection with the *Los Angeles Times* bombing of 1910. McNamara, secretary treasurer of the International Association of Bridge and Structural Iron Workers, was held along with his brother and another man, although labor presumed them innocent. Defense funds sprung up, and Clarence Darrow once more was chosen as defense counsel. "The kidnapping of the McNamaras has established a dangerous precedent," Mother Jones observed. "The workers might get that habit and lay hold of Rockefeller or Morgan."[54] Mother Jones apparently was not as deeply involved in the McNamara's defense as she had been with that of Haywood and Moyer. But when the McNamaras confessed in December 1911, upon stipulation of prison terms rather than death sentences, labor was stunned, and in the public mind, labor was guilty along with them.[55]

Mother Jones's feud with John Mitchell escalated further in 1911 when she joined in a fierce attack on his membership in the National Civic Federation. Mitchell had resigned as UMW president in 1908 and taken a position as head of the federation's trade agreement department, which aimed at promoting collective bargaining. Formed in 1900, the federation sought to bring capital, labor, and the public together in an effort to maintain industrial peace. Samuel Gompers and Mark Hanna were the leaders of the movement, and an impressive roster of political, educational, and ecclesiastical officials were associated with the group.[56]

For some time the more radical elements in the UMW had attacked the federation as a device designed by capital to stifle any real change within the labor movement. Aided by internal politics, the UMW opposition burgeoned at the 1911 convention and was directed against Mitchell, the union's only member who was associated with the federation.

Mother Jones told the miners that the federation was "the biggest, grandest, most diabolical game ever played on labor." Until labor leaders pull out of the federation, she said, "labor never will progress; it cannot as long as they sit down and eat and drink and fill their stomachs and get their brains filled with champagne." Calling the federation "strictly a capitalist machine" and "a menace to the working movement," Mother Jones contributed to passage of a proposal requiring Mitchell to resign from either the union or the federation.[57]

Mitchell, who still held his UMW card from his Spring Valley, Illinois, local, quit the $10,000-a-year job with the federation. Ironically enough, he was at the time facing a nine-month contempt sentence for an action taken by an earlier UMW convention while he was president. Unemployed, Mitchell spent the next few years giving public lectures and holding minor government positions.[58] Also in 1911 Mother Jones spent much time in Westmoreland County, Pennsylvania, long an anti-union bastion, cheering up striking coal miners and their families.[59] Drawn away from the coal mines since the Colorado strike, she was in the years just ahead to compensate for her absence by a flurry of her most dramatic activities.

EIGHT

There sits the most dangerous woman in America.
She comes into a State where peace and prosperity
reign. She crooks her finger—20,000 contented men
lay down their tools and walk out.

—A West Virginia prosecutor[1]

PAINT and Cabin Creeks were the yin and yang of central West Virginia's Kanawha Valley in 1912. Eight miles apart and separated by a razorback ridge, the two streams each extended southward from the Kanawha River for some 25 miles. Through the coal-laden mountains, they carved narrow gorges, just wide enough in some spots for railroad tracks and a road. Thanks in part to Mother Jones, the Kanawha Valley—including the two creeks—had been unionized in the 1902 strike. But two years later, a brief strike by the Cabin Creek miners caused the union to lose all its organization there. Paint Creek remained a union bastion. But on Cabin Creek, the operators hired mine guards to prevent organizers from getting another foothold.[2] Along these two streams, the mines soon would spew out many of their 7,500 miners and in so doing mark the beginning of the state's worst coal war. Before there would be a truce, scores of men would die violently, a heavy economic loss would be incurred, and Mother Jones would fight—and be fought—fiercely.

The aged agitator, now eighty-two years old, was touring the West and the Pacific Northwest in 1912, aiding striking railway employees and addressing mass meetings. Returning to Denver by the first of June, she then went among the copper miners in Butte, Montana, prior to a scheduled speaking tour in San Francisco.[3] But then, labor news from West Virginia broke, as it did on and off for the next decade and a half, onto the front pages of the nation's newspapers. "Now the battle had to be fought all over again," she later wrote, so I "tied up all my possessions in a black shaw—I like traveling light—and went immediately to West Viriginia."[4] Prompting her urgency was a dispute which had been smouldering particularly since 1907 when coal-mine operators in the central competitive field—western Pennsylvania, Ohio, Indiana, and Illinois—reportedly offered financial aid to the UMW for organizing West Virginia. Forced to recognize the union as early as 1898, the central operators continued to face competition from the high-grade, cheaply dug West Virginia coal, especially after the opening of the rich Logan field in southern West Virginia in 1904. The state's coal production rose from 6,000,000 tons in 1888 to 70,000,000 by 1912, and 90 percent of that was sold in competition with the central field operators.[5]

A UMW contract with the Kanawha field operators expired April 1, 1912. When the mine owners refused to agree to improve upon the old contract, the miners struck on April 18 throughout the Kanawha district, except, of course, for nonunion Cabin Creek. For nearly a month the strike was conducted without violence. Soon, all strikebound operators came to terms except those on Paint Creek. They maintained that with unorganzied Cabin Creek so near, they could not afford to jeopardize further their competitive position.[6] With the battle lines narrowed to just Paint Creek, the operators there hired mine guards from the Baldwin-Felts Detective Agency in Bluefield. The first assignment of guards arrived May 7 and began bolstering the companies' defenses. Violence began in late May and escalated until, by July, miners and guards alternately were attacking one another in armylike battles. The threat of civil war gripped the state, and Mother Jones, who arrived about this time, did little to ease tensions. By the Fourth of July, she was reported "working night and day" encouraging the miners' resolve.[7] She also may have encouraged no little violence.

Addressing strikers in Charleston, she denounced Governor William E. Glasscock for not meeting with them. "You can expect no help from such a goddamned dirty coward," she reportedly told them, "whom, for modesty's sake, we shall call 'Crystal Peter.' But I warn this little Governor that unless he rids Paint Creek and Cabin Creek of these goddamned Baldwin-Felts mine-guard thugs, there is going to be one hell of a lot of bloodletting in this hills." On another occasion on Cabin Creek, Mother Jones is said to have held up a bloodsoaked coat discarded by a wounded mine guard and told the crowd: "This is the first time I ever saw a goddamned mine guard's coat decorated to suit me." Then she had the coat cut into pieces which she threw to the audience for lapel emblems.[8]

For weeks the carnage grew in pitch. More than once, the miners attacked Mucklow, five miles up Paint Creek, where the guards had built a fort, complete with a machine gun, and where one of the largest collieries was headquartered. One observer noted that when Mother Jones addressed the miners, she "encouraged them to keep up the shootings and keep up the trouble. If she found some weak-kneed fellow who were [sic] hanging around the tents, she went after him and drove him off into the mountains. In one instance she was heard to say, 'Get your guns, you cowardly sons of b——s, and get into the woods.' "[9]

Viewing the Paint Creek operators' recalcitrance as an attempt to drive a wedge into the state's slender union strength, Mother Jones again veered close to an outright call to violence during an August 1 meeting on the Charleston levee. "I am not going to say to you don't molest the operators," she stated. "It is they who hire the dogs to shoot you. (applause) I am not asking you to do it; but if he is going to oppress you, deal with him."[10]

Socialist editor and IWW leader Ralph Chaplin was on the same program that day with Mother Jones and he later described her speech.

She might have been any coal miner's wife ablaze with righteous fury when her brood was in danger. Her voice shrilled as she shook her fist at the coal operators, the mine guards, the union officials. . . . She prayed and cursed and pleaded, raising her clenched and trembling hands, asking heaven to bear witness. She wore long, very full skirts and a black shawl and her tiny bonnet bobbed up and down as she harangued the crowd. The miners loved it and laughed, cheered, hooted, and even cried as she spoke to them.[11]

Sensing the rapport, Mother Jones grew yet bolder and climbed up on a box in the bed of a wagon. Then she began:

I say to the policemen: "Get all the ammunition you can; get all the ammunition and lie quiet; for one of these days you will come over with us, and we are going to give the other fellows hell." . . . We are law-abiding citizens, we will destroy no property, we will take no life, but if a fellow comes to my home and outrages my wife, by the eternal he will pay the penalty. I will send him to his God in the repair shop. (loud applause) The man who doesn't do it hasn't got a drop of revolutionary blood in his veins.[12]

Mother Jones was born, raised, and buried as a Roman Catholic. But she never missed an opportunity to excoriate the church, any church. The heavily Protestant West Virginians, fiercely independent and at the same time fundamentalist, relished every word. Their antiestablishment fervor, fueled by hardship, ran stronger than their piety. The church, like politics, was an easy target for their frustrations.

Mother Jones told them on the levee: "Jesus don't know any more about you than a dog does about his father. (loud applause) I was in church one day when they raked in $1,600, and at the same time they were robbing the representatives of Jesus to feed them who robbed them. You build churches and give to the Salvation Army and all the auxiliaries of capitalism and support them to hoodwink you."[13] On August 4 in Montgomery, she stated, "No church in the country could get up a crowd like this, because we are doing God's holy work; we are breaking the chains that bind you; we are putting the fear of God into the robbers. . . . What happened on Paint Creek? Did the church make the operators run and go into the cellar? (applause)."[14]

Mother Jones, at least in the early part of this long strike, was not representing the UMW but only herself. To the miners this seemingly made little difference. Still an aggressive organizer, she did not always adhere to the policy of waiting for the optimal opportunity. She told one UMW organizer to stop playing preacher and telling the miners "that silly trash" about justice eventually righting all wrongs. And at one point, when told she could not legally organize a local because she did not have a copy of the UMW ritual, she retorted, "The ritual, hell. I'll make one up!"[15]

The union by late July turned its attention toward persuading Cabin Creek's miners to join the walkout. But by setting up guard stations at strategic spots, the operators had made Cabin Creek virtually inaccessible. In a countermove, Mother Jones scheduled an August 6 speech at Eskdale, a "free" city within the Cabin Creek territory. As one miner put it, "The only thing beautiful about Eskdale was its name. It was smoky, sooty and grimy."[16] But it also was incorporated and thus became a refuge for miners above Eskdale who had been assaulted or driven out. Beyond it was a no-man's-land and organizers so feared the company gunmen beyond the town that union headquarters could not produce a single volunteer to venture past Eskdale on an organizing foray.[17]

Preceding Mother Jones's expeditions, union broadsides beseeched the Cabin Creek men "in the name of the outraged women and murdered miners of Paint Creek to lay down your tools and join your striking brothers." Mother Jones's exhortations apparently were effective. Charles Cabell, general manager of the nearby Carbon Coal Company, later told Congressional investigators that the men on Cabin Creek were peaceful and content until Mother Jones began holding her meetings. After one such August meeting his men came back "very much exercised over the outlook and worried," Cabell said. Some of them left the next day. "After that time there was a great deal of unrest among our men, from that time on."[18]

But if the first Eskdale meeting was successful in persuading the miners to unite, the next one led to the further embellishment of the legend of Mother Jones. When the second meeting broke up on August 13, someone suggested a march to the Red Warrior mining camp in the no-man's-land. Leading the marchers in a buggy, Mother Jones soon ran into a group of 50 or more mine guards with a machine gun pointed at the advancing column. As one miner recalled, Mother Jones drove her rig up to the gun emplacement, and a miner helped her step down. "She surveyed the scene with a critical eye and walked straight up to the muzzle of one of the machine guns and patting the muzzle of the gun, said to the gunman behind it, 'Listen here, you, you fire one shot here today and there are 800 men in those hills (pointing to the almost inaccessible hills to the east) who will not leave one of your gang alive.' "[19]

The hoary bluff worked. Mother Jones later admitted that if there were miners up in those hills, she did not know about them. The basis of some controversy, and perhaps hyperbole, the machine gun incident seemed to grow in Mother Jones's memory. "I realized that we were up against it," she confided, "and something had to be done to save the lives of these poor wretches, so I pulled the dramatic stuff on them thugs. Oh! how they shook in their boots, and while they were shaking in their boots I held my meeting and organized the miners who had congregated to hear me."[20] The machine gun operator, J. H. Mayfield, however, later told a Congressional subcommittee that Mother Jones got out of the buggy and talked quietly with the guards. She "told us that when she left Eskdale that these fellows with the guns followed her up there, hot heads, and she told us she didn't want no trouble."[21] At any rate, a tale was born and Mother Jones was allowed to continue to Red Warrior alone while the crowd had to return to Eskdale.

The joining of the Cabin Creek miners with the strike, whether done out of sympathy or coercion, was a blow to the operators. Cabell, who had about 1,000 employees, distributed questionnaires to his men when it was obvious that the UMW was going to seek to proselytize them. The results, he claimed, showed that 90 to 95 percent of the workers were satisfied with conditions.[22] One contemporary historian said, "Through distortion of facts, the union agitators had so aroused the passions of the miners that men who were usually cool-headed threw all self-restraint to the winds and followed these leaders with the blind faith of children."[23]

Two days after the machine gun incident, Mother Jones delivered an hour-and-a-half address to a throng of miners gathered on the steps of the capitol in Charleston. Following several socialist speakers, she demanded the abolition of the mine guards and berated the establishment in a resolute and imaginative speech which claimed the labor movement to be a mandate from God and stated that the star of Bethlehem had been a portent of the industrial revolution. She pledged that some day the miners would take over the mines, and she poked fun at the operators' wives. They wear $5.00 worth of makeup and have toothbrushes for their dogs, and they say, "Oh, them horrible miners. Oh, that horrible old Mother Jones, that horrible old woman," she chided.

Taking an even harder than usual crack at the clergy, Mother Jones said the operators "give your missionary women a couple of hundred dollars and [they] rob you under pretense of giving it to Jesus. Jesus never sees a penny of it, and never heard of it. . . . I wish I was God Almighty, I would throw down something some night from heaven and get rid of the whole blood-sucking bunch. (Laughter and applause.)" In a stirring climax that moved her audience to both tears and rage, she told them: "And instead of the horrible homes you have got we will build on their ruins homes for you and your children to live in. . . . The day of oppression will be gone. I will be with you whether true or false. I will be with you at midnight or when the battle rages, when the last bullet ceases, but I will be in my joy, as an old saint said:

> O'God, of the mighty clan,
>   God grant that the woman who suffered for you,
> Suffered not for a coward, but oh, for a man.
>   God grant that the woman who suffered for you,
> Suffered not for a coward, but oh, for a fighting man."[24]

Then she asked the crowd to pass the hat for miners in the throng who were broke and needed a glass of beer or who could not pay their way back home. Then a man came out of the audience and told Mother Jones: "Here is $10. I will go and borrow more. Shake hands with me, an old union miner. My children are able to take care of themselves, and I will take care of myself.

"Fight, fight, right," he said. "I have a good rifle, and I will get more money. If I don't have enough to pay my railroad fare I will walk. I don't care if this was the last cent I had, I will give it to 'Mother' and go and get some more."[25] Such was the response Mother Jones got to her impassioned and inflammatory speeches during this long and bloody strike. As an orator, she was at her peak. Lawrence Lynch, a contemporary writer, stated:

Head and shoulders above all the other agitators in ability and forceful-ness stands "Mother" Jones, the heroine of many similar strikes. Her eighty or more years have not dimmed her eye, weakened the strength of her personality or tempered the boldness of her language. She is the woman most loved by the miners and most feared by the operators. Her thoughts are expressed in language both picturesque and striking. She knows no fear and is as much at home in jail as on the platform. In either situation she wields a greater power over the miners than does any other agitator.[26]

And Fred Mooney, a West Virginia miner, described her and her techniques.

With that brand of oratorical fire that is only found in those who originate from Erin, she could permeate a group of strikers with more fight than could any living human being. She fired them with enthusiasm, she burned them with criticism, then cried with them because of their abuses. The miners loved, worshipped, and adored her. And well they might, because there was no night too dark, no danger too great for her to face, if in her judgment "her boys" needed her. She called them her boys, she chastised them for their cowardice, she criticized them for their ignorance. She said to them, "Get you some books and go into the shade while you are striking. Sit down and read. Educate yourself for the coming conflicts."[27]

At the state capitol meeting, Mother Jones presented a demand for the abolition of the mine guards, and she exhorted a group of miners to take the document to the governor's office.[28] But Governor Glasscock, a frail, former school teacher and lawyer, did little to meet the miners' demands. Upon adjourning the capitol meeting, Mother Jones said she told the miners, "We will protect ourselves and buy every gun in Charleston." She later recalled that they "left the meeting peacefully and bought every gun in the hardware stores of Charleston. They took down the old hammerlocks from their cabin walls. Like the Minute Men of New England, they marched up the creeks to their homes with the grimness of the soldiers of the revolution."[29]

By the end of August, shootings were occurring almost every night and sometimes during the day. Assaults, murders, and property destruction were common. The struggle climaxed on September 1, 1912, when union miners on the north side of the Kanawha River armed themselves and began crossing the river to help the beleaguered strikers drive out the guards and the miners who were still at work. Estimated at anywhere from 1,500 to 6,000 men, the combined armies massed near the mouth of Cabin Creek. The mine owners quickly imported more than a hundred extra guards and recruited every employee who could hold a rifle. In all, about 400 well-armed and determined defenders waited behind breastworks to repel the invaders. A monstrous war was in the making.[30]

On September 2, Governor Glasscock declared the entire strike zone to be under martial law, and 1,200 militiamen were rushed to the creeks where they would stay for six weeks. During the first few days of military occupation, the soldiers seized 1,872 rifles, 556 pistols, 6 machine guns, 225,000 rounds of ammunition, 480 blackjacks as well as daggers, bayonets, and brass knuckles from the two sides. Yet of the miners, "the great majority of them followed Mother Jones' advice" and hid their weapons, one observer stated.[31] Despite the martial law, Mother Jones continued to speak with gusto throughout the Kanawha region. At Charleston on September 6, she castigated the miners as "a lot of cowards" without "enough marrow in your backbone to grease two black cats' tails. If you were men with a bit of revolutionary blood in you, you wouldn't stand for the Baldwin guards, would you?" She warned against the bad publicity that grew from destruction of Chesapeake and Ohio railroad trackage. "Don't meddle with the track, take care of it," she advised, "and if you catch sight of a Baldwin bloodhound, put a bullet through his rotten carcass (loud applause)."[32]

Throughout the month she kept up her speeches, and during a talk at Eskdale a few days after the imposition of martial law, she was said to have been seized and detained briefly for reading the Declaration of Independence to strikers at a railway depot. On September 21, she led a protest parade in Charleston of 100 miners' children with banners and a band.[33] Her actions, chronicled closely by socialist magazines and newspapers, won her a growing following, not only among West Virginia coal miners but the metal miners of the West as well. *Miner's Magazine,* the organ of the WFM, said, "A few years more, and 'Mother' Jones will be sleeping in the bosom of Mother Earth, but when the history of the labor movement is written and there is recorded the glad tidings of labor's emancipation, the name of 'Mother' Jones will shed a halo of lustre upon every chapter that portrays the struggle of man against the despotism of capitalism."[34]

For almost two months there was a tenuous peace in the Kanawha Valley. Under martial law, 66 persons were tried and convicted of a range of offenses usually involving short jail terms. The militia left on October 15, but they left behind some soldiers who joined the ranks of the mine guards and helped protect strikebreakers imported from New York, Philadelphia, and Chicago. In a single month, one New York agency shipped 621 men to Cabin Creek.[35] Embittered at seeing their old jobs taken by the scabs, the miners brought their weapons out of hiding, and by early November, open warfare flared again. Trains bringing the strikebreakers into the two creek valleys met such intense fire from the mountainsides that the trips had to be halted. On November 15, Governor Glasscock issued a second martial law proclamation.[36]

A new military tribunal was established, although the civil courts remained open. The military court went so far as to take jurisdiction over offenses committed before martial law began, and it even tried persons arrested by civil authorities outside of the martial-law zone. Civil liberties were pushed aside. The rights to counsel, to refuse to give evidence against oneself, and to separate trials were not recognized. Trials sometimes were notably speedy, but the sentences could be disproportionate, including penitentiary terms for what legally were misdemeanors. This technique, applied with even more fervor than before, again brought a surface calm. Strikers hid their weapons once more and went back to their tent colonies while the flow of strikebreakers resumed, and the strike wore on.[37]

Meanwhile, in November, the governor's investigating commission delivered a report which failed to exonerate either side. While the guard system was "vicious, strife-prompting, and un-American," the union's officers and organizers were guilty of inciting violence and condoning mayhem against nonunion men, the commission said.[38] Mother Jones took advantage of the lulls to tell of what she had seen. In October, for example, she spoke before the Ohio Federation of Labor and pictured the perils for workingmen in neighboring West Virginia. In November, she was in New York where she cautioned workers about the employment agencies which enticed immigrants to accept strikebreaking jobs in the Kanawha region.[39]

Not until January 10, 1913, was the martial-law order withdrawn. Then, as before, some soldiers remained behind to hire out to the mine owners. Mother Jones continued to try to spread the word of the West Virginia situation. She denounced Governor Glasscock in a speech to 2,000 in Wheeling on January 6. Preaching her "doctrine of divine discontent," she urged an end to the mine guards, to the obligatory company store, and to the lack of union recognition. She then made a Cincinnati-Columbus-Cleveland-and-Washington circuit and tried unsuccessfully, at this point, to prompt a Congressional investigation.[40]

In the Washington armory with Frank Hayes, the UMW's vice-president, she again told of the suppression of civil liberties. "If such crimes against the citizens of the state of West Virginia go unrebuked by the government, I suggest," she said, "that we take down the flag that stands for constitutional government, and run up a banner, saying, 'This is the flag of the money oligarchy of America!' " It was agreed that United States Secretary of Labor William B. Wilson, a former UMW secretary-treasurer and comrade of Mother Jones in the eastern Pennsylvania strikes at the turn of the century, would use his influence in seeking an investigation.[41] In truth, though, it would be Mother Jones who would provide the catalyst for the inquiry.

On February 7, West Virginia again exploded into violence. Mucklow again was attacked and a company bookkeeper killed. Then a posse boarded a train mounted with machineguns. The men on the train exchanged fire with the strikers at the Holly Grove tent colony, killing one miner and wounding a woman. The miners retaliated with more attacks on the guard's camp at Mucklow. After two more men were killed on February 10, Governor Glasscock declared martial law for the third time.[42] Scores of strikers and union sympathizers soon were rounded up by authorities. When Mother Jones arrived in the strike district two days after the martial-law proclamation, she was asked by the miners to go to the governor and plead for them. She and a committee of 34 left by train for Charleston with fists full of protest resolutions.

Stepping from the train at the Charleston depot, the group was walking toward the statehouse from the east when, according to committee member Fred Mooney, two men seized Mother Jones, who was "thrown into an automobile and hurried away." In the confusion that followed, the committee learned that a riot call apparently had been sent out and warnings spread that Mother Jones was leading 3,500 men to assassinate the governor and dynamite the capitol.[43] Mother Jones was taken to another train and delivered to the military commission's headquarters at Pratt, where she was confined. Although the civil courts remained open, Mother Jones was charged by the military with conspiracy to murder. Stealing a machine gun and attempting to blow up a train with dynamite also were mentioned as among her possible offenses.[44] The bullpen, where prisoners were put without due process while awaiting trial, was reopened and a new military court was convened. Despite an article in the state constitution guaranteeing that civilians would not be tried by the military "for any offense that is cognizable by the civil courts of the state," the tribunal operated with slight regard for judicial fine points when dealing with the 166 strikers eventually brought before it.[45]

"Because of the deep respect which the miners have of the advocate of their cause," the *Charleston Gazette* reported, "it is the opinion of many that the arrest of Mother Jones and her consequent confinement may be the instigation of another outbreak of violence among the striking miners."[46] Actually, what the arrest did quickly was to furnish Mother Jones with the forum for publicity which she had sought for six months. This cause was furthered when Mrs. Fremont Older, wife of the editor of the *San Francisco Bulletin* and a magazine writer, came to investigate the grounds for detaining Mother Jones and 48 miners who then also were being held. She found the military's provost marshal was also the Associated Press correspondent and was withholding news of Mother Jones's confinement and trial.[47] Mother Jones refused to make a plea, claiming the six-officer military court lacked jurisdiction while the civil courts remained open. She did, however, seize upon the moment for a short speech. "I am 80 years old and I haven't long to live anyhow. Since I have to die I would rather die for the cause to which I have given so much of my life," she stated. "My death would call the attention of the whole United States to conditions in West Virginia. It would be worthwhile for that reason. I fear, though, that I shall not be executed."[48]

Mother Jones's crimes were said to include inciting the miners to murder at Mucklow for which she could be sentenced to death by firing squad. The alleged acts of course, occurred before martial law was re-established. Further, she had been arrested by special constables on a warrant issued by a justice of the peace. She had been arrested in Charleston, within sight of the still-functioning courthouse and outside the martial-law zone. She had been delivered to the military in the strike zone, and she had not received a hearing, a grand jury inquiry, a civil trial nor all that centuries of jurisprudence would seem to dictate.[49] The West Virginia attorney general came to see her, and Mother Jones told him, she later recalled, that the governor "can chain me to that tree outside there and he can get his dogs of war to riddle this body with bullets, but I will not surrender my constitutional rights to him. I happen to be one of the women who tramped the highways where the blood of the revolutionists watered it that I might have a trial by jury."[50]

A petition to remand Mother Jones and three other prisoners to the civil courts for trial was filed February 20 with the Supreme Court of Appeals of West Virginia. In its decision March 21, the court majority held that the governor had authority to set up a military commission and to hold persons without trial. Because, the court said, a "state of war," insurrection, and public danger did exist before such power was exercised, "the detention of these petitioners, although arrested outside of the military district, is, in our opinion, entirely valid and legal." Thus, they refused to turn the prisoners over to civil authorities.[51] But Judge Ira E. Robinson filed a strong dissenting opinon. The majority, he said, failed to note "that this State is a land of constitutional courts, not one of imperial military courts." A dispute between mine owners and miners, he wrote, "can not be considered public war and the participants dealt with as enemies of the State. . . . Yet the majority opinion deals with the citizens of the district as rebels. It deals with a part of Kanawha County as enemy territory. . . . Cabin Creek has not seceded!" Even the "guiltiest man, if he is not an enemy in public warfare against the State, is entitled to all rights as a citizen."[52]

Mother Jones had been in confinement 22 days when she wrote her friend Terence Powderly.

They have me in close confinement There are two military guarding me day and night No one is allowed to speak to me. . . . Neither one of us was was [sic] in the marshall [sic] law zone they picked me up on the streets of Charleston Kidnapped me, marched me with 2 others down the military camp. here I am now for 22 days! Not allowed to speak to anyone or see anyone just think of it I have lived 80 years and never before charged with any crime now I am charged with stealing a cannon from the military inciting to riot putting dimamite [sic] under track to blow up a C-O road. . . . I know they are death on me for I have cost them hundreds of thousands of dollars.

They came to me yesterday wanted to get a lawyer & witness I refused to get either. I said if I have broke the law of the state or nation I do not want any lawyer nor witness. . . . God spare me the heart to fight them. Love to my dear Emma [Mrs. Powderly]. Tell her not to worry I'll fight the pirates

Mother[53]

Mother Jones still was confined on March 4, 1913, when Governor Henry D. Hatfield was inaugurated. The thirty-seven-year-old physician was a Republican backed by the mine operators, yet he was familiar with the situation of the miners and had established three hospitals for them. He also was a nephew of the famed clan leader Anderson ("Devil Anse") Hatfield, a major figure in the Hatfield-McCoy feud a generation earlier along the West Virginia-Kentucky border. Along with the mantle of office, Hatfield acquired the strike which had cost the state government more than $2 million in 1912. Before passing upon a number of military court convictions inherited from Glasscock, Governor Hatfield decided to visit the strike district, despite warnings from his aides who feared he would be killed. Shortly before dawn on the day after his inaugural, Hatfield, alone and armed only with his doctor's satchel, went by train to a miners' tent colony and later to Pratt.[54]

"I noticed a soldier marching to and fro in front of a little cabin on the banks of the Kanawha River," he would recall. "I told the soldier who I was and inquired what responsibility he had there. He told me Mother Jones was being guarded in this little shack and when I entered I found her lying on a straw tick on the floor, carrying a temperature of 104, very rapid respiration, and a constant cough. She had pneumonia."[55] Hatfield ordered her placed under the care of a physician in Charleston, but she remained a military prisoner and was returned to Pratt after her health improved. For Mother Jones, another legal avenue was blocked when a federal appeals judge denied a writ of prohibition intended to win a civil trial for her. While expressing some sympathy with the miners, the judge reaffirmed the governor's authority to declare a part of the state to be under siege and to try offenders by a military board.[56]

Appeal to Reason, meanwhile, launched a campaign "To the Rescue of Mother Jones and Her Comrades." The newspaper warned that if Mother Jones "is railroaded by a bunch of military hirelings, there will be something doing very speedily in this country."[57] Eugene Debs also beat the drums for her release and for a Socialist declaration of war on "the heartless coal barons." In a May Day article in the *Appeal,* he urged a strike of all West Virginia miners, then all West Virginia workers, then all United States miners, if necessary, to force the release of Mother Jones. If Mother Jones, "seamed and scarred as she is in her lifelong struggle to break their fetters," dies imprisoned, her death would be "a foul and indelible blot" on the manhood and self-respect of all miners, Debs said.[58] The state of Mother Jones's health was unclear. In early April, the *Appeal* reported that she was "in fine spirits" and although guarded by two soldiers, she "has a room with a family who are of the striking miners and who are very good to her." But by May 1, she would write: "I have been sick for some weeks."[59]

Fearing her earlier letter had been "held up by the Military sewer rats," Mother Jones wrote to Terence Powderly on her eighty-third birthday.

I have been here 11 weeks, tried by a military drum-head court, kidnapped on the streets of Charleston and brought in to the martial law zone and handed over to the military and I have been held here with 11 others for 11 weeks and don't know what for. No sentence. . . . They have me held up for stealing a cannon from the coal company is one of the charges against me and the other is making incendiary speeches. And . . . no where in the country could you find more brutality than you do here. Men have been shot down in cold blood. The children have been starved to death, some of them.[60]

In April and May, debate over a proposed investigation of the West Virginia conflict split the United States Senate. Indiana's Senator John W. Kern offered a resolution under which an investigation would seek to determine if a system of peonage existed in the strike zone, if immigration or postal laws were being violated, if strikers were being prosecuted contrary to federal law, and if certain other conditions existed. Kern's effort was aided by Mother Jones. On May 14, she smuggled out a telegram to him which he read on the Senate floor. It said: "From out the military prison walls, where I have been forced to pass my eighty-first milestone of life, I plead with you for the honor of this nation. I send you groans and tears of men, women, and children as I have heard them in this state, and beg you to force that investigation. Children yet unborn will rise and bless you."[61] With tariff matters intervening, the debate over the Kern resolution stretched on for weeks. Opponents questioned the assigning of the resolution to the Committee to Audit and Control the Contingent Expenses of the Senate instead of a more functional body. They said much of the debate on the proposal had been one-sided and that other strife-torn states, notably New Jersey with its Paterson silk strike, were not being investigated.[62]

The most vehement opponent was Senator Nathan Goff of West Virginia who saw the proposed inquiry as an assault on the state's integrity and an insult to Governor Hatfield. "You can not conduct a war with kid gloves on," Goff said. "The military commission in West Virginia existed by virtue of proper authority. It tried all cases of all persons caught red-handed in insurrection."[63] A seventy-year-old former Union soldier, Goff had crossed Mother Jones's path once before. His election to the Senate removed him from the United States Circuit Court of Appeals where he had sat since 1892. In 1902, he had sustained the controversial contempt ruling of District Judge John Jackson in the celebrated case of Mother Jones's speech near Clarksburg in northern West Virginia.

Goff was free of any illusion about neutrality in strike situations. Mine owners were, as he put it, "conquering the wilderness" and were deserving of state protection. His biographer wrote: "When 'outsiders,' such as 'Mother' Jones, came into the state, and led the strikers in riots and 'insurrections' that resulted in closed mines, destroyed property, intimidation of mine workers and mine owners, wholesale violations of law, and even the importation of arms for illegal use, they deserved to be restrained by all the power at the governor's disposal. This included martial law and military tribunals."[64] Goff "is not a bad fellow at all," Mother Jones would quip, "but he has been dead for 40 years and doesn't know it." Of her, Goff said, "Grand and good and a friend of the miners she may be—but she certainly has been inciting riot and urging insurrection."[65]

Kern, who had run unsuccessfully for the vice-presidency in 1908 with William Jennings Bryan, told the Senate he was appalled that just 300 miles from Washington "one of the best-known women in America . . . was being tried in this unusual way before this mock tribunal." He was distressed that news agencies failed to report on her trial by the military and that Hatfield had not made the court-martial verdict known. "Whether this old woman is to die or to live," Kern said, "whether she is to spend the remainder of her life in prison or go free is known only to the one man who sets his will above the law of the land."[66]

Much of the debate came after, as Goff pointed out, the strike largely was ended. Hatfield, elected on a pledge to end the violence, had issued what amounted to an ultimatum, and he established a board of arbitration to reach a settlement by May 1. As the board's chairman, he imposed terms on the UMW and the operators in what came to be known as the "Hatfield Contract." It called for nine-hour days, the right to organize, the right to shop at other than the company store, semimonthly paydays, and checkweighmen to act for the miners as the law, written in 1908, required. Many of the miners' demands were met by the Hatfield Contract, but not the important one of abolition of the Baldwin-Felts guards.[67] The governor also reasserted the citizens' constitutional guarantee to a civil trial by jury, and he disapproved pending sentences of the military tribunal, including the 20-year penitentiary term which had been handed Mother Jones. Those already in jail were paroled. The military proceedings had been so confused and fragmented that even the defendants were not sure of the outcome.[68]

Hatfield, however, also took exception with Kern's statements that Mother Jones was in "prison." Mother Jones "is not now nor has she at any time since her arrest been in prison," the governor replied. "She is being detained—and is not in any way confined—at a pleasant boarding house with a private family on the banks of the Kanawha River at Pratt, W. Va. I do not intend to permit Mrs. Jones or any other person to come into West Virginia and make inflammatory speeches that have a tendency to produce riot and bloodshed."[69] But as debate on the Kern resolution heightened, Governor Hatfield released her without comment after 85 days of confinement. He had her sent to a Charleston hotel where, according to Mother Jones, he pledged to see her shortly. He did not appear, however, so she went to Washington to join in the call for an investigation. By May 14, she was sitting in the Senate gallery listening to the increasingly acrimonious arguments.[70]

After conferring with Kern, Mother Jones left on a wide-ranging speaking tour to win public support for the inquiry. To a Pittsburgh throng on May 19 she boasted that the miners had warned her she could be hurt or killed in West Virginia. But instead, she said, "I didn't come out on a stretcher, I raised hell."[71] In a packed Carnegie Hall in New York, Mother Jones shared the rostrum with Big Bill Haywood and radical editors Max Eastman and Joshua Wanhope. The West Virginia conflict had shown the futility of moral suasion, said Wanhope, adding: "There is hope for the laboring class as long as there are in it, as was shown in West Virginia, men who, seeing that it is a case of killing or being killed, are willing to take guns and do a share of the killing." Mother Jones told the crowd that she would have been in prison still if Senator Kern had not called for an investigation. "Cowards! Moral cowards!" she cried. "If you had only risen to your feet like men and said, 'We don't allow military despotism in America.' "[72]

On May 27, the Senate passed the Kern resolution, after some modification and after routing it through the Education and Labor Committee. Arriving in Charleston on June 7, Mother Jones then made a quick tour of adjacent states before returning to listen to the subcommittee sessions June 10 to June 18 in the state capital. The investigation later was resumed in Washington.[73] The senators heard 2,291 pages of testimony but none of it from Mother Jones. It was unlike her not to wish to speak, doubly so given her central role in the creation of the inquiry and the public support for it. Eugene Debs complained of this in a letter to Adolph Germer, a UMW organizer and, along with Debs, a member of a three-man Socialist Party investigating team which looked into the West Virginia strike and Mother Jones's jailing. Debs asked Germer why Mother Jones and others were not put on the witness stand by the miners' attorneys. "I am not so sure that we should insist upon them appearing from the fact that their movements are not known minutely," Germer replied, "and their testimony will not only injure the case that has been established before the subcommittee, but some of the boys might be involved in serious complications." Some were nonunion miners without previous UMW connections and who "would have injured the case rather than help it," Germer said.[74]

But surely Mother Jones's biases were no secret. Why she did not testify remains curious. Perhaps she was discouraged from speaking lest she widen the split between the UMW leadership and some Socialists, who favored a continuation of the strike and rejection of the Hatfield Contract.[75] The Senate investigators did not find, per their mandate, peonage, blocking of the mails, or violation of the immigration laws. But they did find that individuals had been arrested, tried, convicted, sentenced, and punished by military authorities even though civil courts remained open. In a 1914 report, the senators pointed to causes which Senator William Kenyon of Iowa summed up as "private ownership of these great coal properties, with the attendant human greed."

Senator James Martine of New Jersey stated:

> I charge that the hiring of armed bodies of men by private mine owners and other corporations and the use of steel armored trains, machine guns and bloodhounds on defenseless men, women, and children is but a little way from barbarism. . . . I, at the risk of criticism by my many friends and countrymen, unhesitatingly say that Government ownership of the mines is the only hope of solution for those who may come after us.[76]

In another report, the state adjutant said that the national guard had been on duty about nine months in all during the strike. As many as 1,500 troops were present at any one time, and more than 200 persons were tried and sentenced on charges ranging from intimidation of workmen to adultery to disorderly conduct. The guard also collected a mass of weapons from the miners, mine guards, and operators. These included 6 machine guns, 482 pistols, 453 repeating rifles, 84 old-style mountain rifles, 301 small repeating rifles, and 1,136 shotguns.[77] Despite some dissatisfaction with the Hatfield Contract and another brief round of strikes on the two creeks, the dispute was over by late July 1913. "More hungry, more cold, more starving, more ragged than Washington's army

that fought against tyranny were the miners of the Kanawha Mountains," Mother Jones wrote. "And just as grim. Just as heroic. Men
died in those hills that others might be free."[78]

But no one thought that the confiscated guns were but a fraction
of the existing weaponry or that the Hatfield Contract in the Paint
and Cabin Creeks field meant that the battle for West Virginia had
ceased. Some 30,000 shots were estimated to have been fired in the
14-month-long mine war which left perhaps 50 persons dead.[79] Although the strike had cost the UMW $602,000, the union's membership
increased from 2,000 to 5,000 in the state. Further, UMW leaders soon
began organizing the New River district, and by 1915 that field became
union for the first time. By the end of World War I, about one-half
of West Virginia's mines would be unionized.[80] But those in the coal-
rich southern rim of the state—the Bluefield, Logan, and Williamson
areas—remained nonunion. In the effort to win them over, strikers
would shock the nation again, and Mother Jones would play another,
and most unusual, part.

NINE

We don't want Sunday schools. We've had enough
of them. We want to fight.

—Mother Jones[1]

T H E hard-fought West Virginia mine war brought Mother Jones's exhortations to their zenith. Never before and never again would she be so blatant in her appeals to violence and in her pledges to see the law broken. Like her politics, her philosophy of force was highly pragmatic. Hers were the ethics of the situation. With a good feel for psychology, she tailored her outpourings to her audience. When addressing a crowd of armed and angry miners, she could be the aggrieved anarchist spoiling for a fight and spilling over with contempt for the moneyed, powerful classes. When in company with the oligarchs, she could be feistily charming and no less eloquent. And when with journalists, those molders of the public opinion which she sought to sway, Mother Jones could resemble an aged Maid of Orleans.

In one remarkably conciliatory interview during the period, she showed a Mother Jones with a depth far beyond that usually attributed to her. This was the same old agitator who, at a Paint Creek meeting of citizens intent on inducing the miners to lay down their weapons, said, "Don't give up your guns, and if you haven't got good guns, buy them."[2] But in a different setting, she made these observations:

104

I believe no more in thug-statemanship than in thug-economics; either one will breed the other; they are brothers. I am neither Socialist nor Anarchist; I decry them both and, naturally, in decrying them, I must decry their causes. . . .

I do not hate employers. What I hate is the causes of labor troubles. I hate no individuals. There are those among the mine owners in West Virginia who deserve less hate than pity; they deserve more sympathy than I do, more sympathy than any of the striking miners do, for they are going to be beaten into doing right. The man forced into his righteousness is a sorry spectacle. . . .

I do not believe in shotguns for workers any more than I believe in injunctions for employers. Let us eliminate both these fierce enemies of society. We can do it.[3]

Such seemingly simultaneous endorsement of violence and conciliation, as in the West Virginia period, punctuated Mother Jones's career. In the 1902 anthracite strike, for example, she denied weapons to strikers, saying we "had . . . nothing but our hands, because I don't believe in those instruments and don't travel with any organizer who carries them."[4]

In 1916, she would write a socialist jailed for allegedly killing ten persons with a bomb. "I am opposed to violence, because violence produces violence, and what is won today by violence will be lost to-morrow. We must ever and always appeal to reason, because society after all," she said, "has made all the progress it has ever made, by anyalizing [sic] the situation carefully and bringing the matter before the public with reason. . . . The taking of human life has never settled any question. And the wrongs eventually revert back to those who commit them."[5] She added, in what was the converse of many a coal-country politician's pronunciamento: "I am not afraid to say that I probably, in the great industrial struggles that I have been in have prevented more blood shed than any other person in America."[6]

In a *New York Times* interview in a Union Square hotel soon after being released from her West Virginia confinement, Mother Jones stated:

I was never really uncomfortable. But who gained anything? . . . I am not railing against my imprisonment, but against the inefficiency of the system which so sillily imagined that to keep me there could do anybody any good. It accomplished nothing toward the solution of the trouble. To try to do that in that way was like an effort by a doctor who gives you a little morphine, when you ache, so that you won't feel the pain.[7]

While this was a Mother Jones of reserve and of calm insight that few miners or operators would recognize, it showed again that she could and did shape her utterances shrewdly to match the circumstance. Once, when nagged about the prospect of violence in an upcoming strike, she speculated, "I wonder if Washington was peaceful when he was cleaning hell out of King George's men. . . . I want to tell you we're not going to have peace, we're going to have hell. Strikes are not peace. We are striking for bread, for justice, for what belongs to us."[8] That was more nearly the quintessential Mother Jones.

Violence, like the law, was relative in her mind. "I am always in favor of obeying the law," she told the Commission on Industrial Relations, "but if the high-class burglar breaks the law and defies it, then I say we will have a law that will defend the Nation and our people."[9] As she later explained her pragmatism, it went like this: "We use the force of law wherever we can, but if we are forced to use the law of force, if the other fellow makes us, we do; we don't offer any apologies for doing it. We all have a gun, and we know how to use it; we don't do anything with it unless we are called on to do so."[10]

Her whole career was dotted with either a brand of schizophrenia or a deception so calculated that she could appear to a group of disillusioned miners as a radical savior and to a news reporter as a folksy, school marmish heroine. No longer the shrill, incensed voice of the crusader leaping from the small but ample body with arms flailing and fists pounding, but rather, as a *Times* reporter saw her: "Handsome, well dressed, carefully spoken, hospitable, smiling and sympathetic. After two visits to her, aggregating quite 10 hours, I should as much expect her to be violent as to see a matron at a charity ball spring into anarchistic action."

Anticipating the "blood-red flag," the newsman instead got "cabin sociology, interspersed with humor . . . an educated woman careful of her speech and sentiments. If she had a red flag with her she kept it in her satchel with her comb and brush and powder puff. She has a powder puff. That, too, astonished me."[11] But if Mother Jones was unpredictable on the subject of violence, she was steadfast in her views on the church. Her speeches were peppered with references to the Deity. Yet she was bitter at what she considered the shams of the church:

missionaries to solve foreign ills while children at home go hungry; the company-controlled houses of worship in many mining towns; and the clergy's failure to champion the workingman's revolt.

A lifelong Catholic, Mother Jones never claimed allegiance to the organized church. In fact, aside from having a few activist priests as friends, she had little patience with religion and often reserved for it her most vehement scorn. Her distaste for the church followed several themes. For one, there was the church's identification with the mine and mill owners. "I must give the company credit," she said of one child-labor experience, "for having hired a Sunday school teacher to tell the little things that 'Jesus put it into the heart of Mr. _____ to build that factory' so they would have work with which to earn a little money to enable them to put a nickel in the box for the poor little heathen Chinese babies."[12]

She also scorned the church's role as a pallitive which offered visions of the afterlife but slight succor for the worker here and now. The relative wealth of the church and its abandonment of what she said was the revolutionary thrust of the Gospel further raised her ire. "Jesus . . . took twelve men from among the laborers of his time (no college graduates among them)," Mother Jones wrote, "and with them founded an organization that revolutionized the society amid which it rose. Just so in our day the organization of the workers must be the first step to the overthrow of capitalism."[13]

She never clothed her thoughts in niceties for the benefit of churchmen. One progressive priest, later to become her friend, told of meeting Mother Jones on a train. "With her black bonnet and black silk dress, she looked like an old-fashioned New England grandmother," he said, "She was having trouble with a window and I arose to help her. We were passing a new factory; walled in with glass and with its green clipped trees.

" 'How beautiful,' I said. A man of my profession cannot repeat what Mother Jones said. I collapsed in my seat. I agreed with what she said," the priest later recounted, "but I would have said it in a different way."[14]

She sometimes manifested her antireligious bias by meeting with miners on a public road rather than in an available church, although this was often a practical consideration, too. She told them that their "organization is not a praying institution. It's a fighting institution. It's an educational institution along industrial lines."[15] Perhaps her religious philosophy—like her total ideology, based on the workers' short-term needs—was best summed up in her oft-used imperative: "Pray for the dead and fight like hell for the living!" For labor was her religion—with its saints, its martyrs, its promised land, its righting of wrongs, and its lifting up of the sinners. Her speeches often reflected redemptive Christianity, and, like an industrial Jonathan Edwards, she spoke in fiery tones of the individual's failings and how he could win economic salvation by a change of mind, by answering a call to the union.

Thus, the gospel according to Mother Jones: "The labor movement was not originated by man," she told one large West Virginia group. "The labor movement, my friends, was a command from God Almighty. He commanded the prophets thousands of years ago to go down and redeem the Israelites that were in bondage, and he organized the men into a union and went to work.

"And they said, 'The masters have made us gather straw; they have been more cruel than they were before. What are we going to do?'

"The prophet said, 'A voice from heaven has come to get you together.' They got together and the prophet led them out of the land of bondage and plunder into the land of freedom. And when the army of pirates followed them the Dead Sea [*sic*] opened and swallowed them up, and for the first time the workers were free."[16]

As in all things, Mother Jones was, perhaps unconsciously, appealing to the link between the workers' desire for a new industrial freedom and his desire to hang on to the best and most familiar parts of the past. That past, of course, included religion. And Mother Jones skillfully mated these elements.

"This fight that you are in is the great industrial revolution that is permeating the heart of men over the world. They see behind the clouds the star that rose in Bethlehem nineteen hundred years ago, that is bringing the message of a better and nobler civilization," she proclaimed to the miners. "We are facing that hour. We are in it, men, the new day; we are here facing that star that will free men and give to the nation a nobler, grander, higher, truer, better manhood."[17]

TEN

Mother Jones: I want you to come out to Colorado. . . . what you see will make you do things which will make you one of the country's greatest men.
Rockefeller: I am afraid you are inclined to throw compliments.
Mother Jones: Oh, no. I am much more inclined to throw bricks.[1]

THE passing of years seemingly fueled Mother Jones's zeal. She had been jailed without cause before, had marched before, stalked the halls of Congress before, and been a supreme publicist before. But she probably never was as effective in these roles as she was during the Colorado mine wars of 1913–15. Coming soon after the Paint and Cabin Creeks strife in West Virginia, the Colorado conflict drew heavily upon her energy and that of the UMW. But it aroused public opinion as perhaps did no other mining conflict. Mother Jones's frequent jailings and deportations in the Colorado strikes of 1903 and her split with the UMW hierarchy then were, in retrospect, only the backdrop for a fiercer battle on both fronts a decade later.

In Colorado, mining laws were progressive but ignored. Despite long-standing statutes to the contrary, few mines had checkweighmen to ensure honesty on the scales. Nor did they always pay semimonthly and in other than scrip, as required, to reduce the miners' dependence on the company store. Elections in the coal districts often were marred by fraud, and wages were low.[2] Both in and outside of the mines, conditions were hazardous. The number of miners accidentally killed per million tons of coal produced in 1912 was double the national average.

In that same year, poor housing and sanitation bred 151 cases of typhoid fever among the workers and their families at the state's largest mining firm.[3] Furthermore, the coal diggers "were forced not only to depend on the favor of the Company for the opportunity to earn a living," said an investigator for the United States Commission on Industrial Relations, "but to live in such houses as the Company furnished, to buy such food, clothing and supplies as the Company sold them, to accept for their children such instruction as the companies wished to provide, and to conform even in their religious worship to the Company's wishes."[4]

The 1913 strike climaxed a flurry of protests against such inequities which began as far back as the 1880s when eastern capital invaded the state. By 1912, 11 million tons per year was being mined in Colorado, making it the nation's eighth largest coal producer. Sixty percent of the output came from Las Animas and Huerfano counties in the particularly isolated southern field. There, the influx of strikebreakers a decade earlier meant that only about 30 percent of the miners were English-speaking. The strike zone accounted for one-third of the state's illiteracy, and this added to the difficulty of union organizing.[5]

In the late spring of 1907, John Lawson, a UMW national executive board member, arrived in Walsenburg in Huerfano County to set up headquarters for a renewed organizing drive. Walsenburg and Trinidad, 40 miles to the south in Las Animas County, were the centers of a wide area which was said to be governed almost as a subsidiary of Colorado Fuel and Iron Company (CFI), the state's biggest coal producer. Through 40 percent ownership of its stock and bonds, John D. Rockefeller controlled CFI and thus the near-feudalism it imposed over 300,000 acreas of southern Colorado. CFI's 5,000 miners mostly lived in camps where the land and buildings were company-owned.[6] Even a company social worker described some of the houses as "hovels, shacks, and dugouts that are unfit for the habitation of human beings and are little removed from the pig sty make of dwellings." Some camps were hygenic, continued the Reverend Eugene Gaddis, but others were among the "more repulsive looking rat holes [that] can be found in America."[7] Company stores earned up to 20 percent per annum on their investment. CFI passed upon teachers, ministers, elections, juries, movies, magazines, and books. It proscribed not only socialist literature but also such works as *Origin of Species* and *The Rubaiyat of Omar*

Khayyam "to protect our people," the company said, "from erroneous ideas." Sheriffs, working in concert with the companies, made organizers unwelcome.[8]

The resistance of the employers and the government as well as the spin-off of the 1907 financial panic prevented Lawson from making much headway in resurrecting the union from its post-1903 shambles. What locals he was able to create were dissolved, and the enrollees were given international cards so as to try to thwart company spies. Meanwhile, Lawson and his fellow organizers also went to Jefferson, Boulder, and Weld counties in northern Colorado. Although employing fewer men and producing less coal, the mines there lacked the classic isolation. Many miners lived away from the mines, often owned their own homes, and sometimes doubled as farmers. Ethnically, they were more homogeneous and therefore a surer union target.[9] The threat of a strike in July 1908 won a quick agreement from the northern operators. Providing basically for an eight-hour day (already a Colorado law) and a closed shop, the settlement constituted UMW recognition as a bargaining agent and promised brighter days for the union in both sections of the state.

The northern operators, however, balked at renewal and a wage increase two years later. As a result, some 3,000 miners struck. The walkout was remarkably peaceful, but the recalcitrance of the northern companies was reinforced by pressure from their southern counterparts who feared surrender. The mine owners brought in the Baldwin-Felts detectives to help protect their property. That Bluefield, West Virginia, agency, regarded as anathema by miners across the country, was named by a Denver district court judge in the fall of 1910 to enforce an injunction restraining the union from picketing, congregating, or posting notices.[10]

Sixteen strike leaders were arrested and jailed for violating the order, but public pressure forced their release. Yet the injunction remained, and in the spring, after a rash of beatings and the fatal stabbing of a Lafayette, Colorado, official, UMW District 15 Secretary-Treasurer Edward Doyle and 15 other strike leaders again were arrested. Taken to Denver, they were found guilty of contempt and jailed. Meanwhile, Mother Jones had been sent to Colorado to assist Lawson. She soon showed slight patience with what she said were the "damn fool lawyers" and their "sissified mumbo jumbo and pussyfooting" in the Doyle case.[11]

Mother Jones met with WFM officials with whom she had become close during the 1903 strike. Fearing UMW's northern walkout might weaken their union, the WFM leaders apparently devised with Mother Jones a scheme whereby Doyle and the other prisoners would apologize, be freed, and the strike called off. But Mother Jones, acting independently, had not confided in Lawson, who learned of the plan from a lawyer fired by her. The strike, already a year old, was proving costly and perhaps premature. UMW President John White came to Denver intent on the plan and the apology. But Lawson dissuaded him from advocating apology for a noncrime and, instead, he preached the pivotal importance of the northern strike. White then changed his mind, deciding Colorado might well be a union testing ground. He returned to Indianapolis with Mother Jones, who received a rebuke. Shortly afterward, the Colorado Supreme Court released Doyle and the others.[12]

In her first venture into Colorado in several years, Mother Jones again had alienated the UMW leadership, this time by what appeared to be an uncharacteristic turn toward compromise. Again, too, she was linked to the rival WFM. The siding of White with Lawson was a blow which may have spurred her to extraordinary effort and pugnacity in the coming rounds of the Colorado contest. The northern strike continued, and Mother Jones, for her part did what she could to stir up sentiment for a walkout of all the state's coal miners. "You have got to call a strike in the Southern field and lick the Colorado Fuel & Iron Co. out of its boots," she told the 1911 national UMW convention. "You cannot win the Northern field until you take a hand in the Southern field. . . . I am for making a fight on the whole bunch. If you don't want to do it alone, I will go there and take a hand in it and give them hell."[13]

The convention did not order a southern strike, nor did the 1912 convention. But a UMW office was reopened in Trinidad in a drive to organize workers at CFI and the other big colliery, the Victor-American Fuel Company. In December 1912, after the election of Governor Elias Ammons, the union beefed up the southern effort by promising unlimited financial backing to Lawson and by sending Frank J. Hayes, an international vice-president, to help.[14] By sending Hayes, who three years earlier—at age twenty-eight—had been elected to the second highest office in the nation's largest union, the UMW, showed the priority it gave to the task. Although it still sought a negotiated settlement in the northern field, the union had come to agree with Mother Jones's view that the state could not be organized without a full-scale southern effort and probably a strike there. By this time, the UMW already had spent $791,000 on the northern walkout.[15]

Charges and countercharges punctuated the organizing drive. The companies declared the miners were content until the union began agitating. The UMW claimed the operators were trying to provoke a strike so they could wipe out the union. The latter view was underscored by evidence that the Colorado operators had imported some of the same guards and the same guns used in the West Virginia strike from which Mother Jones had just come. Meanwhile, several union attempts to arrange meetings with the operators and avert the strike were rebuffed.[16]

Interviewed in the summer of 1913 in New York, Mother Jones, always something of a natural actress, conveyed this image to a reporter: "She is unique. Short of stature, with a slight limp in her walk, and with curly white hair and 'specs', she resembles almost any grandmother who has lived a peaceful life in the bosom of a happy family. When she talks you forget the happy grandmother smile. . . . But through it all there is wonderful tolerance and moderation. Her voice is a high falsetto, but not harsh. There is also a touch of the Irish, in brogue and oratorical flourish."

The eighty-three-year-old Mother Jones waxed philosophic:

I feel this: If labor would eliminate its violence and capital would eliminate injunctions, the battle would be practically over. We could then go sanely at arranging peace. Common sense, uninflamed, productive, could step in. . . . The capitalist and striker—both men are all right—only they are sick; they need a remedy; they have been mosquito bitten. Let's kill the virulent mosquito and then find and drain the swamp in which he breeds.[17]

Such temperate statements and effusive good will would vanish quickly. Returning to Colorado from a copper strike in Michigan, Mother Jones announced: "I hope there is no war in Trinidad for it will cause suffering, but if the war has to be made that the boys in the mines may have their rights—let it come on!"[18] She then joined Lawson and Hayes in meetings at Walsenburg, Hastings, Ludlow, and Trinidad the day before a September 15 district UMW convention was set to discuss the recalcitrance of the southern operators.

Holding the floor for more than two hours at the Trinidad West

Opera House, Mother Jones urged the governor to compel the operators to meet with the union and settle their differences. But "If it's strike or submit," she implored, "why, for God's sake, strike—strike until you win." Lunging from their seats, the miners were said to have "shouted until they dropped back exhausted."[19] And the convention in Trinidad the following day heard Mother Jones give an hour-long harangue including the imperative:

> Rise up and strike! If you are too cowardly to fight for your rights there are enough women in this country to come in and beat hell out of you. If it is slavery or strike, I say strike until the last one of you drop into your graves. Strike and stay with it as we did in West Virginia. We are going to stay here in Southern Colorado until the banner of industrial freedom floats over every coal mine. We are going to stand together and never surrender.[20]

The convention voted to strike in a week. "I was never more hopeful for success than I am in this strike," Hayes told the miners. "I do not think it will last long. . . . I think we shall realize in Colorado the greatest victory in the history of our organization." But as the UMW delegates dispersed, the operators were meeting in Colorado Springs to pledge undying resistance to the miners' demands. Both sides already had bought arms and ammunition, and 326 deputies had been commissioned indiscriminately in Huerfano County alone before the struggle began.[21]

With wagons full of furniture, utensils, bedding, and family, about 9,000 southern Colorado miners struck on September 23 and made their way from the company houses through rain and mud to nearby tent colonies. Eighty to 85 percent of the miners had quit work. They sought a 10-percent wage increase, an eight-hour day, pay for work incidental to mining such as removing of impurities, elected checkweighmen, freedom to shop at other than the company store, abolition of the mine guards, and union recognition. A majority of the demands already were state law.[22]

Ethelbert Stewart, chief statistician of the Bureau of Labor Statistics, arrived in Trinidad the first day of the strike as an emissary of President Woodrow Wilson. Stewart toured the mining camps with state officials, and together they were able to free some miners being held on company property against their will. But the officials' suggestion for a meeting of the disputants went unheeded.

"The thirst for blood was unmistakably evident," the national guard commander later would recall. CFI deployed its defenders in trenches adjacent to the mining property and equipped them with searchlights, machine guns, and an armored car nicknamed the "Death Special." Over a two-year span, the company bought more than $30,000 worth of arms for the strike district. The union purchased weapons openly, too. About $7,100 worth of arms were acquired for the miners, and most of them were stowed near spots where strikebreakers would have to pass.[23] Serious violence began almost immediately. First, a company detective and a union organizer lost their lives in separate shootings. The Death Special killed a miner at the Forbes tent colony. CFI men broke up a Walsenburg meeting, killing three, and the miners slew four company men at La Veta.[24]

Arriving from a brief trip to Texas, Mother Jones got a taste of the coming bitterness. "They are sending me all sorts of threats here," she wrote in a letter. "They have my skull drawn on a picture and two cross sticks underneath my jaw to tell me that if I do not quit they are going to get me."[25] Instead, Mother Jones got quickly to work, holding meetings and demonstrations to elicit strike support. As she often did, she attempted to shame the strikers into bold action with dollops of sarcasm and thinly-veiled sexual allusions. She told a Walsenburg audience:

> You men, you great, strong men have been enslaved for years. You have allowed a few men to boss you, to starve you, to abuse your women and children, to deny you education, to make peons of you, lower and less free than the Negroes were before the Civil War. What is the matter with you? Are you afraid? Do you fear your pitiful little bosses? Are you great, strong men, with so much latent power in you, afraid of your masters or the Baldwin-Felts thugs hired by your masters? I can't believe it. I can't believe you are so cowardly, and I tell you this, if you are, you are not fit to have women live with you.[26]

When Governor Ammons came to Trinidad to investigate the strike situation, Mother Jones lined up the women and children from nearby tent colonies for a parade to the hotel where he was staying. Failing in an attempt to charter railroad cars for the demonstration, she marched the group, with a brass band in the lead, to the hotel, into its lobby, and through the hallways. The governor refused to come out. "Unlock that door and come out here," Mother Jones shouted, beating on the door. "These women aren't going to bite you." All this amused the crowd but did not diminish the governor's inhibition.[27]

The operators refused to meet with the union for fear this would connote recognition of the UMW as the miners' representative. This was the central and nonnegotiable issue in the strike, the companies contended. Ammons, who tried to be neutral, at least at first, was subject to intense political pressure from the coal interests. On October 26, he called in the state militia. Arriving in Trinidad two days later, they were told to permit neither union intimidation of those willing to work nor the importation of strikebreakers. But after continued mediation efforts failed, Ammons a month later rescinded the second part of the militia's charge.[28] "From that time things went from bad to worse," a former United States senator told investigators later. "Crimination and recrimination, the operators insisting that all violence was committed by the miners and the miners insisting that there was ample provocation for whatever violence they resorted to."[29] The troops were led by Brig. Gen. John Chase, an affable optician in civilian life, whom even a Congressional committee called "overbearing" as a commander. He deployed his troops on a line about 120 miles long through Las Animas and Huerfano counties. Arriving at the large Ludlow tent colony, midway between Trinidad and Walsenburg, he ordered saloons closed and strikers, guards, and detectives disarmed.[30]

Mother Jones meanwhile, complaining of fatigue from her arduous early efforts, went to Washington, D.C., for both a rest and an attempt at spurring a proposed federal inquiry into the Colorado industrial scene. Hayes wrote her from Colorado, saying, "I appreciate very much the good work you have done in Washington, especially in the halls of Congress, and feel sure you have aroused a splendid sentiment in favor of our cause."[31] Intermittent violence in Colorado continued, and the neutrality of Chase's troops wore thin. Some of the soldiers from Denver left after seeing that the duty promised to be more than a brief outing. Mine guards were enlisted to fill the ranks. Chase took to riding in a CFI automobile and to restricting the right to habeas corpus and the jurisdiction of the still-functioning civil courts. Another officer was retained as legal adviser to the Colorado Mine Owners' Association while he was still in the field.[32]

Mother Jones returned to the state and was quickly deported by the militia. But she slipped back into Denver and appeared at a special convention of the state federation of labor on December 16. She told the women who were among the 500 delegates that they "could bring Governor Ammons to time double quick. . . . A lady is a female whose skull is adorned with four feet of feathers. A woman is one whose skull is full of gray matter—studying the conditions beneath the surface." The convention went on record in favor of a statewide sympathy strike if called by its leaders, and it requested that Governor Ammons remove General Chase and also transfer military prisoners to the civil courts.[33]

Mother Jones, who also was said to have recommended that the governor be hanged, challenged the delegates to follow her in a march to the state capitol building and demand withdrawal of the troops. She later would claim that the march was just a diversion to prevent the calling of a general strike of which she disapproved.[34] In any event, about 2,000 unionists, with Mother Jones and Trinidad strike leader Louis Tikas in the lead, met with Governor Ammons in the chamber of the House of Representatives. He told them he had no evidence of misconduct by the troops, but suggested the delegates appoint a committee and report back to him. They did, and in January 1914 they issued a searing indictment of the militia, including mistreatment of prisoners, enlistment of mine guards and detectives, drunkenness, robbery, unwarranted arrests, and debauchery. The committee report also singled out the seizure in the meantime of Mother Jones. "Has it come to this," said the committee headed by James Brewster, a University of Colorado law professor, "that men so fear the truth that they must unlawfully imprison and silence this woman of eighty-two years?"[35]

After the state labor convention, UMW President White had sent Mother Jones to El Paso, Texas, to see if she could help halt the importation of Mexican strikebreakers into Colorado. Mother Jones contended that troops were escorting the scabs from the border. While across the border in Juarez, Mother Jones also met Pancho Villa.[36] Encouraged by the failure of the militia to remove her from Denver as pledged, she soon announced that she would return to the southern coal fields. "She will be jailed immediately if she comes to Trinidad," General Chase said. "I am not going to give her a chance to make any more speeches here. She is dangerous because she inflames the minds of the strikers." Naturally, Mother Jones had a retort. "Tell Genl. Chase that Mother Jones is going to Trinidad in a day or two and that he'd better play his strongest cards—the militia's guns—against her. He had better go back to his mother and get a nursing bottle," she said. "He'll be better there than making war on an 82-year-old woman in a state where women vote."[37]

She went to Trinidad, was arrested, and was ordered out of the coal fields. Placed on a Denver-bound train under military escort on January 4, she shouted that she would return "when Colorado is made part of the United States." As the train passed through Walsenburg, it was greeted by Lawson and other labor leaders singing "The Union Forever." Carrying an American flag, the contingent stood under Mother Jones's car window during the train's brief stop there. "I didn't get off the train," she later explained, "because I thought I would not create any excitement. I just went to the window and shook my handkerchief at them."[38]

Although General Chase pledged to hold her incommunicado if she returned to the strike zone again, Mother Jones told the Denver Trades and Labor Assembly: "I serve notice on the governor that this state doesn't belong to him—it belongs to the nation and I own a share of stock in it. Ammons or Chase either one can shoot me, but I will talk from the grave." While in Denver she bought $500.00 worth of shoes at wholesale prices for the strikers and their families. Then she again left for Trinidad on January 12.[39] Learning that detectives were posted in Denver's Union Station to prevent her boarding, she walked through the railroad yard and got on the train there. Early next morning, the Colorado and Southern train made a quick, unscheduled stop north of Trinidad. Mother Jones got off and walked into town while militiamen scanned debarking depot passengers. She spent three hours in a hotel across the street from militia headquarters before her presence became known.[40]

Again the troops confronted her. "There were 150 cavalry, 150 infantry, 150 horses with their heads poked at me," she later recalled with some likely hyperbole, "150 gunmen of the Standard Oil Co., and the old woman." General Chase offered to deport her again. "Nothing doing, general," she is said to have replied in stating her right to go "where I damned please."[41] Where she went, under the governor's orders, was into military confinement. She was taken to Mt. San Rafael Hospital, run by the Sisters of Charity, on the eastern outskirts of Trinidad. Five guards were assigned to a 24-hour watch over her. "I never got a line, never got a newspaper, never had a book," she would recall. "I never saw a human being" except for the union's attorney.[42]

Mother Jones soon was the focus of a public clamor, with miners threatening to free her by force and women demonstrating against General Chase and the state. "I am not making war on women," Governor Ammons said, "but since Mother Jones is not a resident of the county she insists on going to, she has no business there." It was never clear if martial law had been declared. General Chase acted as if it had, but the governor never made an explicit statement on the matter, and the attorney general said he did not know.[43]

A UMW attorney filed a writ of habeas corpus petition in Las Animas County district court, but it was denied. The union, however, had an active publicity campaign and made the most of her imprisonment. On one occasion, a union doctor was sent to see Mother Jones. A militiaman guarded her room where the door was ajar. She could be seen sitting in bed, propped up with pillows, and "smiling merrily." The guard blocked the doctor's path, so the physician called Mother Jones and asked her if she was ailing.

"The old girl let out a groan, cried in a piteous voice: 'Oh, doctor, help me, I'm dying . . . I'm dying . . . ,' " the doctor later noted. The following day, previously prepared cartoons appeared in sympathetic newspapers across the country. They showed an old woman stretched out in a hospital bed while an unshaven soldier stuck a bayonet in the doctor's stomach and snarled, "Get out of here. No admission to you no matter how sick th' old woman is."[44]

As such efforts churned public opinion, General Chase and the governor came under mounting pressure to explain her detention. Mother Jones was told she could leave the strike area, Chase explained, "but she pertinaciously and with great contumacy insisted on remaining in imprisonment." She did this to create sympathy, he said, adding that she was angry at having been "so nicely restrained at the hospital, instead of being confined in a common jail." The general said that "most of the murders and other acts of violent crime committed in the strike region have been inspired by this woman's incendiary utterances." Ammons, too, believed Mother Jones "largely responsible for the riot and bloodshed."[45]

Actually, however, her role in this strike was less as an agitator than as a focal point of prolabor sympathy. Imprisonment of a kindly looking old woman was a poignant theme. She did not have to make fiery speeches to raise the public ire. In fact, she had little chance to. Her treatment at the hands of the militia, with the governor's endorsement, was more than enough to make her a unifying symbol. Nine hundred Fremont County miners told the governor they would march to Las Animas County and free Mother Jones if Ammons would not. A hundred women invaded Trinidad's Columbian Hotel, brushed aside guards, surrounded Chase, and futilely demanded the release of Mother Jones. Then, on January 23, 1914, a group of Las Animas County women paraded up Trinidad's Commercial Street carrying banners which said "God Bless Mother Jones" and "We're for Mother Jones." The marchers turned onto Main Street and met a line of cavalry with sabers drawn.[46]

Chase later said that the women broke their pledge not to start toward the hospital. Instead, he stated, with their striking husbands nearby, the women set out for the hospital "with loud shouts of their intention to liberate Mother Jones by force." Chase ordered them to turn back. He rode up to block one surging protester when his horse backed into a buggy and he fell off. The women roared with laughter. Chase got up and reportedly ordered his men to ride down the women. The demonstration turned to horror. Slashed with sabers and knocked by the horsemen, the women beat a disorderly retreat in the midst of a troop riot which further aroused feelings against the militia.[47] Six women were hurt, and the press and the UMW naturally seized upon the incident. The 1914 UMW national convention received a graphic wire report from Lawson: "Woman carrying American flag knocked down with butt of gun and flag torn from her hands by militiamen. Cavalryman slashed another woman with a saber, almost severing an ear from her head. Militiamen jab sabers and bayonets into backs of women with babes in their arms and trample them under the feet of their horses. Mothers with infants thrown into military prison. Feeling is intense. Union officers doing everything to pacify the people."[48] Chase, on the other hand, claimed the parade was broken up "promptly and effectually" due to the "self-restraint and patience" of the guardsmen.[49]

In either case, Mother Jones remained in the hospital-prison. The experience there did not diminish her long-held distaste for organized religion's role in the class conflict. She wrote Terence V. Powderly that the "sisters permitted their religious institution to be turned into a military prison. I never saw more moral cowards in my life than those sisters. . . . They are simply owned body and soul by the Rockefeller interests." She did, however, condescend to allow the sisters to bring her meals because she feared the military was poisoning her food.[50] Miners, angered at Mother Jones's continued incarceration without charge, without trial, and without bond, were said to be planning retaliation against the militia when word arrived from Washington that the House of Representatives had authorized its Mines and Mining Committee to investigate the Colorado coal strike and the Michigan copper dispute. The committee began its sessions in Denver on February 9, 1914, and by the end of that month, Ammons withdrew 800 of the 1,000 troops from the strike zone.

On March 6, the investigation moved to Trinidad. General Chase refused to testify. Meanwhile, the UMW sought Mother Jones's release through another writ of habeas corpus. It was denied. Then the union prepared a challenge of the so-called Moyer rule of a decade earlier in which it was held that since the militia did not intend to try an imprisoned strike leader, the right of habeas corpus did not apply. Arguments were set for March 16 before the Colorado Supreme Court.[51] The day before that Mother Jones was released after nine weeks in confinement. She was freed only after what she described as a harrowing auto ride through the back streets of town with a military officer. "It was the one time in my life I thought my end had come; that I was to say farewell to the earth," she said, "but I made up my mind that I would put up a good fight before passing out of life!"[52]

She was put on a train for Denver where she was told the governor waited to see her. According to Mother Jones, the governor told her to leave the strike zone and she refused. According to the militia, she had asked to be released and taken to Denver, ostensibly to see the governor but really to leave Colorado on some face-saving excuse of her own. But upon reaching Denver, "she promptly repudiated the rest of her proposal," General Chase said, and soon prepared to return.[53] The UMW charged that her release was timed to forestall an imminent ruling by the supreme court. In any case, she remained in Denver several days, conferring with mine union officials and making speeches against military despotism. By March 22, she left for Trinidad again.

Mother Jones never got that far. "If she remains" in the strike zone, Governor Ammons declared, "it will be in direct defiance to the State, and it seems hardly fitting that the State should be insulted by the very people who have made it necessary for the State to spend more than $500,000 to keep peace and order." Militiamen thus boarded the train at Walsenburg at 5:30 A.M. and ordered Mother Jones off. "Will you take my arm, Madam?" a lieutenant asked. "No, I won't," she snapped. "You take my suitcase."⁵⁴ Mother Jones was placed in a cell in the cellar of the Huerfano County courthouse in Walsenburg. The orders: imprisonment until she is ready to leave the strike zone. The charge: none.

She remained there 26 days without due process although the courts remained open. "It was cold, it was a horrible place," Mother Jones said, "and they thought it would sicken me, but I concluded to stay in that cellar and fight them out. I had sewer rats that long every night to fight, and all I had was a beer bottle; I would get one rat and another would run across the cellar at me. I fought the rats inside and out just alike."⁵⁵ The opportunity to win a few propaganda points, however, was not missed. In an open letter dated March 31, she wrote of her capture and added:

I want to say to the public that I am an American citizen. I have never broken a law in my life, and I claim the right of an American citizen to go where I please so long as I do not violate the law. The courts of Las Animas and Huerfano are open and unobstructed in the transaction of business, yet Governor Ammons, and his [former Governor James] Peabody appointee, General Chase, refuse to carry me before any court, and refuse to make any charge against me. I ask the press to let the Nation know of my treatment, and to say to my friends, whom, thank God, I number by the thousands, throughout the United States and Mexico, that not even my incarceration in a damp underground dungeon will make me give up the fight in which I am engaged for liberty and for the rights of the working people. Of course, I long to be out of prison. To be shut from the sunlight is not pleasant but John Bunyan, John Brown and others were kept in jail quite a while, and I shall stand firm. To be in prison is no disgrace.

In all my strike experiences I have seen no horrors equal to those perpetrated by General Chase and his corps of Baldwin Feltz [sic] detectives that are no[w] enlisted in the militia. My God—when is it to stop? I have only to close my eyes to see the hot tears of the orphans and the widows of working men, and hear the mourning of the broken hearts, and the wailing of the funeral dirge, while the cringing politicians, whose sworn duty it is to protect the lives and liberty of the people, crawl subserviently before the National burglars of Wall Street who are today plundering and devastating the state of Colorado economically, financially, politically, and morally.

Let the nation know, and especially let my friend General Francisco Villa know, that the Great United States of America . . . is now holding Mother Jones incommunicado in an underground cell surrounded by sewer rats, tin horn soldiers and other vermin.[56]

Both the violence and the propaganda onslaught continued unabated. The jailing spurred Eugene Debs to describe Mother Jones a bit floridly as "the flaming incarnation of the world's proletarian revolt against capitalism's bloody misrule" and to contrast her with Ammons. "Behold them both," he said, "the one the inspired liberator of the masses, the other the servile lackey of the princes of plunder and assasination; the one as glorious in her guarded cell as the other is despicable in his guarded sanctum."[57]

General Chase submitted a 119-page report to the governor which labeled Mother Jones "an eccentric and peculiar figure. I make no mention of her personal history [i.e., alleged prostitution]," he said. But her speeches "are couched in coarse, vulgar, and profane language, and address themselves to the lowest passions of mankind." With indisputable truth, Chase also noted that Mother Jones used her age and her sex as a shield as well as a means of winning popular sympathy.[58] For Mother Jones, meanwhile, "the hours dragged underground. Day was perpetual twilight and night was deep night." She said she watched people's feet from her cellar window. There were "miners' feet in old shoes; soldiers' feet, well shod in government leather; the shoes of women with the heels run down; the dilapidated shoes of children; barefooted boys. The children would scrooch down and wave to me but the soldiers shooed them off."[59]

Mother Jones's mention of Villa in the open letter she smuggled out of the Walsenburg jail referred to the Mexican's offer to bargain with President Wilson. Villa said he would release Luis Terrazas, a wealthy Mexican landowner, if Wilson would "show the same regard for humanity toward one of your own citizens, a woman past eighty years, who is being illegally deprived of her liberty. . . . I refer to Mother Jones." The Villa appeal actually was published while Mother Jones was between jailings—after the hospital confinement but before

Walsenburg. But, at any rate, his concern pleased her. "Villa . . . gave Wilson and the Democratic party a terrific slap," she wrote to Powderly.[60]

Professor Brewster later testified before a federal commission that the arrest of Mother Jones "without a warrant, without any suspicion of crime, was one of the greatest outrages upon civilized American jurisprudence that has been perpetrated."[61] But the woman, whose function was publicity, probably succeeded better in jail than out of it. Her confinement, as un-American and criminal as it was, however, came to be just a prelude to one of the greatest catalysts of public opinion in the nation's history—the Ludlow Massacre. Long trips and longer jail terms, treks over the mountains, and the anxieties of a fiercely fought battle had worn Mother Jones down. When released after 26 days in the Huerfano County Jail, Mother Jones left Colorado. She went to Massachusetts, New York, and Washington, D.C., where the House Mines and Mining Committee had resumed hearings.

John D. Rockefeller, Jr., reaffirmed for the committee his opposition to unionism and pledged vast sums to retain the open shop while expressing boundless confidence in the CFI officers. "I have been so greatly interested in the matter, and have such a warm sympathy for this very large number of men that work for us," he said, "that I should be the last to surrender the liberty under which they have been working and the conditions which to them have been entirely satisfactory, to give up that liberty and accept dictation from those outside who have no interest in them or the company."[62] The committee, though, found his interest and sympathy less than complete. He had not, he told the legislators, visited the Colorado coal camps in a decade. He had not even been to a CFI directors meeting in ten years, although he was in charge of his father's properties there. His statements that he was fighting for the workingman's freedom to work for whom and on such terms as he pleases "will not bear investigation," a House report later said. "One must conclude he would rather spend the money of the company for guns, pay of detectives and mine guards and starve the miners into submission."[63]

Mother Jones followed Rockefeller to the witness stand. She was hardly a recalcitrant witness but not always a coherent one, either. Her anecdotal testimony leapfrogged from this dispute to that bit of repartee with fluid, if frustrating grace. After recounting her role in the strike, she told the committee that President Wilson should order the governor to "dispose of those gunmen" and industrial peace would follow. Saying she did not think the Colorado strike could be settled without recognition of the UMW, Mother Jones added that she favored Rockefeller's open-shop ideas only "when the government owns the machinery of production."[64] She was asked by the investigators if she did not urge the southern miners "to strike or do violence of any kind" in the convention just before the walkout began. Mother Jones replied, "Never in the world. That is false." Such statements surely did not enhance her credibility with the Congressmen. However, she may have disarmed them when, after hearing some of her inflammatory West Virginia speeches read, she answered, "That is not half as radical as Lincoln. I have heard him make a great deal more radical speech."[65]

On April 17, about the time of Mother Jones's release from the county jail, the governor had removed the remainder of the troops, except for two ill-chosen companies. Those two, through attrition and connivance, had come to be composed of mine guards, pit bosses, adventurers, and professional soldiers who chose to remain on strike duty. Of the 130 men in the two militia companies, 122 were said to be coal-company employees.[66] The result was a backdrop for atrocity. By April 20, each side at Ludlow was rumored to be planning an attack. The largest of the miners' tent colonies, with about 1,000 people and 200 tents, Ludlow was also the most strategically located and housed strikers of 22 nationalities. Hysteria and confusion have clouded the sequence of events. But it appears a rather minor difficulty led the commander of the two companies to set his troops drilling on a nearby hill as a precautionary measure. In response, the strikers dispersed to their defensive positions.

Then the commander ordered two bombs exploded as a signal to his men that the miners apparently were preparing for an attack. But the union men viewed the signal as the beginning of a barrage by the soldiers. In any event, each side claimed the other had opened fire first.[67] All day the battle raged. One soldier and at least five strikers were killed, including Louis Tikas and two other men who had been captured by the militia. A young boy also was shot in the head as he ate dinner in a tent. The miners were driven away, but their families, overestimating the chivalrousness of the soldiers, stayed in pits dug beneath the tents. But the tents were raked with machine-gun bullets and set afire by the militia. "During the firing of the tents, the militiamen became an uncontrolled mob and looted the tents of everything that appealed to their fancy or cupidity," said an investigator's report.[68]

Not until the next morning was the "Black Hole of Ludlow" discovered. In the charred remains of a tent site were found two young mothers and their 11 small children, the youngest being three months old. Although some soldiers had tried to rescue the colony's women and children, even a militia investigation concluded that the troops ceased "to be an army and had become a mob" as they looted and destroyed.[69] The killings shocked the nation and sparked ten days of open rebellion in the state. Uniting in armed fury, the miners, aided by other outraged citizens, seized Trinidad and pounced on mines in assaults as far as 250 miles from home base. Company buildings were set ablaze, and CFI holdings for 30 miles around were destroyed. The workers' army controlled vast areas of land and clashed in war-scale battles with state and industry forces. The militia abandoned Trinidad to the strikers, and the sheriff and his deputies barricaded themselves inside the courthouse to prepare for a seige.[70]

Pursuant to a broadside entitled "The Call to Arms," the Colorado labor movement began mustering a statewide army. At one point the UMW considered calling out every union miner in the United States. "There were several days when there was positive danger of a national revolution growing out of this Colorado strike," members of the Commission on Industrial Relations later suggested.[71] Governor Ammons, like Mother Jones, had been in Washington, D.C., when the incident occurred. But he soon called upon President Wilson to put down the "open insurrection against the State," and on April 29, the first contingent of 175 soldiers from Fort Russell, Wyoming, reached Denver and continued toward Trinidad.[72]

Ammons agreed, over General Chase's objections, to withdraw the remaining state militia. The federal troops then began their occupation by declaring their absolute neutrality. They authorized strikers to rebuild their tent colonies, and they forbade strikebreakers to enter the district. About the same time, more than 5,000 people gathered on the capitol grounds in Denver. They were addressed by George Creel, a newspaperman who later would head the wartime Committee on Public Information. Creel denounced the state government and the Rockefeller interests as "traitors to the people" and "accessories to the murder of babes."

Other speakers followed, and then Mother Jones arrived from the Union Station upon her return from Washington. "The crowd screamed its approval when she appeared. . . . She took off her bonnet and threw up a clenched fist in welcome," one observer wrote. But in a remarkably conciliatory speech, she seemed to be adhering to her Congressional pledge of rationality.

Here I am again, boys, just back from Washington, and you aren't licked by a whole lot. Washington is aroused and there is help coming. Just keep your heads level and don't do anything to disgrace the state. The state is all right. It is just a few fools at the head of things that are bad. . . . Don't commit any depredations. We'll make some laws to put the Colorado Fuel & Iron Co. out of business, and Mr. Rockefeller who's probably teaching his Sunday school class right now.[73]

The strike dragged on into the summer of 1914. President Wilson's conciliators worked zealously in efforts that probably made this the most intensely mediated strike of its time. The government mediators suggested a three-year truce; rehiring of all miners not found guilty of lawbreaking; adherence to the state mining laws; posting of wages, rules, and regulations; establishment of a grievance committee at each mine; and the naming of a three-man commission by the president to serve as a court of appeals. The UMW agreed, contingent upon approval by a miners' convention in Trinidad. Having already spent some $3 million on the strike, some leaders saw acceptance of the plan as both a means to further consolidate public support and move toward an end to the dispute.[74]

Mother Jones, soon after returning to Colorado in the wake of the Ludlow Massacre, took to the road again. She barnstormed the country seeking food and clothing for the strikers and telling their story. She also remained determined to convince Rockefeller of the deeds being committed in his corporate name. In New York in May, she again took a slam at him for returning unopened her registered letter and writing "Refused" across the envelope. "I could hardly hope that John D. Rockefeller, Jr., would listen to a woman in her 83rd year," she said, "who has given her whole life to the interests of the people he is exploiting." She also called for Congressional action to seize the Colorado mines, a theme to which she would often return.[75]

By the time the rank-and-file vote came on the president's proposal, on September 15, Mother Jones was back in Colorado. In fact, she was on her feet several times during the convention to urge acceptance of the plan. "You must remember that we have in Washington today a type of statesman we have not had since the days of the immortal Jefferson and Lincoln," she told the miners. "The President of the United States, when he found you could not settle your difficulties, sent the Federal troops here to defend you, and now if you don't accept this proposition what more can he do? John D. Rockefeller owns the resources of a nation, but one man arises against the power and says to the miners of Colorado, 'I will be with you if you are fair.' "[76] The truce passed 83 to 8. But the coal operators stalled and did not give their approval.

In October, Mother Jones was in Washington, D.C., again where she had an audience with President Wilson. She explained that Colorado state officials were unable to cope with the situation there, and she urged the president to close the mines if the operators failed to accept the proposed settlement. She further recommended he keep the federal troops there to ensure protection of the miners from the company-dominated militia.[77] Wilson replied that he was doubtful of his authority to close the mines. This led the *New York Times* to comment the following day, October 20: "Once there was a President [Theodore Roosevelt] who said that he was prepared to settle a coal strike by taking the mines and operating them by a Major General. The army is not now commanded by that sort of President."[78]

In November, Mother Jones "in an extended speech" at the AFL convention in Philadelphia deplored internal union strife, jurisdictional disputes, and dissension among organizers. She urged that the convention attempt to get President Wilson to speed up a resolution of the Colorado conflict.[79] Time was runnning out for the union. As often occurred in the face of defeat, bitterness developed within UMW. The leadership split over whether to accept Wilson's proposal if the operators finally did.

Illustrative of this schism, one District 15 official had made an oft-voiced criticism of Mother Jones. She was invaluable as an organizer in the early stages of a strike because she excited the men. But she had always proved embarrassing to the union in the latter stages, particularly when the UMW chiefs were seeking a compromise or adjustment, he said.[80] In this case, her all-out championing of the Wilson proposal may have limited union flexibility. While the criticism was un-

This 1909 photograph shows Mother Jones with Terence V. Powderly, who, in spite of their differences, was to remain one of Mrs. Jones's closest friends. Powderly as one of the leaders of the idealistic Knights of Labor held strikes to be barbaric—in stark contrast to Mother Jones who felt that the strike was virtually the only way to bring about changes in the relationship between labor and capital.—Courtesy of the Catholic University of America Libraries. Department of Archives & Manuscripts. Terence V. Powderly Papers

This view shows Mother Jones in the strikers' parade during the Michigan copper strike of 1913–14. The parade depicted here took place in Calumet on August 10, 1913.—Courtesy of The Archives of Labor History and Urban Affairs, Wayne State University

This illustration shows three of the main figures involved in the 1913–14 Colorado coal strike. Horace Hawkins, United Mine Workers union attorney, left, Mother Jones, center, and John R. Lawson, international organizer for the union, right.—Courtesy of the Archives of Labor History and Urban Affairs, Wayne State University

Mother Jones (with hat) in the miners' tent colony at Ludlow, Colorado, before the infamous massacre in which the National Guard became a mob and killed not only men but also women and children.—Courtesy of Mrs. Adolph Germer, from the collection of the author

During the period 1913–14 Colorado was the scene of extensive mine warfare which climaxed in the bloody 1914 Ludlow Massacre. This illustration shows a women's demonstration in Trinidad around the time of the massacre.—Courtesy of the Denver Public Library, Western History Department

After a High Requiem Mass in Washington, D.C., the body of Mother Jones was transported to Mt. Olive, Illinois, for the funeral and burial. This view shows the casket lying in state December 5–7, 1930, in the Odd Fellows' Hall, where many filed by to pay their last respects.— Courtesy of Mrs. Adolph Germer, from the collection of the author

Mother Jones Memorial at Mt. Olive, Illinois. Several years before her death Mrs. Jones asked to be buried in the miners' cemetery with the Virden martyrs, men killed in an 1898 union-management battle at Virden, Illinois. This imposing granite monument was erected by the Progressive Miners amidst controversy and in the face of strenuous opposition by the United Mine Workers. It was dedicated on October 11, 1936.—Photograph by the author

For a time this handsome bust of Mother Jones by Jo Davidson graced a foyer of the Department of Labor building in Washington, D.C. Later it was put in storage there.—Photograph by the author

doubtedly true, it was used by General Chase and other of Mother Jones's opponents to bolster their arguments that she was "undoubtedly a most dangerous factor in the peace problem."[81] After more than two months without company response to the Wilson plan, the international UMW board asked the president to have the federal government take over the mines. He refused. But on November 29, he did appoint the commission named in his proposal. This, in essence, was a face-saving measure on behalf of the union.[82]

With the national union treasury near exhaustion, copies of Wilson's statement were sent to each Colorado local with a note:

> In view of this urgent request, coming as it does from the Chief Executive of the Nation, we deem it the part of wisdom to accept his suggestion and to terminate the strike. In our opinion, to wage the strike further would not mean additional gain to our members. . . . We recognize no surrender and shall continue to propagate the principles of our humanitarian movement throughout the coal fields of Colorado. We advise all men to seek their former places in the mines, and to those who are refused employment we shall render assistance to the best of our ability and shall provide every legal protection to those of our members who are being prosecuted by the hirelings of organized greed.[83]

On December 7, 1914, the miners met in Denver and decided to end the strike three days later. It had lasted almost five years in the northern fields and fourteen months in the south. Having spent more than $4 million on the strike and in litigation, the union recognized that many of the mines were working at near-capacity with scabs. Still, ending the strike was opposed by Lawson and Doyle, and their recalcitrance contributed to an eventual suspension of the District 15 charter. As the strike ended, more than 400 indictments were returned against the strikers.[84]

Again, as happened so often during Mother Jones's career, a massive offensive by labor had been turned back. The miners lost, she told a crowd in New York's Cooper Union in January 1915 because the union "had only the Constitution. The other side had the bayonets. In the end, bayonets always win."[85] But although nearly eighty-five years old and having endured jails, threats, marathon marches, and the excesses of her own enthusiasm, Mother Jones had succeeded in her part. The conflict probably was the most demanding and violent strike in which she played a part. The struggle, too, had never been for wages and conditions as much as it had been against arbitrary power.

More lasting than the failure to organize the state was the evoking of the national indignation. The horrors committed by the guards and the militia were made known. The need for industry reform was acknowledged. A United States House of Representatives report said, "The constant oppression and neglect and arbitrary conduct of the officials of these companies were prolific causes of the dissatisfaction which resulted in this disturbance and the consequent destruction of life and property." The governor and General Chase also were criticized in the report for not having better "discipline and a clearer conception of their duty" than did many of the militiamen, who were so obviously "on the side of the operators in this controversy."[86] So, the image of the union member as a subversive was mitigated, and some headway may have been made in dispelling the antiunion feeling which swept the nation after the 1910 *Los Angeles Times* bombing.

In January 1915 Rockefeller also testified before the nine-member Commission on Industrial Relations which had been created two years earlier by Congress to seek the underlying causes of labor strife. A crowd of spectators, including Mother Jones, jammed into the hearings in the New York City Council chambers. When he saw her in the audience, Rockefeller came over to her. "I wish you would come to my office and tell me what you know of the Colorado situation," he said. ". . . I can see how easy it is to misjudge you," Mother Jones replied, apparently flattered by his attention. She promised to come and to bring Frank Hayes along also.[87]

In the first day of questioning, the commission heard Rockefeller plead almost total ignorance of the specifics of CFI's policies. He was not opposed to trade unionism, Rockefeller added, but only to violent disputes. He was for free speech, against corporate control of elections, blacklists, and some other CFI practices documented by the commissioners. But he evaded categorical support or condemnation of CFI's labor measures and said his knowledge of the firm was sketchy.[88] Nevertheless, Mother Jones, like some members of the commission, proved susceptible to the young Rockefeller's charm. "I don't hold the boy responsible," she said afterward. "When I have a good motherly talk with him I believe I can help him take another view of the situation among his miners out west."[89]

The talk came the next day, January 27, 1915, at his office in 26 Broadway—the aerie at which Mother Jones so often had slung her verbal shots. "I misjudged that young man sadly," she reported afterward.

"I called him a high-class burglar. I told him so this afternoon. I said, 'Mr. Rockefeller, my name for you has been "the high-class burglar." ' He laughed and I must say he took it good-naturedly. But I know him better now, and after talking with me he knows more about his father's mines in Colorado, too.

"I said: 'Mr. Rockefeller, the people in those mining camps should have the right to trade at any store they want to patronize. They have the right to schools run by the State. The company should pay them in cash, not scrip and leave them free to spend it where they like,' ' Mother Jones stated.

"I think you are right," Rockefeller replied, according to her account.[90]

But Mother Jones's comrades thought her comments a bit too saccharine. Upton Sinclair, for example, wired her: "We are sure you will not let yourself be overcome by the sweet odor of the American beauty rose."[91]

Industrial Relations Commission Chairman Frank Walsh demolished Rockefeller's facade of innocence—and dented Mother Jones's reputation for toughness—when he mercilessly grilled the magnate and then contradicted his answers with correspondence to the Colorado mine officials signed by Rockefeller. But Mother Jones, while showing some personal affection for him, did nevertheless express reservations about his Colorado Industrial Representation Plan, or Rockefeller Plan.

It was developed for Rockefeller by W. L. MacKenzie King, a former Canadian labor minister and later prime minister, and it proposed a management-worker committee to hear grievances. The plan also granted several of the miners' strike demands, such as checkweighmen, the right to trade where one pleased, and the right to join a union. The forerunner of many a company union, the plan was launched in a blaze of publicity in the fall of 1915 when Rockefeller came to Colorado. Dancing with the miners' wives and bouncing their children on his knee, he inaugurated the plan which was an aid to the workers, but not to the UMW.[92] "Benevolent feudalism," Frank Hayes called it. "A sham and a fraud," said Mother Jones. "You can't fool my boys," she added, "they know that this kind of scheme is a hypocritical and dishonest practice."[93] She remained hostile to company unions the rest of her life. They just would not work, she maintained, without a strong and independent union with the power and the money to carry out a strike in pursuit of just demands.

Mother Jones, too, had her hour before the Industrial Relations Commission when it met in Washington in May of 1915. She was, the *New York Times* said, "one of the most entertaining witnesses that could have been brought before that body. Not a question interrrupted her and she proceeded in her quaint way without being tied down to geography or continuity of events."⁹⁴ Although she had not been there, she related the tragic events of a year earlier in Ludlow, and she recommended that the government eliminate unemployment, regulate detective agencies, and take over the coal mines. "No operator, no coal company on the face of the earth made that coal," Mother Jones declared, "It is a mineral; it belongs to the nation; it was there down the ages, and it belongs to every generation that comes along." She added that she also favored nationalization of "all other industries, and then we can get the hours of labor down and put men to work." Inaction on grievances and the continued use of the militia, she asserted, were producing "anarchists out of men who would otherwise be the very best and orderly sort of citizen."⁹⁵

As the Colorado conflict shifted from the battlefield to the courtroom, Mother Jones returned to whip up sympathy for those sentenced for their strike activities. Lawson, indicted for murder, was sentenced to life imprisonment at hard labor. Presiding at his trial in July 1915 was a newly-appointed Las Animas County judge who formerly had been a coal-company attorney and who had assisted in preparing cases against the strikers. Much of the evidence against Lawson came from detectives retained by the coal companies, and the jury was selected by the county sheriff whose sympathies were quite clear.⁹⁶ Labor bodies across the nation protested the sentence, and Mother Jones loosed her still-volcanic rhetoric in Kansas City, Chicago, Columbus, Cleveland, and Washington on Lawson's behalf. In Seattle, she even took time to visit striking coal miners in British Columbia. There she addressed their meetings in Victoria after winning a dispute with Canadian immigration authorities who would have kept her out of the strike zone. Lawson eventually was freed by the Colorado Supreme Court, and many of the other cases were dropped, reportedly at Rockefeller's request.⁹⁷

As in West Virginia, unionization would not come fully to Colorado until the 1933 National Industrial Recovery Act and its progeny, the Wagner Act and the Fair Labor Standards Act. But in what may have been in part a delayed reaction to the strike, the Victor-American Fuel Company in 1917 signed a three-year UMW contract unionizing its dozen large mines in Colorado and two in New Mexico. In this strike Mother Jones, as was her aim, had centered public outrage on the injustices heaped upon her and her fellows. She told the House Mines and Mining subcommittee just after Ludlow, that "if I had been in Colorado now and the governor had left my hands loose, their tragedy would not have taken place. . . . I believe in the brain instead of the muscle," she said. "I believe in the pen instead of the sword."[98]

It is unlikely that Mother Jones would have prevented the Ludlow debacle or its aftermath. Both were spontaneous. Both may have happened even sooner or on a larger scale if she and her incendiary rhetoric had been there. But in a limited sense she was correct in saying that she was a force for education, if in an unorthodox way. Her opponents' fear was her best weapon, and she used it shrewdly. Her legend, her impassioned speeches, perhaps her charisma led the opposition in Colorado and elsewhere to blatantly stupid acts. She was omnipotent to those who feared what she stood for, and they reacted blindly. And when they did—like riding down women, or locking up an old lady, or saying that people should not cross county lines—Mother Jones became the educator, telling the world.

ELEVEN

If I pray I will have to wait until I am dead to get anything; but when I swear I get things here.
—Mother Jones[1]

L IK E social zealots before and since, Mother Jones was the target of persecutions, public and private. She was, as has been noted, jailed without charge, deported for slight cause, threatened with her life, and tried for dubious crimes. The Bill of Rights seemingly applied to more timid souls in less troubled times. Calumny, too, could be the iconoclast's reward.

On a pleasant, sunny morning along the Tug River in southern West Virginia, a man standing in a gondola car casually tossed leaflets along the Mingo County countryside. But as the train rumbled slowly through the town of Matewan, West Virginia, a group of miners darted out and jumped aboard. The leafleteer, when he saw the men coming, leaped off the train and ran for the river. But before he could get 50 yards, he was caught. A short while later, a doctor in Williamson, about eight miles away, received an anonymous call asking him to pick up the beaten, castrated victim. The broadsides he had been distributing called Mother Jones a former prostitute. Antiunion propaganda often was thrown from the trains as they passed through mining towns. But this message, designed to sway the religious people of the county, was anathema to those who admired her.[2]

134

Because she was a spectacular woman in a dangerous occupation, because she was articulate, given to occasional hyperbole and because hers was an obscure background, Mother Jones naturally gave rise to legends. These grew, and depending on her mood or impishness, she accepted some by not denying them. The "prostitute" tag endured, and despite outrage shown by some of her associates, Mother Jones never did much to refute it. At one point, she obliquely acknowledged it—but whether for devilment or candor we may never know. Her early years—after the loss of her family and before her known labor activities—are clouded, and she did little in her speeches or writings to clarify. The vacuum, however, was not lost on her detractors. The prostitution charges had their beginning in January 1904 when Mother Jones was involved in her first major strike effort in Colorado's southern fields. A Denver weekly newspaper, *Polly Pry,* published a two-page article purporting to detail Mother Jones's background.

When Mrs. Leonel Ross O'Bryan (then Mrs. George Anthony) began her paper in September 1903, the former *New York World* and *Denver Post* newspaperwoman promised readers "a dose of that unpalatable and evanescent bug-a-bear known as the—Truth." She added that the paper "will have no malice in it and no scandal. . . . It will never intentionally injure any man or woman even if it sometimes says the thing that sounds unkind."[3] A January issue, however, quickly sketched Mother Jones's labor involvement, citing "her battle cry of 'We'd rather fight than work!' " and stating that Mother Jones "Has a record of never advocating peace, nor arbitration—but always being for strife and war." *Polly Pry* then went on to give "a few of the facts" said to be gleaned from secret files down at the "Pinkerton office."[4] "A vulgar, heartless, vicious creature, with a fiery temper and a cold-blooded brutality rare even in the slums," Mother Jones had been an inmate of the Jennie Rogers house on Denver's Market Street until she bribed all the girls into leaving for a house in Omaha, the newspaper stated. Mother Jones is also mentioned as working for three other "madams" and as taking "a prominent part in the Denver preparations" for the care of Coxey's Army, a contingent of the unemployed who marched on Washington in 1894.

The article went on to forecast gloomily what political power Mother Jones could have. "Not content with owning and controlling the United Mine Workers of America and that sister organization, the

Western Federation of Miners, she sighs for new worlds to conquer. One of these new worlds is to be politics and the political ownership of the State of Colorado—and 'Mother' Jones is going to own it." The following week, *Polly Pry* added to the charges. In 1899, Mother Jones leased a building at 2114 Market Street, refurbished it, and then opened it as a "house" that soon "became one of the most notorious in the city." Its seven inmates were making Mother Jones rich, the paper reported, until a "friend" called "Black-leg" deserted her. After that, Mother Jones "went to the bad." She "took to drink, and was arrested several times on the charge of drunkenness and disorderly conduct." Within two months, she had squandered $15,000 and became an inmate of another house of prostitution. Said *Polly Pry:* "And this is the woman the wives and children of the deluded miners call 'Mother.' Interesting, isn't it?"[5]

These articles, reprinted in many other papers, became the basis of attacks from across the nation. The allegations gained their most widespread circulation when George Kindel, a Colorado Congressman allied to the mining interests, read the *Polly Pry* pieces into the *Congressional Record* during the height of the 1914 Colorado strife.[6] This highly irritated Terence Powderly, who wrote to Kindel. "My acquaintance with her began at a time when part of this alleged record of her by *Polly Pry* was being made up, and at that time to my certain knowledge, she was not the keeper of a house of ill fame, nor an inmate of such a house, neither, was she a procuress for any such institution," Powderly said of Mother Jones. "It seems to me to be your duty to ask Congress the privilege of erasing from the record the stain fastened upon it on June 13, 1914, when you made use of that record to assail a white-haired, aged, defenseless woman."[7]

John Mitchell also had been asked to refute the charges soon after they appeared in 1904 and not long before he and Mother Jones split irrevocably. But he replied that he had not known her prior to 1899, "although no person on earth would give more than I to be in a position to deny the charges mentioned."[8] In fact, Mitchell wanted Mother Jones to file suit against *Polly Pry,* and his insistence may have added to her disenchantment with him, one report indicates. However, a UMW attorney in Denver who examined the newspaper articles and the state's libel laws advised against a suit because of the weakness of the case.[9]

Mother Jones's silence on the matter, even though the allegations hounded her for years, is curious. Certainly, she was silent on little else. Certainly, the picturing of her as a "heartless, vicious creature" with "a cold-blooded brutality" was cut from the whole cloth. Certainly also, the dates—if not the acts—that *Polly Pry* asserted were in part obviously wrong. In 1899, thousands of eastern Pennsylvania coal miners could attest to her whereabouts.

But where was she and what was she doing before that?

Perhaps Mother Jones did not wish to lend any more attention to the charges than they had received already. Perhaps an air of mystery, a murky past, was to her not altogether unattractive. Perhaps, although Denver records yield no such evidence, the substance of the allegations was true. Duncan McDonald, an Illinois miner and warm admirer of Mother Jones, said that when he asked about her reluctance to rebut the charges, she replied: "Don't you think whatever my past might have been that I have more than made up for it?"[10] This appears to be the closest she came to admitting the truth of the reports. Upton Sinclair, however, said that Mother Jones told him that the story spread from her early days as a seamstress. She did some sewing for a prostitute who soon died and was denied burial by a Catholic church. Mother Jones then wrote to a newspaper to protest the church's policy and, in return, was herself castigated as being a "madam."[11]

Mother Jones was the frequent object of other vituperations as well. A McDowell County, West Virginia, pamphlet in 1915, for example, asserted: "It is generally known that Mother Jones is an Athiest. . . . She is as profane and foulmouthed as any dive keeper and rarely ever makes a public speech that she does not swear and take the name of God in vein [*sic*]." The pamphlet went on to quote verbatim from the prostitution charges of *Polly Pry*. It then implied that Mother Jones was at fault, when, as reported by a Chicago newspaper, striking union teamsters refused to drive carriages to pick up the injured at the 1903 Iroquois Theater fire. Mother Jones wasn't said to have been there or even to have been the inspiration. But the anecdote was carried under a headline: "Typical Results of Her Work." The article concluded that Mother Jones "is the worst enemy to poor and laboring men for she teaches false standards of organization and infuses only a spirit of lawlessness, anarchy, and results which make the poor deluded workers poorer and more miserable. From such as she they should flee as from the plague."[12]

Similarly, the wages earned by Mother Jones and other organizers often were exaggerated in an attempt to discredit the union leadership. An operators' bulletin in Colorado, for example, said that Mother Jones, "whose sole duty was to agitate," received $2,668.62 as salary in a nine-week period, or about $42.00 a day. Actually, she did receive $2,668.62 but for the entire year 1913 and not all of it in salary. The sum consisted of $940.00 in UMW salary and $1,728.62 in expenses. The daily rate, then, was $2.57, not $42.00.[13]

As she proved again in Colorado, Mother Jones had an unequaled emotional power over workers, especially miners and their famililes. Like her hero John Brown, she had an intensity and a commitment which put backbone into the hesitant and fear into the opponents of change. Brown "committed murder in his day. . . . He was a criminal in the eyes of the court and in the eyes of many of the Nation," Mother Jones told a UMW national convention. "But he was a hero in the eyes of God. He started the war on chattel slavery. We have to carry on the war on industrial slavery."[14] But rather than John Brown—or Carrie Nation, Joan of Arc, or even Peter the Hermit, with all of whom she was at times compared—she more nearly resembled Wendell Phillips or Louise Michel, the "Red Virgin of Montmartre."

Unlike Mother Jones, Phillips, an abolitionist and reformer, had an Ivy League education. But like her, he was an awe-inspiring speaker whose direct and colloquial manner won him a fond following. He did not back away from abolitionism when Brown was excecuted. Instead, he persevered by personal fearlessness and a willingness to sacrifice. He, too, at times split with the leaders of the movement. He refused in large part to link the cause with political action, much as Mother Jones disdained politics for work directly with the poor and the oppressed. Again like Mother Jones, Phillips was considered extremely radical at the time but hardly so in retrospect after his death at the age of 73 in 1884.[15]

Louise Michel, a revolutionary French socialist, was, like Mother Jones, born in May 1830. Although the illegitimate daughter of a housemaid, she received a liberal education and, again like Mother Jones, became a teacher before involving herself in social work and revolutionary ideas. A soldier of courage in the 1871 Commune, she was in and out of prisons for much of her life, but she never recanted her radicalism. She was a woman of humanity as well as zeal who condoned violence, like Mother Jones, when it was seen as indispensable to her own inflexible purpose. Louise Michel won notoriety for leading protests and received six years in jail for one in which she incited a mob to rob bakeries during a hunger march. She died, however, in Marseilles in 1905, about the time Mother Jones was reaching her stride as an agitator.[16]

Mother Jones had an education which then was well above the ordinary for a woman, certainly for an immigrant worker's daughter. She occasionally quoted Kipling and other classics of literature and was alert and informed about national and international affairs even as she approached her hundredth year. But while she preached to miners about the merits of education, she, publicly at least, preferred to obscure her own background. She could be something of an anti-intellectual at times.

She told a West Virginia audience:

"A doctor said to me in Cincinnati, 'Did you ever graduate from college, Mother Jones?'

"I said, 'I did.'

"He said, 'Would you mind telling me?'

" 'No,' I said, 'I graduated from the college of hard knocks.' That is my college; I graduated from that college—hunger, persecution, and suffering—and I wouldn't exchange that college for all the university dudes on the face of God's earth. (Loud applause.)"[17]

All her life she would deal in such retorts and epigrams. Succinct flippancies mated with poignant reality appealed to her and to her roughhewn audiences. Such was the staple of her speeches. "Don't bother about politics," she would caution UMW delegates, "keep close to the economic struggle; don't allow politicians to interfere with your business. . . . Don't let the ministers bother you, we know the Lord Jesus Christ as well as they do."[18] But she had a more philosophic side as well. Despite the barbs at religion, she held a basic faith in man's ability to improve himself. The anti-intellectual facade notwithstanding, she recognized education as a needed tool in the evolution of the workingman.

"The people of this country must learn to choose their leaders—political, industrial, and social—not because they are good fellows but because they are intelligent students of the great questions," she said another time. "No job is too small to put a thinker into. . . . There are such men for every situation. When they get into the offices, we will begin to hurry on the upward path. Politics, economics, and sociology should link arms."[19] Naturally, she told this to a news reporter, not to a mob of miners.

Eighty-four-year-old Mother Jones's zeal didn't end with the Colorado combat but carried over into a variety of causes and conflicts soon to attract her. In them, she showed not only the deep empathy which made her loved by the workers but also the sporadic veering toward violence which made her name an epithet among keepers of the established order.

Flitting from West Virginia's striking miners to those of Colorado in 1913, Mother Jones rallied thousands in the coal fields. But in bettween, she also returned to Upper Michigan, after an absence of eight years, to attempt to fan the flames of a fierce struggle there. In 1905, she had preached unionism and the class struggle. By 1908, the WFM had won a foothold, and membership grew in size and militancy until in July 1913 union officials were forced to call a strike they had hoped to delay until the following spring. But 98 percent of the miners voted to present demands to the copper companies and strike if concessions were not won.[20]

It was the WFM's largest walkout. About 15,000 men stayed out for eight months from the 42 copper mines in the three-county district. Taking a cue from the history of its western counterparts, the conflict included vigilante committees and deportations. In producing ore worth more than $33 million in 1912, the copper miners worked underground 10 to 11 hours daily and for less money than their Montana equals who worked only 8.5 hours. Union recognition and abolition of the new one-man drill, a back-breaking, dangerous tool called the "widow-maker" by the miners, also were at issue in Michigan.[21]

Adding to the bitterness after the strike began on July 23 was an almost immediate call-up of 2,400 National Guardsmen after early but minor violence against nonunion workers. Deputization of up to 1,700 men, many of whom were imported from New York, and the hiring of private detectives as mine guards further heightened tension, "More than anything else that happened during the strike," a government inquiry later concluded, these importations incensed the strikers.[22] At first there was little violence and strikers held parades and meetings in large halls. Labor leaders, including former UMW President John Mitchell, WFM President Charles Moyer, AFL Treasurer John Lennon, and

Mother Jones gave speeches of encouragement which were translated into several languages for the miners.

To the greetings of 3,000, Mother Jones arrived in Calumet on August 5, declined an auto ride from the railroad depot to the union hall, and declared, "These strike movements are the greatest fun in the world." In her speeches, she criticized use of the troops and promised to "get the women lined up to keep up their nerve and I'm going to make some of these weak-kneed men buck up and fall into line. I'll take them back into the game instead of letting them sneak out into the grass."[23] But if the strike was "fun" and a "game," the mirth soon dissipated in bloodshed when, first, deputies killed two strikers by opening fire on a boarding house. Then, on Christmas Eve in a crowded union hall, a false cry of "fire" caused a stampede which trampled to death 11 adults and 62 children of the miners. When Moyer refused to accept $25,000 in relief from the Citizens Alliance business group for the tragedy, in which he implied they were the cause, he was beaten, shot in the back, and deported to Chicago.[24]

Blame was never fixed in the Christmas Eve disaster, although the WFM said a man with a Citizens Alliance lapel button incited the panic. Moyer and 38 others, however, were indicted by a grand jury on charges of violence and conspiracy, although they were not brought to trial.[25]

The Michigan strike, to the accompaniment of broad injunctions, the importation of strikebreakers, and offers of arbitration refused by the companies, dragged on for eight months. With their strike fund lagging, WFM members in April 1914 voted to end the walkout since the eight-hour day and rehiring of most of the strikers had been conceded by the operators.[26] The Michigan fight was the last upsurge of the militant WFM spirit. The 1903 Colorado strike and the Haywood-Moyer-Pettibone trial had drained it financially, and the 1907 split with the IWW rent it ideologically. Mother Jones's brief appearance in the second Michigan strike was but a reminder of earlier days which would not return.

Just prior to testifying before the Industrial Relations Commission about her Colorado adventures, Mother Jones stopped off in Roosevelt, New Jersey, to bolster striking workers at the Williams and Clark chemical plant. Two days earlier, a pair of strikers had been shot and killed by plant guards, and a county prosecutor's investigation revealed they were shot in the back and when not on company property. Community sentiment in the town, including that of public officials, went over-whelmingly to the side of the strikers.²⁷ Addressing the 900 strikers on January 21, 1915, Mother Jones advised them to hold out "to the last ditch" but to remain calm and not use guns regardless of the provocation. "Stick to your husbands," she later told the women. "Don't let them go back as scabs. Help them stand firm, and, above all, keep them away from the saloons."²⁸

Early the next month, she spoke before 7,000 New York City members of the Ladies' Waist and Dress Makers Union which voted to strike if its demands were not met. "I would rather raise hell in this country than anywhere else on earth," she told them. "I have just fought through a 16-month strike in Colorado and it ended in our forcing J. D. Rockefeller to admit that we were right. I have been up against armed mercenaries in labor troubles all over the country, but this old woman with a hatpin scared them."²⁹

Later, she was in Chicago, telling striking waist and dress makers "it's an honor to go to jail when your cause is just." Her arrival, called "explosive" by the Chicago press, may have helped win this first victory of the city's dress and white goods workers. The walkout, which began in protest of the discharge of several glove workers, resulted in a cut in hours to 50 a week, union recognition, higher pay, and an arbitration plan.³⁰ A few weeks later, Mother Jones also joined protests in Chicago by 15,000 strikers who belonged to the Amalgamated Clothing Workers of America.³¹

Returning also to Arizona in 1915, Mother Jones worked in rare concert there with a politician. Governor George Wiley Paul Hunt had been struck by both poverty and wanderlust as a youth. He became a prospector, ferry boat operator, waiter, rancher, delivery boy, and banker. An eight-term territorial legislator of modest achievements, Hunt, a Democrat, presided over the consitutional convention when Arizona became a state in 1912. As the state's first governor, he would win the praise of labor in general and of Mother Jones in particular.³²

Three times during 1915 the WFM struck in parts of Arizona, and by October about 5,000 copper miners in the Clifton district were off the job. Mother Jones said she joined the fray and was impressed by the way Hunt kept down the violence by prohibiting the importation of professional strikebreakers and mine guards. After five months, the dispute ended with the miners receiving a wage increase of from 20 to 70 percent and an improved arbitration procedure, although no union recognition was won.[33] Soon afterward, as labor voiced its enthusiasm for the governor's handling of the dispute, Mother Jones arrived in Phoenix where Hunt dispatched his car to meet her at the railroad station. He also sent a bouquet to her hotel "as a reward for declaiming Governor Hunt to be the greatest governor that the country has ever produced," a newspaper reported.[34]

"The governors of several states," Mother Jones later said, obviously flattered, "have sent their militia to meet me at the stations and they always brought a bouquet with them, but it was always a bouquet of bayonets. And if there was any inquiry about my health, it was always with the hope of finding me dead."[35] But Governor Hunt needed more than accolades. He was up for reelection soon. His positive stand during the strike probably prevented bloodshed, but it also created angry criticism. A movement to recall him actually had been started during the dispute.

After a trip to California, Mother Jones returned to the state in August 1916 to stump for Hunt's third-term campaign. On August 8, she spoke before the Arizona State Federation of Labor convention in Tucson and shared the platform with a university president. The anti-Hunt *Arizona Daily Star* called this a "striking contrast" since " 'Mother' Jones used profanity, while the learned educator used the most chaste of language. The contrast, however, was evidently lost upon their hearers, who cheered both impartially." Mother Jones traveled northward through Phoenix and Prescottt before leaving the state again for California.[36]

In the election, however, Thomas Campbell, a former mine owner, defeated Hunt by 30 votes out of 55,000 cast, although Hunt contested the results. The state Supreme Court seated Campbell without pay until the issue could be settled.[37] In analyzing the presumed defeat of Hunt, the *Arizona Daily Star* found the crux to be "the people as a whole versus union labor and its selfish programs." A vote for Hunt was for continued labor strife, the newspaper said, and "Mother Jones, the notorious firebrand, was also a factor . . . for she insulted every decent element in the State by her foul expressions."[38]

However, the court ultimately gave Hunt the majority of the 30 disputed votes and Campbell was deposed after serving about half of the two-year term. During that period, though, Arizona's labor troubles grew. In June 1917 a walkout of about 2,000 miners in the Bisbee area seriously crippled production and spawned a wave of wartime hysteria. An IWW "scare" blossomed, and in several mass deportations, strikers and strike sympathizers were shipped off to the desert. Hunt, appointed as a federal conciliator, met little success in ending the dispute. But a federal mediation team, including William B. Wilson and John H. Walker, both friends of Mother Jones, finally won an agreement.[39]

Hunt maintained that the "IWW menace" was camouflage by the operators to attempt to destroy all of organized labor in the state. Having been characterized as George "Wobbly P." Hunt, he was defeated in 1918 and then appointed United States minister to Siam. He served there from 1920 to 1921 before returning to win four more terms as Arizona governor.[40] Although Mother Jones was not active in the state after 1916, she and Hunt corresponded and remained good friends. In 1927, Fred Mooney, a West Virginian who had heard Mother Jones mention Hunt with fondness, dropped in on him in Phoenix, armed with a letter of introduction from Mother Jones. After chatting for a while, Hunt motioned Mooney over to a "lace covered frame hanging against the wall" in the governor's office. "You know, boy," Hunt said, parting the lace curtain and revealing a large, inscribed photograph of Mother Jones, "I think she is unquestionably the greatest woman this nation has ever produced."[41]

Others, too, if less generous in their praise, nonetheless sought Mother Jones's powerful presence. In December 1915, Tom Mooney, a San Francisco socialist, had written to her, asking her to come to California to help the three-year-old International Workers Defense League pay off the debts it incurred in acquitting Mooney of a charge of illegal possession of explosives.[42] The League was organized to help radicals in court. It publicized their cases, raised funds, and hired counsel. Local leagues were formed for specific cases, and the San Francisco branch, for example, helped raise legal and moral questions about Mother Jones's repeated imprisonments in West Virginia and Colorado from 1912 to 1914.

Apparently, she didn't go to California at this time. But she did remain close in spirit to Mooney, secretary of the San Francisco league, and events soon were to place her once again on the fringes of a major national issue. On July 22, 1916, a bomb exploded at Steuart and Market streets in San Francisco, killing ten spectators watching a Preparedness Day Parade. Forty were wounded and, as in the Haymarket after-math, anarchists and other radicals were rounded up quickly as possible suspects. Even more than the Haymarket affair of 30 years earlier, the San Francisco incident had wounded the national psyche, shattered the cohesiveness—real or imagined—of a nation bent on expunging the European evil.[43] Tom Mooney and his wife, Rena, claimed to be watch-ing the parade from the top of their residence at 975 Market Street, more than a mile from the explosion. They produced a photograph taken by a friend which showed them on the rooftop and revealed, under magnification, a nearby clock at a time just minutes before the explosion. Mooney never wavered from this explanation.[44]

"For Mother Jones," wrote a Mooney scholar, "the significant fact was Mooney's struggle against the Pinkertons and corporation lawyers, not his guilt or innocence according to the law. He was on the fighting line in the class war."[45] Mooney, who was to be tried in January 1917, again wrote Mother Jones the month before the trial. "I hope you will find time to give what ever help your health and energy will permitt [*sic*] you." She replied with a lecture on the evils of violence and added, "I felt in this case, as I read it, there was a hidden wire somewhere, that has not come to the surface. I cannot believe that the workers of California would resort to any crime of the kind.

"The people have a right to have a preparedness parade, if they wish, without being molested, or interfered with in any way. And we must be generous enough to concede every citizen the rights we claim for ourselves," she told Mooney. "I feel that you boys have been the victims of this diabolical crime and are innocent from the beginning. I will do everything that I can do to help you. . . . I am yours in the struggle for a nobler civilization."[46]

Mother Jones went within a few days to the AFL Executive Council meeting in Chicago to present Mooney's case, and when Mooney was sentenced in May to be hanged, she was in California claiming he had been prejudiced by a hostile court.[47] Indeed, there were some very un-reliable prosecution witnesses and a great deal of conflicting testimony. During the spring of 1917, the Mooney case became a national labor cause, gaining momentum as the irregularities in the trial were high-lighted. Protest meetings were held in cities from coast to coast, and unions joined in to broaden the earlier radicals-only base of the Mooney defense movement.

The AFL, which had been humiliated by its help in financing the McNamara defense in 1911, was reluctant to become involved. Its 1916 convention took no action, and in the two succeeding years, the convention limited itself to passage of resolutions appealing to California and federal officials. But the AFL did not raise funds or approve coercive measures, such as a general strike. After several prosecution witnesses were exposed as perjurers, however, some middle-of-the road labor leaders, including AFL President Samuel Gompers, increased their support from behind the scenes. For a year, Mooney remained on Death Row.[48]

Mother Jones was active in the Mooney protest movement and apparently even sought support from the Women's Christian Temperance Union (WCTU), a group whose aims she normally held in slight regard. "The great issue now before Organized Labor and the thinking American people is the integrity of the courts," she wrote to a WCTU official. "They are the bulwark of our institutions and their integrity must be preserved, for once the workers lose faith then all hope is blasted and no one can be responsible for the outcome."[49]

This hardly sounded like the judge-baiting Mother Jones of old. But she did work hard for Mooney as did leaders of various other persuasions. Finally, spurred by worldwide protests, the governor of California in April 1918 commuted the sentence to life imprisonment. That, of course, did not quell the voices of dissent. Many still considered Mooney the target of right-wing, militaristic hysteria and a man whose only "crime" was being a radical labor leader. Throughout the 1920s, the labor movement appealed for his release. The embittered prisoner, never swaying from his claim of innocence, wanted nothing short of unconditional freedom. In late 1927, Mother Jones wrote to a friend: "I understand that the Governor offered a parole to Mooney but he would not accept it. He wanted a full pardon. If he does not accept a parole I am inclined to think he will spend his time behind prison bars.

"It is sad to think you have such men to deal with," she wrote, "and that one has to put forth their best efforts to get their freedom, and then not to be appreciated any more than he appreciates it." Mother Jones added that if she could get J. P. McNamara, convicted in the *Times* bombing case, and several others out of jail, "I would not bother with Mooney until he got tired of his boarding place."[50] But though disenchanted at times, she remained loyal to Mooney. On her hundredth birthday—May 1, 1930—she would appeal to California Governor C. C. Young to redeem his state's reputation by freeing Tom Mooney.[51] As it happened, Mooney was released, but not until nine years later by Governor Culbert L. Olson. Ill and near death, Mooney led a victory parade up San Francico's Market Street.

In October, 1916, a few months before the Mooney trial and just before Mother Jones's recitation to Mooney on the evils of violence, she spawned no little strife of her own, taking part in a strike of street-car operators in New York City. She arrived there October 3, the same day as the strikebreakers appeared. More than 11,000 carmen had struck on subway, surface, and elevated lines in the city of five million. They were protesting the discharge of hundreds of union members in violation of contract, and they had strong support from 400,000 other unionists.[52]

Mother Jones told the men on October 4 how violence had succeeded in many of the past strikes she had been in, and the following day, she gave an inflammatory speech to 200 wives of the strikers in Mozart Hall. "You ought to be out raising hell. This is the fighting age," she said. "Put on your fighting clothes. America was not discovered by Columbus for that bunch of bloodsucking leeches who are now living off us. You are too sentimental."[53]

As the women filed out of the hall, a streetcar, run by a scab, passed the door, then stopped for a stalled truck. The women crowded around. Many carried babies which they left on the sidewalk, and then they began throwing paving blocks and attacking the police "with their fists, finger nails, bricks, and other missiles," newspaper reports said. The conductor and his passengers fled as the mob broke every window in the streetcar and attempted to take apart the seats and the woodwork. A crowd of thousands was attracted by the skirmish. Several women were clubbed by the police and six were arrested, and one ample woman required four patrolmen to carry her to the paddy wagon.[54]

Mother Jones's armchair philosophy of nonviolence once again had crumbled in a burst of passion. As she once confided to a friend: "I am not greatly worried by methods, but I want results."[55] Editorialized the *New York Times:* "It would be a pity to interfere with the diversion of so gentle and fragrant a personage as Mother Jones, but her charter of speech will not be suffered to cover an attested case of incitation to disorder or worse."[56] Undeterred, however, she spoke to 5,000 strikers the following day, describing the police as "uniformed murderers." She pledged not "to make any apology" for the riot. "If the police are organized to shed our blood we are to organize to shed the other side's blood. Tell the Mayor and your Councilmen and Police Commissioner that if they want to hang me, let them hang me, but when I am on the scaffold I'll cry 'Freedom for the working classes' and when I meet God Almighty I'll have Him damn them."[57] She threatened to bring in an army of women from outside the state to stop what she said were the police outrages, and she denounced the press for taking the strike stories off their front pages. The day of her first speech, police reported 29 other attacks on surface or elevated cars.[58]

In something of a similar sequence, Mother Jones was reported in Raleigh County, West Virginia, in the fall of 1917 where a strike for recognition had begun about a month before her arrival. However, a sizeable bloc of nonunion workers continued on the job at the Glen White operation. At a mass meeting, Mother Jones is said to have told the strikers: "You goddamned cowards are losing this strike because you haven't got the guts to go out and fight and win it. Why the hell don't you take your high-power rifles and blow the goddamned scabs out of the mines."[59]

A few days later, on November 16, strikers armed with high-power rifles opened fire from a hillside on a group of nonunion miners who were being hoisted to the surface in an elevator. The hoist operator quickly lowered the cage, and no one was injured. But more than 300 rifle shots were reported fired in the fusillade. Six men were indicted for attempted murder and received sentences of up to five years in prison.[60] Again it was clear that Mother Jones's preachments were not necessarily her principles in the field. She was consistently inconsistent in her views toward violence, and, most assuredly, toward politics.

TWELVE

I am a Socialist. Why shouldn't I be?
—Mother Jones, 1913
I am neither Socialist nor Anarchist.
—Mother Jones, 1913[1]

MOTHER Jones's love-hate relationship with the Socialists was in fullest bloom in the frenetic years just before World War I. She often agreed with them on policy. She befriended them and borrowed money from them. But at the same time, she often discounted them in aggregate as having more "sentiment than sense." The bitter feelings may have been caused in part by a dispute over money. Living as she always did without property, bank accounts, or even a place to call home, Mother Jones forever was borrowing or lending for assorted causes. Letters to and from her are filled with mention of debts and of money delayed in the mail or through personal plight. Furthermore, she never trusted banks. Instead, she turned over her cash—when she had some—to her friends for safe-keeping.[2] When she did not have money, she borrowed.

Mother Jones claimed to have told John D. Rockefeller, Jr.: "If you gave me your institution, I would wreck it tomorrow; it would not last a month after I was in. All I want money for is to use to lick the other fellow." With some accuracy she prophesied that she would not "take any money to the grave. I didn't bring any here," she said, "and I don't want to go up to God Almighty as a high-class burglar."[3]

149

Despite her inexact financial affairs, Mother Jones normally steered clear of party disputes over money. But on February 28, 1911, an investigating committee of the Socialist Party reported on charges leveled against its national secretary. Among the allegations was a complaint by Mother Jones that J. Mahlon Barnes, the secretary, had acted dishonestly. Charges filed against Barnes by others included drunkenness, immorality, inefficiency, and incompetency. In 1905, Mother Jones had loaned Barnes $250.00. He claimed to have repaid it the following year, but Mother Jones denied this and threatened suit to force payment. Barnes replied that although he had already paid, he could not find the receipt but promised to pay a second time in installments.

Mother Jones told the investigators that she received no money either time. But at the hearing, Barnes's position was backed by a witness who said he saw Mother Jones receive $100 from Barnes in the national office. Receipts for the remainder were received by Barnes from third persons who were to pass the repayment on to Mother Jones. The party investigators, who included Oscar Ameringer, James H. Maurer, and her friend Adolph Germer, found Mother Jones's charges to be "wholly without foundation." Further, they said the allegation "was indeed a most frivolous one" which was "instigated maliciously" by attorney Thomas J. Morgan on Mother Jones's behalf to embarrass Barnes. The other allegations were dismissed similarly.[4]

The action must have hurt Mother Jones, who so diligently nurtured her image of honesty and who usually remained so scrupulously aloof from just such tragicomic machinations. John O'Neill, editor of *Miner's Magazine,* the organ of the WFM, blasted the findings and said there was not "a single shred of positive evidence" that Barnes had repaid the loan. O'Neill rejected the idea that Mother Jones was "a blackmailer," and he printed a series of letters from her and Barnes which purported to show nonpayment.

The report was a "white-wash," ONeill said. Barnes escaped conviction because "he knew the weakness and frailities of the National Executive Committee" and "would squeal upon others" if exposed. In his continuing defense of Mother Jones, O'Neill said the party needs to get rid of the "professional parasites and soulless slanderers" because if it does not "the party will be submerged in a cesspool whose stench of 'free love' and moral rottenness will nauseate even the callous stomach of the Brotherhood of Libertines."[5] O'Neill's rebuttal in *Miner's*

Magazine continued for months, although Mother Jones herself apparently said little about the episode. She continued to speak aggressively for the cause, making no secret of her socialism as individually endorsed by herself. She was a revolutionary in the vague sense that she believed in the dawning of a new system.

But she was also, and perhaps more fundamentally, a unionist which meant winning here and now a better life for the workers. She wavered between the two ideals, never excluding one for the other. In an interview in the summer of 1912, she best explained her position.

I am simply a social revolutionist. I believe in collective ownership of the means of wealth. . . . Sooner or later, and perhaps sooner than we think, evolution and revolution will have accomplished the overturning of the system under which we now live, and the worker will have gained his own. This change will come as a result of education.

My life work has been to try to educate the worker to a sense of the wrongs he has had to suffer, and does suffer—and to stir up the oppressed to a point of getting off their knees and demanding that which I believe to be rightfully theirs. When force is used to hinder the worker in his efforts to obtain the things which are his, he has the right to meet force with force. He has the right to strike for what is his due, and he has no right to be satisfied with less. The people want to do right, but they have been hoodwinked for ages. They are now awakening, and the day of their enfranchisement is near at hand.[6]

To a group of cheering West Virginia miners, she phrased her dream less abstractly. "One of these days we are going to take over the mines," she said, "that is what we are going to do; we are going to take over those mines. The Government has a mine in North Dakota. It works eight hours—not a minute more. There are no guards, no police, no militia. The men make $125 a month, and there is never any trouble at that mine. Uncle Sam is running the job, and he is a pretty good mine inspector." (Cries of "Tell it, mama; I can't.")[7]

The internationalism of the Socialists sometimes was more than Mother Jones could fathom. They were "too busy eulogizing their political dictators," she said, to hear "the screams and groans and heartaches of women and children as the military tear their loved ones from them, throw them into prison cells and tell them they must submit or perish there."[8] The Socialist cry of "universal brotherhood" alienates many, she stated, presumably including herself. Socialism has "too much sentiment in it—far too much, I'm sure of it. It's mostly sentiment, and that's why it will not work. What we want is not sentiment, but sense," Mother Jones told a newspaper in 1913.[9] Her words, when thrown to a cheering crowd or carefully measured for a journalist, differed dramatically.

The Socialist Party, although officially against America's entry into World War I, came to be badly split. Mother Jones saw Germany as a threat to the Russian Revolution and thus reluctantly recognized the need for the Allies to hand the Kaiser a defeat. The *Appeal to Reason* threw its support to Wilson and his Fourteen Points, and by June 1918 Mother Jones announced for the first time that she was urging working men and women to buy government bonds.[10] On the question of war she split from some of her radical friends like Bill Haywood and Eugene Debs, who paid severely for their opposition to what they said was a capitalist-inspired conflict.

Mother Jones could count among her admirers some of the most well known Socialists of the day. One, for example, was Kate Richards. The daughter of a well-to-do Kansas rancher who was ruined in a drought and panic, she came to reject the temperance movement in which she was involved and instead became a machinist and a union member. When she heard Mother Jones speak at a local cigar makers' ball, she "hastily sought out 'Mother' and asked her to tell what Socialism was." Talking to the old agitator was "one of the milesposts" of her life. Subsequently married to Frank O'Hare, Kate Richards was with him editor and publisher of the *National Rip-Saw,* a popular Socialist monthly in St. Louis.[11] Another admirer, but of a different status, was Mrs. J. Borden Harriman, a socialite turned social reformer and a member of the Commission on Industrial Relations. To her Mother Jones was "the most significant woman in America though her life has been alien to everything comfortable American womanhood is supposed to stand for."[12]

Over the years, Mother Jones also remained close to Gene Debs and to the *Appeal.* She occasionally stopped in at Debs's Terre Haute home, and in one incident particularly she sided with him in the furor which resulted when he took an outcast girl into his home. The daughter of an old friend of Debs, the girl had been arrested for "immorality" and taken to the city jail. Debs, who as Terre Haute city clerk had refused to levy fines against streetwalkers, persuaded authorities to appoint him as temporary probation officer and give the girl a home. Mother Jones, who had felt the sting of a somewhat similar lash, commiserated: "That poor girl was a victim of a horrible system that is more brutal than the world has ever known, and God grants [sic] that we have more Eugene Debs, to protect such people from the depraved lions of capitalism."[13]

In 1916, the paths of Mother Jones and Debs crossed again and with less warmth. After presidential races in 1900, 1904, 1908, and 1912, Debs ran for Congress from Indiana's fifth district. He flung himself into the effort with vigor and campaigned from a Model T against the agents of capitalism and their European war. He was receiving encouraging support and financial help. But as the campaign neared its peak, Mother Jones appeared in the state as an active campaigner for John Kern, the Democratic senator who had been instrumental in freeing her from her West Virginia confinement.[14] Barnstorming for Kern under UMW auspices, Mother Jones also supported Wilson for another term as president. "Wilson will be reelected and I think he ought to be be," she told one Indiana crowd. "I don't know of anyone we could put into the White House who would do better. Socialism is a long way off; I want something right now." Mother Jones was especially fond of Wilson for his championing of child-labor legislation.[15]

The Indiana campaign was one of the few times she was an active advocate of Democratic Party candidates, and Debs supporters were chagrined. Only three years earlier Debs had been among members of a Socialist Party investigating team which went to West Virginia to probe Mother Jones's imprisonment. The two had been friends and comrades. But now Debs backers felt she was purposely damaging his chances on the Socialist ticket. Marguerite Prevey, a pioneer Ohio Socialist, was one who questioned Mother Jones's motives. Mrs. Prevey apparently suggested that Mother Jones entered Indiana at the urging of an anti-Debs faction among the Socialists. Mother Jones bridled at the accusation. "I went to the mining districts of Indiana to have Senator Kerns [sic] returned to the Senate, because he saved me from serving five years in the state penitentiary of West Virginia with twenty-one of my fellows," she replied. "I had nothing to do with Debb's [sic] campaign. I was not sent there by the National office to interfere with any party affairs." The Socialists, she continued, "are not running my affairs and they don't own me and they had better learn to quit slandering people if they are going to revolutionize the nation. They had better revolutionize their own brains first."[16]

Debs ran ahead of the Democratic incumbent but the Republican candidate for Congress won an easy victory. Senator Kern, too, was defeated. In any event, Mother Jones's rancor about her treatment at the hands of fellow Socialists was not uncommon. When she was in the Pratt, West Virginia, confinement in April 1913, Mother Jones wrote a letter to Mrs. Ryan Walker, a friend and the wife of the editor of the New York *Call*. Mother Jones criticized the lack of concern on many fronts for her plight and for the others who were imprisoned. She also revealed her growing antagonism toward many Socialists.

Ironically, when Mrs. Walker forwarded the letter to the *Appeal to Reason,* the Socialist newspaper seized the opportunity for a three-column, front-page spread headlined as "A Stirring Letter from Mother Jones." Readers were urged to "read it from the housetops." But what they could not know was that an *Appeal* editor, probably Fred Warren because Wayland had shot himself to death a few months earlier, had expurgated and altered the message. The censoring reveals the uneasy alliance between Mother Jones and the Socialists. In the letter Mother Jones claimed that "no word of protest has gone out from our dear Socialists" about her imprisonment. But if it had been Victor Berger, or some other prominent Socialist who had been held "what a howl would go up." This was deleted by the *Appeal*.

She spoke of the "groans and sobs" of a prisoner's wife outside the military jail "but the dear well fed socialists don't care for that." The editor substituted the word "people" for "socialists." Mother Jones complained in another expurgated section about the socialists who "can tell us what they are doing the Balkan war or something of that kind, they are very much like the capitalists they will take us many miles across the ocean to see misery and overlook the horrors at home."[17]

In short, Mother Jones was a socialist but not a good Socialist Party member. She was ill-designed, as her UMW affiliation also showed, to be an obedient member of any rank-and-file. She believed, with the Socialists, in the collective ownership of the means of production, at least in the critical and embattled industries. But the concept was not the keystone of her thought—economic betterment by whatever means was. And whatever her ideology, it was shaped by a strong strain of native individualism and a distrust of political institutions, left or right or middle-of-the-road. She found the Socialist Party's aims too diffuse and its leaders often too dreamy. No doubt they found her quaint and occasionally useful, but also embarrassing at times.

THIRTEEN

The press groveled at the feet of the steel Gods.
The local pulpits dared not speak. Intimidation
stalked the churches, the schools, the theaters. The
rule of steel was absolute.

—Mother Jones[1]

EVENTS and time had eroded what little remaining confidence Mother Jones had in the mettle of labor's leaders. "Going over the country as I do, if a revolution started tomorrow I don't know where they would get a leader," she wrote to Terence Powderly.[2] But while scurrying up and down the Pacific Coast to aid Tom Mooney, Mother Jones learned of what would be her last major strike and one in which she would find her doubts allayed. Stopping first for speeches in Illinois and West Virginia, she proceeded to Pittsburgh, heart of the area in which a coalition of AFL unions would seek to shut down the nation's steel industry. "Never had a strike been led by more devoted, able, unselfish men," Mother Jones later would attest.[3] But the task they faced was mammoth.

After World War I, textiles, meatpacking, and other traditionally nonunion industries began succumbing to organization. But steel, the key to the mass production field, did not. There, the open shop—more than wages or hours or conditions—would be the key issue. Yet, conditions were not good. In 1910, 30 percent of the steel workers put in a seven-day week. Nearly 75 percent worked a 12-hour day. Wages were not pegged to productivity, and from 1890 to 1910, the cost of labor as a part of steelmaking shrank from 22.5 to 16.5 percent. Labor was seen as an item of expense, like any other, to be reduced steadily. The Amalgamated Association of Iron, Steel, and Tin Workers agreed in large part to cut wages per ton as technology improved. But the Amalgamated, perhaps the strongest union in the United States at the end of the 1880s, also had work rules which capital found cumbersome.[4]

In 1892, the Carnegie Company, led by general manager Henry Clay Frick, had fought the Amalgamated with a lockout, strikebreakers, fortresses, and Pinkertons. The dispute began when skilled workers refused a pay cut and were supported by the other employees at the Homestead, Pennsylvania, mill. On July 6, armed strikers and bargefuls of detectives clashed in an all-day gun battle there. Ten men died, and a few days later, 8,000 state troops marched in to put Homestead under martial law. With the militia shepherding the scabs into the mill and with strike leaders indicted on charges ranging from murder to treason, the union largely was destroyed. Only about 800 of the original 4,000 employees got their jobs back. The Carnegie Company pledged it would "never again recognize the Amalgamated Association or any other labor organization." Other industry leaders followed suit, and, by 1903, the Amalgamated lost its last big mill.[5]

In the coming struggle, though, industry's standard was to be carried by United States Steel. That firm, controlling more than 60 percent of the basic steel industry, was led by Methodist moralist Judge Elbert H. Gary, who dispensed his paternalism iron-handedly. World War I changed the steel industry. It shut off the supply of immigrant labor, dropped real wages, forced the mills to operate at full capacity, and led to the setting up in August 1918 of the National Committee for Organizing Iron and Steelworkers. A weakly funded, awkward coalition of ultimately 24 unions, the National Committee was led by John Fitzpatrick, a friend of Mother Jones and the president of the Chicago Federation of Labor, and by ex-"Wobbly" William Z. Foster.

It was to Foster that Mother Jones reported in preparation for the strike which aimed, she said, to "bring back America to America."[6] Her role, as usual, was less with the necessary nuts and bolts of planning a strike than with publicizing the workers' plight and the police interference. Largely, she marched. She first led 10,000 workers in a protest at Monessen, claiming an absence of free speech and assembly in the town where city officials were controlled by the steel firms. By August

12, she was reported speaking to crowds of more than 3,000 steelworkers in Pittsburgh's southside.⁷ On August 20 in Homestead she gave
her view of the issues: "We are to see whether Pennsylvania belongs
to Kaiser Gary or Uncle Sam. Our Kaisers sit up and smoke seventy-five
cent cigars and have lackeys with knee pants bring them champagne
while you starve, while you grow old at forty, stoking their furnaces.

"You pull in your belts while they banquet," she told the steel workers. "They have stomachs two miles long and two miles wide and you
fill them. . . . If Gary wants to work twelve hours a day, let him go
into the blooming mill and work. What we want is a little leisure, time
for music, playgrounds, a decent home, books and the things that make
life worth while."⁸

But Mother Jones and three other organizers were pulled from the
automobile from which they were speaking and jailed for not having
a street-speaking permit. They had moved from a hall to Fifth Avenue
because of an overflow crowd.⁹ However, after the arrest, "a great mob
of people collected outside" the jail and demanded Mother Jones's release. The jailer, fearing he might be lynched, tried to pacify the crowd
by letting her out to speak to them. She urged them to return home,
saying she would be released soon.

Mother Jones was freed on $15.00 bond, and six days later, she
claimed innocence and told the magistrate she did indeed have a street-
speaking permit. "Who issued it?" he asked. "Patrick Henry, Thomas
Jefferson, and John Adams," she claimed to have replied. In any event,
she was released without penalty, and the others were fined $1.00.¹⁰
It was a sequence to be often repeated in the months just ahead.

As a result of the publicity stemming from the arrest of Mother
Jones, Homestead officials began allowing meetings of union organizers
"for the first time" in 20 years, another participant stated. Still, the con-
stabulary censored the gatherings and decreed they could be only in
English.¹¹ Officials of the city of North Clairton, sensing the changing
tide of public opinion, left Mother Jones alone. But Duquesne Mayor
James S. Crawford banned speech and assembly in the Pittsburgh area
town. The AFL could not even rent an office, let alone a hall. The
brother of the president of a nearby tin-plate company, the mayor
"naturally saw the strike through steel-rimmed glasses," Mother Jones
quipped.¹² When asked for a speaking permit, Crawford told organizers
that "Jesus Christ himself could not speak in Duquesne for the A. F.

of L.!" Mother Jones claimed to have replied: "I have no doubt of that, not while you are mayor. You may remember, however, that He drove such men as you out of the temple."[13]

Again arrested for public speaking on September 7, Mother Jones was taken along with Foster to jail. A group of citizens, town officials, and ministers supposedly came to her cell and asked: "Why don't you use your great gifts and your knowledge of men for something better and higher than agitating?" She told them that George Washington, Abraham Lincoln, and Jesus Christ were agitators, and one could not aim higher. Again, she was released without penalty, although other organizers were fined.[14]

Violence and intimidation were common even before the strike began. Fannie Sellins, another prominent woman organizer, was shot and bludgeoned in Brackenridge, on the Allegheny River north of Pittsburgh. Active in a miners' strike in the area—as well as in preparation for the steel walkout—she was trying to shield several children from the sight of a coal picket who had just been killed by gunmen. The gunmen again opened fire and killed her, too. Union leaders claimed she was murdered by henchmen of the steel trusts in revenge for her activism on behalf of the mill workers.[15] Mary Heaton Vorse, a magazine writer covering the strike, said one day she found Mother Jones staring at a picture of the battered Fannie Sellins. "I often wonder it wasn't me they got," Mother Jones said to her. "Whenever I look at the picture of her I wonder it's not me lying on the ground. . . . Bending over them children with her head turned, they shot her."[16]

But repression didn't work in countering the organizing drive. In fact, the conflict kept erupting before the National Committee desired. Before the Pittsburgh area was more than half organized, the rank and file began to demand action. AFL President Samuel Gompers on June 20 wrote to Judge Gary stating that more than 100,000 men had been unionized and suggesting a conference. The invitation was ignored, and the National Committee saw that the men were likely to drift away unless it acted. On July 20, 1919, it had voted 12 unions to 2 to take a strike vote. The result: 98 percent of the members were for a strike if the companies continued to refuse to negotiate. An eight-hour day, a six-day week, a wage increase, double time after eight hours, reinstatement of men fired for union activity, dues checkoff, and an end to company unions were among the demands formulated. And, of course, the right to bargain collectively would be a pivotal aim. But Judge Gary rejected further attempts of the unions to meet with him, and President Woodrow Wilson's attempt to arrange a meeting was rebuffed similarly. Calling Gary a "pirate" who "insults the whole nation" by spurning the president's offer, Mother Jones made a rambling appeal at the miners' convention for UMW support of the steelworkers. With some truth, she called the coming strike "the crucial test of the labor movement in America."[17]

On September 22, the smoke ceased from many of the mills in Pueblo, South Chicago, Wheeling, Gary, Johnstown, Cleveland, Lackawanna, Youngstown, Pittsburgh, and other steel towns around the country. The first great strike in the industry saw a purported 365,000 workers leave their jobs in 50 towns spread over 10 states. While the number of strikers may have been closer to a quarter-million, it amounted to a remarkable one-half of the industry's work force, and it shattered management's claim that the union cause lacked popular support.[18]

The walkout was not complete. Production in the South and in the Lehigh Valley hardly faltered, and elsewhere, as in Pittsburgh, for example, the effect was mixed. But from the beginning, a remarkable solidarity characterized the strike, despite the myriad unions and the score of nationalities involved. The workers had demanded the strike, and their commitment ran deep. Probably twice as many walked out as had actually joined the union. In the western Pennsylvania steel communities of Homestead, Braddock, Rankin, McKeesport, Monessen, and Pittsburgh, there was said to be not a single vote cast against the strike.[19]

Establishment reaction to the strike's surprisingly successful start was to create a "Red Scare." This fed on postwar fears about Bolshevism abroad and worker anarchy at home. It wasn't a strike so much as a revolution, said the newspapers, the military, the politicians, and industry leaders. They began equating the foreign-born—many of whom worked in the mills—with radical causes. And they found a scapegoat in William Z. Foster. Eight years earlier, Foster, an international organizer for the Brotherhood of Railway Carmen, coauthored a fiery tract, *"Syndicalism."* It included such statements as "The thieves at present in control of the industries must be stripped of their booty and society so reorganized that every individual shall have free access to the social means of production. This social reorganization will be a revolution." Although Foster had not yet embraced Communism, as he later would, he did refuse to renounce fully the pamphlet, even at the behest of Gompers.[20]

The radical issue sidetracked the unions' hope for wide public support. Could the average citizen blame Judge Gary for refusing to bargain with Reds? The hysteria also fueled repression. Western Pennsylvania mill towns, particularly, became the site of attacks on civil liberties. "American Cossacks," the hated Pennsylvania Coal and Iron Police, on horseback literally cleared the streets of Clairton and other steel towns. Vigilante groups sprung up. Four thousand troops under General Leonard Wood patrolled Gary, Indiana. In all, thousands were arrested, hundreds injured, and some 20 persons killed during the strike.[21] "The soldiers broke up the picket line," Mother Jones said. "Worse than that, they broke up the ideal in the hearts of thousands of foreigners, their ideal of America. Into the blast furnace along with steel went their dream that America was a government for the people—the poor, the oppressed."[22]

Mother Jones made her base with the other organizers in the old Monongahela House hotel overlooking the river in Pittsburgh. Mrs. Vorse also lived there and sometimes went along with Mother Jones on her forays. She described the eighty-nine-year-old agitator as "a tiny, very clean little old lady in a black silk basque with a lavender vest and lace around the neck, a bonnet on her snow-white hair. She hadn't altered her style of dress in twenty years."[23] But if her costume was unaltered, so, too, had her fervor not been diluted by time. "There's a terrible bitter tide rolling up and welling up in this country," she told Mrs. Vorse. "There's gall mixed with the mud that's churned under the workers' feet in the city alleys. . . . Look at those towns. . . . I say to you there has never been a crueler despotism than there is in this country today. . . . Look at the blast furnaces and smoke as far as your eye can reach, and the wealth that comes out of it made by the blood of slaves."[24]

Operating free-lance, Mother Jones visited Pittsburgh area mill towns as well as those in eastern Ohio and the Midwest. She wrote that she "traveled up and down the Monongahela River. Most of the places where the steel workers were on strike meetings were forbidden. If I were to stop to talk to a woman on the street about her child, a cossack would come charging down upon us and we would have to run for our lives. If I were to talk to a man in the streets on Braddock we would be arrested for unlawful assembly."[25] Particularly during the latter part of the organizing campaign and in the first two months of the strike, "Mother Jones lent great assistance to the steel workers," Foster said. She labored "dauntlessly, going to jail and meeting the hardship and dangers of the work in a manner that would do credit to one half her age."[26]

Foster, who was liked by Mother Jones, wasn't alone in his vulnerability to charges of radicalism. In Gary, on October 23, Mother Jones gained some notoriety in making a public appeal to violence. She addressed 1,200 strikers in Turner Hall after having been refused permission to speak in East Side Park. "So this is Gary," she began. "Well, we're going to change the name and we're going to take over the steel works and we're going to run them for Uncle Sam. It's the damned gang of robbers and political thieves that will start the American revolution and it won't stop until every last one of them is gone.

"I'll be 90 years old the first of May," she exclaimed, "but by God if I have to, I'll take 90 guns and shoot hell out of 'em." To the soldiers guarding the hall, she shouted: "You went abroad to clean up the Kaiser, and the bones of 60,000 of your buddies lie bleaching on the battlefield of France. My God, ain't you men enough to come over and help us get the Kaisers at home? . . . We'll give Gary, [J. P.] Morgan, and the gang of bloodsuckers a free pass to hell or Heaven.

"You can arrest me," she taunted, "but I'll be free. I can raise more hell in jail than out. If Bolshevist is what I understand it to be, then I'm a Bolshevist from the bottom of my feet to the top of my head." She was cheered for a full five minutes by the strikers.[27]

No doubt many took Mother Jones at her impassioned word. In any event, both the press and industry continued to beat the drums about the pervasive foreign "isms." The effect was felt, and the strike began to falter by its sixth week. By the end of October 1919 strikebreakers, mostly Negroes, began to be imported in large numbers. The Chicago district collapsed first. By November 21, the mills were operating with 75 percent of their work force in Gary, 85 percent in Indiana Harbor, and 80 percent in South Chicago. Soon, other steel centers like Johnstown, Youngstown, and Wheeling were weakening.[28]

The National Committee called for mediation, but Judge Gary said there were no issues to be discussed. On December 13, the strike leaders estimated that 109,300 workers were still out. Over the protests of the

Amalgamated Association, the committee voted to continue the strike. But waning morale, lack of funds, AFL hesitancy, company repression, strikebreakers, and the approach of winter all took their toll. Soon, the walkout remained effective only in Pueblo, Lackawanna, Joliet, and scattered steel mills in the Cleveland and Pittsburgh areas.[29]

On January 8, 1920, the National Committee, while accusing the steel companies of "arbitrary and ruthless misuse of power," announced the inevitable: "All steelworkers are now at liberty to return to work pending preparations for the next big organization movement."[30] The ever-militant tone amounted to whistling in the dark. Neither side was anxious to do battle again. Less than six months later, the National Committee would disband. And the "next big organization movement" would not come for 16 years.

Public opinion churned up by the strike did soon end the seven-day work week, and about three years later, the eight-hour day came to the steel mills. But some strikers were blacklisted and never got their jobs back, and, of course, open-shop advocates had triumphed. Collective bargaining had been stymied in the nation's most important industry. Labor's paralysis in the 1920s might have been averted if the strike had been won. But having shown surprising early strength, the steel workers had suffered their second crushing defeat in 28 years.[31] "At headquarters, men wept," Mother Jones recalled. "I wept with them."[32]

FOURTEEN

I have never had a vote and I have raised hell
all over this country! You don't need a vote to raise
hell! You need convictions and a voice!

—Mother Jones[1]

SOON after the steel strike, Mother Jones left for a respite in
California. There she would go repeatedly in her later years to
seek relief from rheumatism, an affliction she blamed on her imprisonment in the "black hole of Walsenburg" which crippled her hands. But
if she withdrew briefly from the strike scene, Mother Jones took no
leave of the issues. The year 1920, for example, saw the coming of age
of both Prohibition and women's suffrage. Strangely, Mother Jones was
against them both.

Her progressivism ended with suffrage despite the fact that for
decades she had ridiculed workingmen for lacking the strength of
women. Perhaps overcompensating for her own family's tragedy, she
felt strongly that women belong in the home with their children. Her
logic was simple and steadfast.

She said:

In no sense of the word am I in sympathy with woman's suffrage.
In a long life of study of these questions I have learned that women are
out of place in political work. There already is a great responsibility upon
woman's shoulders—that of rearing rising generations. It has been in part
their sad neglect of motherhood which has filled reform schools and which

163

keeps the juvenile court busy. . . . The average working woman is unfitted for the ballot. She will rarely join an organization of the industry she works in. Give her the vote and she'll neglect it. Home training of the child should be her task, and it is the most beautiful of tasks. Solve the industrial problem and the men will earn enough so that women can remain at home and learn it.[2]

Mother Jones's aversion to suffrage divorced her ideologically from most of the other female activists of her day. But she apparently could not or would not distinguish between the woman agitating for political rights and the one pulled away from her children by the demands of work.[3] "The human being is the only animal which is neglected in its babyhood," she stated. "The brute mother suckles and preserves her young at the cost of her own life, if need be. The human mother hires another, poorer woman for the job. Of course, the race must suffer for it."[4] In part, Mother Jones's attitude sprang from her traditionalism. Apart from the quest for economic equity, she was a little fearful of change. Moreover, suffrage and other niceties, to one who had for so long been an ascetic, seemed unlikely to breed successors equal to the struggle. Freedom for women connoted frivolity and that Mother Jones could not countenance. "We are standing on the eve of that mighty hour when the motherhood of the Nation will rise," she told a West Virginia crowd, "and instead of clubs or picture shows or excursions, she will devote her life to the training of the human mind, giving to the Nation great men and great women."[5]

She spoke at one meeting where most of the women were "crazy about women suffrage. They thought that Kingdom-come would follow the enfranchisement of women." But Mother Jones told them, "I have been up against armed mercenaries but this old woman, without a vote, and with nothing but a hatpin has scared them." Furthermore, she said, "women of Colorado have had the vote for two generations and the working men and women are in slavery." A coal operator claimed, she added, that if it had not been for the women's vote, the Colorado miners would have defeated the operators long ago.[6] It was one of Mother Jones's stranger manifestations, this paradox about women's power and its circumscription. In an unenlightened age she was a female who fought fiercely and with some success for social change. As has been shown, she often used women in strikes to rally dejected strikers or even physically to assault the scabs. But she would have denied women the right to political clout, if not the wallop of the broomstick. Perhaps her own suspicion of politics was pivotal. For in areas other than voting, she had not this underestimation of women.

At one miners' convention, for example, a delegate challenged Mother Jones's being in the employ of the union and on the payroll. She replied that "the most valuable person on the staff of President Lincoln was a woman. . . . and if you had twenty women in Europe they could stop" World War I. "Twenty women with a consciousness of what it means to the children yet to come could stop that war. Don't you think they have as much sense in Europe as you have?"[7] On another occasion she contended that what Congress needed was at least one woman to shake it up.[8] Suffrage, however, somehow suggested inaction or sloth. To Mother Jones these were the most loathsome of vices, the folly of the bourgeoisie. A lady is "the last thing on this earth I want to be," she told congressmen who questioned her behavior. "A lady is a parasitical outgrowth of the system we live under. How many of the 'wretches' in Colorado have lost their lives in the mines to send one society girl to a finishing school, give her a trip abroad, marry her off—that is, make a 'lady' of her?"[9]

Mother Jones judged women—and men, organizations, and movements—by a single standard. For her, the economic battle was the only battle. All were judged by their valor and strength in that struggle. Non-participants were irrelevant and were liabilities. "We must realize that the woman is the foundation of government and that no government is greater or ever can be greater than the woman," she told the 1911 UMW convention. But, she hastened to add, "as along as the women are unorganized, as long as they devote their time to women's clubs and to the ballot, and to a lot of old meow things that don't concern us at all and have no bearing on the industrial battle" the men will have to make the fight alone.[10]

Mother Jones never would be able to disassociate suffrage from Sybaris. On her hundredth birthday, a decade after passage of the Nineteenth Amendment, she would rail against the capitalists for sidetracking women into clubs and politics. Nobody wants a lady, she said, "they want women. Ladies are parlor parasites."[11] On the Eighteenth Amendment she was no less opposed. Drink, like the role of women, played a large part in Mother Jones's conception of the workingman's milieu. She knew how little pleasure there could be in the short life of the miner. To her, all else was secondary to improving that life. Often, during her speeches, she would ask for donations to buy beer for some of the poorer men in the crowd. "It's a wonder that we are not all drunk all of the time" because of the misery in the mine and mill towns, she stated.[12] She saw the saloon as a social asset, as a gathering place whose doors were open when others were not. Mother Jones also felt Prohibition was something of an affront in the class war, designed by middle-class politicians but bearing most heavily on the working man.

Mother Jones's views, as peculiar as they sometimes seemed—especially in the case of suffrage—were an integral facet of her wide appeal. Whether natural or contrived, her complex personality closely matched the early twentieth-century workingman's own bewilderment. She gave him faith, and he returned admiration, even worship. In the 1916 UMW convention, for example, she performed spectacularly. The gathering was marked, not uncommonly as the miners' meetings went, by acrimonious debate and claims of personal misconduct. This time, rank-and-filers from Illinois who were often at the core of dissidence, accused President John White of improper handling of funds. Amid fiery dialogue they sought an internal investigation.

Led by Adolph Germer and Duncan McDonald, the critics claimed that White encouraged lavish expense accounts and high living, while the president claimed the pair were plotting against him. Rebuttals and counterclaims fueled more of the same. Allegations of nepotism, mismanagement of the UMW *Journal,* padding of expense statements, and other offenses followed for three days. Then Mother Jones entered the fray. Although she was a delegate without credentials, President White told the convention, "You can't stop her from talking." And talk she did. She told of her battles in West Virginia, of the bullpen and the mine guards. She told the convention that the past four years were the "most strenuous years that this organization has ever gone through" and that its international officers had been under much pressure. She went on at length, her often irrelevant monologue a respite from the bitter controversy which preceded it.

Then in a gesture which had its precedent in scores of mine and mill towns, she said: "Now, boys, let Mother talk to you, and let's put a stop to this thing. Let's take a vote on the whole thing and squash it. Let Duncan McDonald and Adolph Germer come up here on the platform and shake hands and bury the hatchet with President White."

She continued, "The corporations have got their paid tools here. . . . There is not a single move you make in this convention that is not registered to the big interests as soon as it is made. Now, then, put a stop to it and shake hands and say, 'Here there is no power of the high-class burglars will ever separate us, the miners of this country! . . . we must stand before the world and show that we have got a common sense and judgment and no spite at each other.'"[13]

The record shows that "Delegates McDonald and Germer complied." Mother Jones continued her speech, talking of projects she planned or dreamed of and giving her usual biting anecdotes about the enemies of the working class. When she finished, Vice-President Hayes, who was chairing, concluded succinctly: "There is only one Mother Jones."[14] Her marathon speech quieted the convention and removed some of its sting. The rebels sheepishly shook hands with White, Frank Hayes, and Secretary William Green, their combatants a brief while earlier. The source of the conflict—the centralized UMW to which power had accrued during the bitter strikes of the past few years—had not been dealt with. But Mother Jones had scorned these hardened men, as she had their constituents across the land, and given them, if but for a time, more humility, a different perspective, a reason for unity. She probably was more tolerated than heeded, but still she was not without effect.

What was this charm? Why should an aged but eloquent old woman have a hold on half a million miners? She claimed to have worked "on the night shift and the day shift in Pennsylvania from Pittsburgh to Brownsville."[15] But she had not really been a miner or a miner's wife or even a miner's daughter. How could she, often without benefit of credentials, move into myriad disputes and not be spurned by the clannish miners? Why was she known as "Mother" and the oppressed as her "boys"? It was because she was a woman and because she was so intensely personal in a culture which cherished these qualities. Miners have always been a tough and fatalistic breed. As John L. Lewis once noted, "The public does not know that a man who works in a coal mine is not afraid of anything except his God; that he is not afraid of injunctions, or politicians, or threats, or denunciations, or verbal castigations, or slander—that he does not fear death."[16] But fearless and violent though they may have been, the miners' families were matriarchies. Mother-centered families occur when the continuation of the father's role is threatened. Such was the case in the highly dangerous job of mining. During the union mine wars, the hazard was multiplied.

Herman Lantz's *Coal Town,* a study of a mining community of 2,300 people, showed this plainly. In interviewing townspeople, the investigators found the wives often interrupting the husband's answers and criticizing his judgment. But when asked who was the boss of the household, the women withdrew quickly, and said, "My husband, of course." Generally, too, women were found to be the joiners of social organizations, the victors in family arguments, and the guardians of the purse strings. The town's culture showed "historical patterns of violence and death for the males an ever-present danger," and this, the study said, accentuated the mother's role.[17]

Mother Jones fitted nicely into the matriarchal pattern. Miners, whether they admitted this or not, were used to being told what to do by their mothers and by their wives. When a woman as matronly, as strong-willed, as articulate, and as compassionate as Mother Jones told them they ought to be fighting, they caught the spirit. When she told them they ought to be ashamed of themselves, they often were. In large part, as one friend pointed out, Mother Jones was to the toilers almost like a biological mother who "goes through the shadow of death in order to endow her child with life."[18] She also was the mother of the revolt which simmered within them. Even men who could not understand her words understood her anger and her impatience with wrong. Brave and fatalistic men, they shared her defiance and her fearlessness. She was far more eloquent than they. But her words stuck to the fiery essentials and bridged the gap.

As Carl Sandburg would write in "Memoir of a Proud Boy":

> He had no mother but Mother Jones
> Crying from a jail window in Trinidad:
> "All I want is room enough to stand
> And shake my fist at the enemies of the human race."[19]

Mother Jones also had a rare understanding of the miner. Her bawdy tone lashed the operators, the pulpit, and the press. But she saved her sharpest scorn for the miners themselves. "Damn you," she told a Williamson, West Virginia, crowd, "you are not fit to live. Of every ton of coal so much was taken out to hire professional murderers to keep you in subjection, and you paid for it. You stood there like a lot of cowards, going along chewing scab tobacco and you let yourself be robbed by the mine owners—and then you go about shaking your rotten head. Not a thing inside."[20]

In Mother Jones's meager papers is a telegram, apparently without significance save for the poignancy of its faith. It shows something of the blind allegiance she elicited. It reads merely:

SHAMOKIN, PA.

MOTHER MARY JONES

CARE UNITED MINE WORKERS

MOTHER THERE IS A STRIKE AT THE SILK MILLS HERE WILL YOU COME [A]T ONCE I KNOW YOU CAN DO LOTS OF GOOD COME IF POSSIBLE

FROM A MINER[21]

According to one anecdote, Mother Jones was once sought out by a group of men in Mt. Hope, West Virginia, who were half-carrying a coughing miner. "I thought I'd like to die organized," he told her. Three weeks later he was dead from consumption.[22] Unwittingly or not, Mother Jones meshed into the coal culture. In addition to her vigor, her endurance, her eloquence, and her perception, this must be considered a basis of her success. Furthermore, her intensely personal brand of organizing and agitating—where she told tales of her past imprisonments, of outrages she had seen, of hopes for the future—met the miners' needs.

Unlike factories, coal mines were not some convenient distance beyond a town. If there was not a city near the shaft, and there usually was not, the mine operator built a town and ran it. Thus the miner and his family, as has been shown, were almost always on the employer's property—where they worked, ate, slept, shopped, and even where they worshipped or sent their children to school. Mother Jones's methods, while simple and not always successful, added a new flavor to the miners' life. On occasion, she held her meetings in a creek bed or on a public road—the only public land around—and damned the operators. In an era when employers fought with no holds barred, so did she. She did not hesitate to impugn the president, the church, the governor, the military, or all of these. She was an unencumbered gadfly who spoke the coal-diggers' language, knew their plight, and won their admiration.

The miner, like the industrial wage earner elsewhere, desired to strengthen his sense of worth in a sterile setting. Unions filled that need, and Mother Jones contributed an extra surge. She also was a throwback to another era, and thus a comfortable sensation for the miners. Many said she reminded them of their boyhood. She came from a simpler century. In her time, the American presidency would pass from Andrew Jackson to Herbert Hoover. Electricity replaced kerosene, and the automobile supplanted the horse. She saw the railroads bridge the continent and witnessed the coming of the telephone, the radio, and the airplane. She had been in a hundred battles for her class. Why, she remembered Lincoln and was in the Knights of Labor. She spoke of Haymarket as if it were just yesterday. Her youth, as she was not reluctant to tell the Celtic miners, was punctuated with tales of Irish rebellion and family martyrs. Moreover, she was against these new fangled movements—like suffrage and Prohibition.

The new ways of work were no better. Henry Ford, she said, was a man who "would drive men mad with his system and throw them on the scrap heap. He makes machines of men" through his assembly-line techniques, she contended.[23] And installment credit was another modern blight which Mother Jones labeled as "the worst thing the laboring man allows himself to be deluded into."[24] These were frills, she said, playthings of the boss class and not something for which we miners or mill hands, bred of another era and constructed of stronger stuff, have any need.

Furthermore, she preached the stamina and self-reliance of the old-time America. Her method always was to denounce her audience, much as did the fundamentalist preacher, and place the blame squarely on the workers' own shoulders. Her message, not always inflammatory, was aimed at bringing the miners into consciousness of their own dignity as human beings with something to say about the conditions under which they lived. All we need is a fair shake economically, she would tell them. All we need is to square off with the coal barons or the steel trust. This may mean socialism. For sure, it will mean fighting like hell. But we can do it, Mother Jones said in effect. We can preserve the past and still win a new economic future. We can make this system human.

Mother Jones was not always, or even most of the time, a force for serenity within the mine workers' union. In fact, 1920 also marked the beginning of the Alexander Howat insurgency, a struggle in which she would become intensely involved. Postwar labor militancy in general and that of the coal miner in particular led Kansas Governor Henry J. Allen to push through approval of a compulsory arbitration law in 1920. It featured an Industrial Relations Court, appointed by the governor, which would settle labor disputes in certain industries and thus preclude strikes. At one point, it appeared to be gaining impetus as a nationwide model.[25]

Howat ran as an antiorganization candidate for the UMW vice-presidency in 1920. On the opposing and winning ticket was UMW president John L. Lewis. Howat's subsequent refusal to obey the Kansas law gave Lewis the chance both to lessen Howat's influence and to centralize further the union's power in the national headquarters.[26] When a strike did break out in Kansas, Lewis ordered Howat to obey the law or forfeit the district's charter. When Howat refused to heed the new law and went to jail in October 1921, the Kansas miners struck in sympathy over a wider area of the state. As a result, Howat was expelled and 81 locals loyal to Howat lost their charters.

All this made a hero out of Howat as far as Mother Jones and the Illinois miners—the UMW's largest and most radical element—were concerned. Their resentment was compounded by Lewis's refusal to persist in a nationwide coal strike, begun in late 1919, once a federal court ruled it illegal. "I will not fight my government, the greatest government on earth," Lewis said, despite a defiant stand earlier.[27] John Walker, the Illinoisan who was among Mother Jones's closest friends and admirers, had sought the UMW presidency three times. He told her that Lewis's "surrendering and bowing in abject submission [to the court order], allowing the men to be driven back into the mines like cattle, without a fight at all . . . makes the decent Mine Workers, who understand what it means, blush with shame."[28]

Howat appealed his expulsion through both the UMW machinery and the civil courts. With Mother Jones's urging, Howat's followers got him out of jail long enough to attend the reconvened UMW convention in February 1922. But there was a credentials fight which the Kansan lost, and by a vote of 2,073 to 1,955, the convention voted not to reopen the matter despite Howat's addressing the group over Lewis's opposition.[29] At the stormy convention, Mother Jones interrupted as the vote was being taken on whether to allow Howat a hearing on his expulsion. She "did not ask permission to speak but walked quietly up to the front of the stage and held up her hand," a correspondent wrote. "Absolute quiet prevailed as she remonstrated with 'her boys.' She begged her beloved coal diggers to save the Kansas miners' union, to quit fighting among themselves."

Mother Jones, who had journeyed to Kansas to organize and speak in support of Howat, compared Howat to another Kansan, John Brown. "I wish to God that the American labor movment had one million Alexander Howats," she said, predicting that some day labor would build a monument to him for fighting "that damnable slave law of Governor Allen's." As she finished, a reporter said, "the crowd seemed to have gone mad as they cheered this wonderful old soldier of theirs that has been in the front line of every battle in the miners' union. It was with difficulty that order was obtained and the calling of the roll continued."[30]

But as usually was the case at the UMW conventions, Mother Jones was more a diversion than a compelling force, and the delegates upheld Howat's expulsion. The same convention was marked by savage debate and even attempts at physically capturing the podium as anti-Lewis factions sought a general strike over contract matters. Mother Jones, who usually sided with the dissidents, admonished the delegates. "Stop howling like a lot of fiends and get down like men and do business. . . . You ought to be ashamed of yourself. Quit this noise," she scolded.[31] Ancient Mother Jones, now almost ninety-two again haranguing the nation's most powerful union in her best matronly fashion was spectacular if not effective. The Howat dispute ran on for years and included his being thrown bodily from the speaker's platform at the 1924 convention. The Kansan continued his fight against the state law, which was ultimately declared unconstitutional, and against Lewis, to whom he consistently lost.

Howat, like his backer Mother Jones, was not given to compromise. He was among the founders, along with Walker and Adolph Germer, of the short-lived UMW Reorganized in 1929. But unlike Mother Jones's prediction, Howat's ultimate fate was not reverence but obscurity, despite his front-line fight against compulsory arbitration. To Mother Jones, Howat, like Tom Mooney, deserved support because he was "fighting the enemy of labor," even if he made tactical errors.

"When your own national officers stand behind the enemy and put you behind the iron bars, it is not very encouraging for men or women either to fight the battle of labor," she asserted.[32]

Such themes won her attentive audiences anywhere, including Mexico City where Mother Jones attended the Third Pan-American Labor Congress in early 1921. Aimed at protecting the hemisphere's workers from predatory capital, the Pan-American Federation of Labor had a tainted birth. Its origin was linked with the United States government's attempt to get Mexico to abandon its neutrality in World War I. But the war ended just before the group's first congress in November 1918 and thus destroyed the federation's secret aim. That first conference in Laredo, Texas, elected Samuel Gompers as chairman. There was a second congress in New York in July 1919 and then a third in the Mexican capital January 10 to January 18, 1921.[33]

Throughout its life, the federation had to cope with deteriorating relations between the United States and Mexico, its two main members. Problems with immigration, United States intervention in the Mexican revolution, the rights of American firms, and the frequent and violent succession of Mexican leaders provided the backdrop for the federation's efforts. In fact, the third congress met only a few weeks after Álvaro Obregón became president after having taken up arms against Venustiano Carranza the year before. It was Obregón who invited Mother Jones to the congress.[34]

On January 4, Mother Jones left Charleston, West Virginia, with Fred Mooney, UMW District 17 secretary-treasurer. They stayed a day in Laredo before continuing on in a Pullman car expropriated from a British railway a few years earlier in the Mexican revolution. After passing through Monterey, Saltillo, San Luis Potosí, and Querétaro, the train halted abruptly about 40 miles from the capital city. "When I looked out there was a string of taxi cabs blocking the railroad tracks," Mooney recalled. "About 40 strikers from a jewelry factory had motored out to meet 'Madre Yones.' They used red flags to stop the train, then boarded it. . . . They threw crimson carnations and blue violets around Mother until only her head and shoulders could be seen. While throwing the flowers they continuously yelled 'Welcome to Mexico, Madre Yones.' "[35] Revered for her crusade on behalf of the Mexican refugees in 1910, Mother Jones received boundless hospitality. She and Mooney had all their expenses paid beyond Nuevo Laredo and were given a book of tickets which could be presented for food, lodging, and drinks. Two servants and a taxi were made available for her.

She also made the usual good newspaper copy. She told the Mexican press that labor conditions in the United States were getting worse, not better and that she "considered Soviet rule in Russia good, but expected better things to grow out of that movement." Soviet-type rule might be possible in the United States someday, she added. Russia "had dared to challenge the old order, had handed the earth over to those who toiled upon it," she later explained, "and the capitalists of the world were quaking in their scab-made shoes."[36] Prohibition, she told the Mexicans, took away the workers' only social club. The rich have their private clubs but the "only club the workingman has is the policeman's. He has that when he strikes." To Mother Jones, the Eighteenth Amendment had come "through a combination of business men who wanted to get more out of their workers, together with a lot of preachers and a group of damn cats who threw fits when they saw a workingman buy a bottle of beer" but who were undisturbed by the misery of the worker and his family.[37]

Mooney and Mother Jones used their taxi often, venturing several times as far as 40 to 50 miles from the capital. They even visited the scene of a coal miners' strike in the state of Coahuila where Mother Jones concluded that "the life of the miner is the same wherever coal is dug and capital flies its black flag."[38] Mooney climbed the Popocatepetl volcano, and Mother Jones urged him on, saying she was not able to do such things anymore. "I have been to the top of the hill and am now approaching the valley for the last time," she told him. Mooney tried to make light of such statements and told her she would easily live longer than a century. Mother Jones replied that she was willing "to stay here that long if I can do any good for the wretches and do not become a burden on someone in my last days."[39]

Such moroseness soon left her, however. A festive mood prevailed at the congress, and a particular highlight was a dinner given by Mexican General Plutarco E. Calles at the San Angel Inn on the outskirts of Mexico City. There the "most colorful" speech was said to have been given by Mother Jones.[40] She was in good form, too, when she formally addressed the delegates on the fourth day of the congress in the amphitheater of the National Preparatory School. Teamsters President Dan Tobin, presiding in the brief absence of Gompers who was still federa-

tion chairman, introduced Mother Jones as "one of the noblest charac-
ters that we have in the great masses of the workers in the United
States."[41] She spoke passionately of a growing solidarity among the
world's workers and of a glowing affirmation of her economic faith. "It
is a great age; it is a great time to live in. Some people call us Bolshe-
viks," she said, "some call us I.W.W.'s, some call us Reds. Well, what
of it!

"If we are Red, then Jefferson was Red, and a whole lot of those
people that have turned the world upside down were Red." There is
worldwide labor unrest, Mother Jones stated, "because the world's workers have produced the enormous wealth of the world, and others have
taken it."

She added:

This may be my last visit to Mexico. My days are closing in. I want
to say to you, young men, there is a mighty task to perform. The world
never before had such a mission for you as it has now. It has granted
that opening for you to enter a new civilization that will make the millions
and thousands happier. . . . And in the days to come when you have
departed the loved ones left behind will come over to your grave and
with the birds above they will sing that beautiful song: "He did well;
he did his work for us; because of what he did we are here to kiss the
ground he is in."[42]

Mother Jones was wrong. She would return again, and her prophecy
of posthumous praise for the delegates seemed more aimed at her memory than theirs. But, in any case, she promised to "come down to South
America some day," and she made another prediction: "We are going
to take over the industry. We are going to take the money from the
robbers that have robbed; yes, we are going to do business."[43] In characteristic hyperbole, Mother Jones called the congress "the greatest event
in history."[44] Actually, it was a personal paean. It was a stirring valedic-
tory perhaps or even something of a reward for a lifetime of sacrifice.
She did have an audience with United States Ambassador Dwight Mor-
row, and one day a package arrived from President Obregón. "With
love, respect, and devotion" read the note which was attached to 25
American double eagles—$500.00 in gold.[45]

The Mexico City congress did protest against the United States pro-
tectorate in Nicaragua and also demanded United States withdrawal
from the Dominican Republic. But, in truth, even at age ninety-one,

Mother Jones would outlive the Pan-American Federation of Labor. Gompers, its guiding force, would die in 1924, and only one more congress—the fifth, in 1927—was held after his death. Although the federation met some success in establishing among its members common aims such as the eight-hour day and an end to child labor, it failed to become a truly hemispheric body. Relations between United States and Mexico may have been improved by the group's efforts. But the Depression and consequent lack of funds wrote the final chapter for the federation, which also suffered an ideological rent.

Gompers had adapted to capitalism; many of the Pan-American labor leaders had not. The federation failed to see the surge of radicalism which sought political control, not just the limited economic gains which might satisfy labor in a different, more stable setting. Some countries never joined, and others, still skeptical of the federation's origins, could not accept the conservative flavor lent by the AFL.[46] Mother Jones's florid rhetoric, then, was not to be confused with reality. Throughout her career, she dealt in overstatement. Her grandiose pronouncements in Mexico City were, as often was the case, little more than garnish on a bitter dish.

Nevertheless, the attention and admiration she commanded in Mexico buoyed her immensely. So much that within a few months she returned again. Powderly, fearing such exertion would weaken her, wrote just before her return. He did not try to dissuade her, but rather quaintly said: "By this time you will be ready to start for Mexico and I ask you to always bear in mind that there is only one Mother Jones. I doubt if the world has seen her like before and while I hope for the future, sadly feel the world will not see her like again. Be careful then of her health," Powderly wrote, "remembering that the covering of the soul you carry is frail, that time has not dealt too kindly with it and every precaution of yours should be taken to guard it carefully and well."[47]

Again the welcome mat was out for Mother Jones in Mexico. "We are expecting you down within a few weeks," wrote Roberto Haberman, who represented Mexico's labor organization in the federation. "Gen. Villarreal has a house ready for you, and a prettier place cannot be imagined. Also servants, and an automobile."[48] Mother Jones stayed more than two months, impressed by what she saw as a swelling of proletarian pride among the Mexicans. In contrast to the creeping lethargy of the American trade-union movement, she found in Mexico the reverence for old battles and old battlers that she shared.

In a May 16 letter to John Fitzpatrick in Chicago, she wrote glowingly of a labor gathering she addressed in Orizaba. There was a fine band, a new municipal building, and a crowd totally free of police. The latter was "something marvelously new to me," Mother Jones said, "because with us in the United States, in the great American Republic, you know the outside and the inside would have been multiplied [sic] by the uniformed representatives of the high class burglars."[49] Furthermore, the Mexican laborers erected a banner to the memory of the Haymarket martyrs, and it was brought in side-by-side with the Mexican flag. "Everyone of you would have been put in jail for the next ten years if that occurred in Chicago," she told Fitzpatrick. "The tribute paid to that banner as it entered that hall was the most remarkable demonstration I had witnessed in all my years in the industrial conflict."

The next morning, on the train back to Mexico City from Orizaba, the workers paraded through the car and urged Mother Jones to come back again. She felt rejuvenated after witnessing "the beautiful conception of industrial freedom that is taking possession of the souls of the workers." Mother Jones also spoke fondly of a Mexican demonstration in which the workers strode into the House of Deputies, planted a red flag, and made demands on their representatives. Yet there was no shouting and no violence. "If such a thing had happened in Washington, all the machine guns within a hundred miles would be called in and turned on them," she asserted.[50]

Mother Jones went also to the Yucatán and stayed over in Mexico City for a labor convention around the first of July. But Powderly was right: the efforts were arduous and took their toll on her. In May she complained of not feeling well, although she later wrote Fitzpatrick that she was "beginning to get back my old fighting qualities."[51] The Mexican sojourns were a delightful respite for the ninety-two-year-old Mother Jones. She lingered because the American labor scene in which she had been so long and unsparingly engrossed looked exceedingly dimmer to her. While praising the hemispheric movement, she privately bemoaned what she saw at home. But upon returning in 1921, she found in at least one engagement a militance which even she could not fathom.

FIFTEEN

There is never peace in West Virginia because there
is never justice. Injunctions and guns, like morphia,
produce a temporary quiet. Then the pain, agoniz-
ing and more severe, comes again.

—Mother Jones[1]

THE Latin sojourn of Mother Jones proved to be but a pause
between acts of another violent drama in which she would play a
rare role. The two armed marches against Logan and Mingo counties in
West Virginia rank among the most awesome, and least known, episodes
in American labor history. In them, the ninety-year-old Mother Jones
would bring to a curious conclusion her three zealous decades in the
Mountain State.

After the tumultuous strike in the Paint and Cabin creeks district
of the Kanawha Valley in 1912–13, Mother Jones left for other conflicts
in Colorado and Michigan. In 1917, however, she returned briefly to
West Virginia to join an organizing jaunt with Fred Mooney, who mar-
veled at her energy and resourcefulness. In one meeting at Lumberport,
Mooney spoke first and droned on for some 40 minutes about the policies and principles of the UMW. Getting no audience reaction, he became disgusted, cut short his talk, and introduced Mother Jones. As
they passed each other on the way to the speaker's platform, he mut-
tered about the lack of response. Said the old woman, as Mooney later
recorded it, "Yuh damn fool, don't you know that not one of them un-
derstands a word of English?" Laughing at his expense, she talked to

178

the miners in her peculiar mixture of gestures, jargon, broken English, and "French classics." Five locals were organized that night and their officers installed, Mooney recalled.[2] Later, at a Fairmont restaurant, Mooney was about to order French fries when Mother Jones berated him. "Potatoes, hell," she said, "order you one of those T-bone steaks, you have earned it." The indulgence was uncommon. Something of an ascetic, Mother Jones took special effort to live not unlike her "boys." The other organizers, Mooney recalled, were cautious to avoid her wrath "for filling their stomachs with beefsteak at the expense of the wretches."[3]

Mother Jones's instinct for reform quite naturally extended to the jails. In July 1919, just before the first armed march on Logan, she visited the Sissonville, West Virginia, road camp operated by Kanawha County. With Fred Mooney and another organizer, she talked to the inmates, some of whom worked in ball and chain under the hot sun. She found many of them had been sentenced for minor crimes, such as possession of liquor, and then had their prison terms extended for trivial violations of the camp rules and again extended if they tried to escape. "At night the miserable colony were [sic] driven to their horrible sleeping quarters. For some, there were iron cages. Iron bunks with only a thin cloth mattress over them. Six prisoners were crowded into these cages," she said. "The place was odorous with filth. Vermin crawled about." The cells lacked proper sanitation, medical care was non-existent, and veneral disease was common.[4]

She claimed to have gone "straight to Washington" seeking an investigation. In any event, the West Virginia governor soon issued 13 pardons to Sissonville inmates after the state pardon attorney, a judge, and a private attorney visited the camp and confirmed the unsanitary conditions also noted earlier by the governor himself.[5]

According to the coal operators, Mother Jones's wanderings also imperiled the World War I preparedness effort. One Raleigh County mine manager wrote his boss that the "Old Hag" was encouraging the nearby miners to organize, then strike. "She states that the Operators are receiving six ($6) dollars per ton for their coal and the pitiful 20% raise is a mere bagatele, when by organizing and striking they could receive so much more. In your communications with the National Defense Council it might be well to call attention to this, as it does not look well for greater output of coal to have such characters going around the country," he stated.[6] But if the operators viewed her as irascible and critical, so did her fellow organizers. "Each of us put forth every effort to avoid Mother's ire," Mooney said. "For several years we were successful, but there came a time when we disagreed."[7] Mother Jones was never so far out of step with her miners, or vice versa, than in the events surrounding the Logan marches, spectacles so romantic and fanciful that they might have seemed ludicrous had not so many dangers and injustices been swept up in them.

Coal production had soared in West Virginia during the World War I years, especially in Logan County, one of the world's richest soft-coal areas and into which steel rails first penetrated in 1904. The state's output rose 23 percent from 1914 to 1921 while Logan County's production climbed 95 percent in the same period. Absorbing more of the markets and employing ever-greater percentages of the state's miners, this southern field had to be organized if the UMW was to remain a potent force in West Virginia.[8] But the problems encountered earlier and elsewhere were, if anything, tougher there. With an edge over their competitors, the mining companies in southern West Virginia subscribed uncompromisingly to the succinct tenet of Garyism: "We do not deal with labor unions." Isolated and in effect their own law, the companies exercised nearly complete control over their employees, and the area achieved dubious renown as the last great stronghold of feudalism.

The southern West Virginia operators saw their role as that of civilizing what before had been "almost unbroken forest." As they reported:

> With the advent of the coal operator in this region came the modern community life. Coal mining demands labor in quantity. None being available, the operator had to carry his workmen with him. He had to provide for them all the creature comforts—houses, food, clothing, water supply, light, medical attention, sanitation, and later, roads, schools, churches, recreation, and amusement. . . . These items entail a heavy fixed charge upon the coal companies for which the only compensation is satisfied and contented employees.[9]

Evidence would seem to indicate, however, that the "creature comforts" sometimes were lacking and the employees less than satisfied and contented. The United States Coal Commission in a study of 713 company-controlled towns, most of them in West Virginia, found great variation, but added:

In the worst of the company-controlled communities the state of disrepair at times runs beyond the power of verbal description or even of photographic illustration, since neither words nor pictures can portray the atmosphere of abandoned dejection or reproduce the smells. Old, unpainted board and batten houses—batten going or gone and board fast following, roofs broken, porches staggering, steps sagging, a riot of rubbish, and a medley of odors—such are the features of the worst camps.[10]

Such situations "are a reproach to the industry," said the commission, which also found that as late as 1922–23, 80 percent of West Virginia's miners lived in company houses compared to less than 10 percent in Illinois and Indiana. The investigators further found that food in West Virginia's New River and Kanawha districts cost more than it did in the capital city of Charleston.[11]

Not only was the condition of the house contingent upon the company's generosity, the renter's continued occupancy depended on his agreement with the firm's philosophy, which meant opposition to the UMW. The coal operators could and did have teachers discharged who developed prounion biases. Doctors were chosen by the company, although their salaries were paid by deductions from the miners' paychecks. The selection of preachers and town officials also could be company-influenced.[12] The result was a closed society which clung to the status quo and eyed outsiders suspiciously. Also resulting was an almost continuous striking for recognition in the Logan and Mingo mines during the postwar years. The crack of a rifle often settled issues in southern West Virginia. The response to a renewed District 17 organizing drive would be no different.

Strong opposition to the union was led by Logan County Sheriff Don Chafin. A lover of classical literature and moonshine liquor, he was elected county assessor by the time he was twenty-one. In overwhelmingly Democratic Logan, he soon became county clerk and then sheriff when Logan was at its violent zenith. Chafin increased his deputy mine-guard force to as many as 300 and also had justices of the peace appoint "special constables." The two groups, the miners said derisively, constituted "the standing army of Logan."[13] As one story had it, a foreigner who sought the right to vote after obtaining his citizenship papers appeared before the Logan County board of registrars to establish his qualifications. He was asked to name the president of the United States. Without hesitation, he replied, "Meester Don Chafin." He was, of course, duly enfranchised as a result either of his amusing ignorance or his canny understanding of the local power structure.[14] Chafin kept an eye on each railroad station in the county to discourage the arrival of union organizers. J. L. Heizer, chief clerk of the state Department of Mines, told of taking a train to Logan where he was to induct new members into the Knights of Pythias fraternal organization of which he was grand chancellor. Apparently, however, the Knights sounded like just another labor organization to the ever-vigilant deputies. Heizer said he was pulled from the train depot, beaten with blackjacks, and ordered out of the county.[15]

Yellow-dog contracts and broad antiunion injunctions further impeded the union's path. Philip Murray, a UMW vice-president dispatched to the area, said, "The character of the towns—the generosity or lack of generosity of the operators—that is not the fundamental point. The fundamental point is that this whole territory, with thousands of inhabitants, is absolutely under the control of the operators. The individual is helpless."[16] Attempting to break out of that cycle, miners along the Tug River in Mingo County in the spring of 1919 applied for a local UMW charter from C. Frank Keeney, the District 17 president. The predictable result: discharge and eviction. A series of bloody strikes and lockouts followed in Logan, Mingo, McDowell, and Mercer counties, comprising the southern rim of the state. With fall, the strikers became increasingly restless and their leadership uncertain as pressure mounted for radical action. Again, a major issue was the mine-guard system. Probably no other single factor contributed more heavily to the deep-seated and nearly continuous industrial warfare in the state. The Logan County operators association, for example, paid $2,275 a month to the sheriff, who named deputies to be stationed in the coal fields to prevent organizers from entering.[17]

Mother Jones spent part of the early summer of 1919 in West Virginia. On August 6, just before leaving for Pittsburgh, she participated in a celebration at Eskdale, where seven years earlier she had ventured into the then so-called no-man's-land and begun an organizing drive among the Cabin Creek miners. Mother Jones also spoke at a spectacular meeting in Whitesville with Keeney and Mooney, District 17 secretary-treasurer. Mooney had introduced her, and as she was speaking, a constable rushed into the building, drew his pistol, and chased an armed man from the audience. Scrambling up to the stage, the man, who had threatened to assassinate the union leaders, was killed by the constable in a gun battle. "During this episode Mother Jones kept speaking and only once did she turn around and that was when the shot was fired," Mooney reported.[18]

By late August 1919 union miners in the Kanawha and New River fields, inflamed by assaults on their organizers and sympathizers, decided to march over the mountains to Logan and Mingo counties. There, presumably, they would shut down the nonunion mines and intimidate the guards. By September 1, the army assembled at the head of Lens Creek, some ten miles from Charleston. Feeling ran so high among the 5,000 coal-diggers that one preacher in a union town supposedly gave his parishioners, who were arming themselves, a blessing which concluded: "Now I lay down my Bible and take up my rifle in the service of the Lord."[19] The starting point of the march was "dark and the moon [was] shining and the camp fires were there, and there were in that crowd about 5,000 rifles," Keeney said. "It looked more like Dante's inferno than anything I can think of, with the moonlight shining on the rifles." Keeney apparently sought the help of Governor John J. Cornwell when the miners' army refused to disband. Cornwell, a Democrat elected in 1916, drove at night over unpaved, unlighted mountain roads to reach the gathering. He later described the encounter as his "toughest spot."[20]

Cornwell took the position, also held by business and many newspapers, that "radical labor" intended to overthrow the government. Telling the miners they had broken their contracts by leaving their jobs to join the march, he defined their Lens Creek assemblage as unlawful. "I concluded by saying that I could not permit them to carry out this unlawful expedition," he later wrote. The miners asked him how could he stop the march. He could have told them a federal regiment was on call in eastern Ohio, but the governor feared "the crack of a high-powered Army rifle might have been the rejoinder, for there in the crowd were more than 500 ex-servicemen in uniform, fresh from the bloody battlefields of France." So Cornwell instead evaded the question, saying "I can show you better than I can tell you." He did, however, promise to investigate their grievances.[21]

As a result, some disbanded, but the bulk of the marchers continued into Boone County where Cornwell threatened them with federal troops and treason charges if they crossed the river into Logan County. At that, they halted, and special trains brought them back to the Charleston area. "Notwithstanding it was the Sabbath Day as they returned," Cornwell noted, "many of the men were poking their guns out of the windows of the cars, some of them firing their pieces and declaring the next time they would go on." And they would. But for now the effort which the governor described as "a deliberate plan to discard the work of Washington and Jefferson, of Madison and Monroe, of Lincoln, of Cleveland, of Roosevelt and to substitute the ideas of Karl Marx, of Nicola Lenin and Leon Trotsky" was halted.[22]

In the southern counties the deadlock remained over the winter of 1919–20, and tensions increased, culminating in the "Matewan Massacre." On May 19, 1920, Albert Felts, head of the Baldwin-Felts detectives, came to Sheriff Sid Hatfield's town of Matewan with 11 armed agents to evict miners who had joined the union strike. Hatfield, a former miner and a local folk-hero, had refused to do the evicting. During a conversation between Hatfield, the Matewan mayor, and Felts, someone pulled a gun and shot Felts, who, in turn, killed the mayor. Sharpshooting mountaineers sprang up from planned hiding places and slaughtered the detectives who struggled to put together their disassembled rifles. In all, seven detectives, the mayor, and two union men were killed. The outbreak sparked further violence, and during July and August, more than 40 men died in Mingo County alone. After a bizarre two-month trial, Hatfield and the other miners were acquitted of the Matewan murders for lack of evidence. But on August 1, 1921, when he was subpoenaed to appear in Welch in neighboring McDowell County on charges arising from another shooting incident, Hatfield was assassinated on the courthouse steps by mine-guard deputies. The murder of this popular figure heightened feelings and led to a second march on Logan.[23]

Mother Jones was involved in the steel strike at the time of the first Logan march. But after the Hatfield assassination she asked Keeney and Mooney to call a mass meeting "somewhere in the Kanawha Valley." They refused, claiming it would only add to the strife. As Mooney later recalled it, Mother Jones then "became abusive, and going into the assembly room where 25 or 30 miners were congregated, she proceeded to read our pedigrees in true Mother Jones style. She told them that 'Keeney and Mooney have lost their nerve; they are spineless and someone must protect these miners!' "[24]

In any event, Mother Jones prevailed, and a meeting was held on the capitol grounds in Charleston on August 7, 1921. For nearly an hour Mother Jones harangued the gathering, assailing Governor Ephraim F. Morgan as a "tool of the goddamned coal operators" and recounting alleged mine-guard atrocities. Keeney reportedly told the crowd of 5,000 that since the governor refused to lift martial law, "you have no recourse, except to fight. The only way you can get your rights is with a high-power rifle, and the man who does not have this equipment is not a good union man."[25] Afterward, Mother Jones bawled out another union leader for calling the meeting, according to Mooney.[26] A week later, however, the call apparently went out for the union miners to arm and assemble near the old rendezvous on Lens Creek on August 20. Their purpose was to release more than 100 strikers held in Mingo County jails, crush Chafin's power, avenge the death of Hatfield, and, presumably, try to unionize the south.[27]

The role of the District 17 leadership is eternally clouded. It was wedged between the employers' demands that existing contracts be honored and the deep desire of its members for protection, physical and economic. There is little doubt that the union hierarchy did not discourage the march, at least at first. That thousands of miners from scores of communities could assemble spontaneously seems unlikely at best. Some observers have reasoned that this gathering, like the earlier march, was engineered by the leadership to underscore the gravity of their grievances and to show that they were ready to win rights of assembly apparently not otherwise attainable in the southern counties. Capturing front-page headlines for days, the preparations for war continued in deadly earnest. The miners, estimated to number anywhere from 3,000 to 12,000, began to move in the general direction of Logan and Mingo counties by way of Boone County. Accompanying them was a cavalcade of doctors and nurses, ambulances to carry the wounded to surgically-equipped field hospitals, and trucks laden with food and supplies.

Governor Morgan had no state troops because the national guard had been mobilized during World War I and had not been reorganized. He issued orders for a quick reorganization and the accepting of all volunteers for emergency duty. He also appealed for federal troops, "including airplanes armed with machineguns."[28] Don Chafin organized the area's defenses, and more than 5,000 volunteers were reported pouring into Logan. Ex-servicemen hastily formed companies and began drilling. Special trains with arms and ammunition arrived from Charleston to bolster the defenders. Machine guns were posted at strategic points.[29]

As the attackers grouped, though, there were second thoughts. Among the doubters was Mother Jones. She had joined the marchers August 24 at Marmet, and the main body was halted the following day. Keeney and Brig. Gen. Harry Bandholtz, sent by the White House to investigate, asked the miners to return home. And Mother Jones, whose views on the march apparently had changed several times, did another turnabout. She ordered the miners to disband, and she produced a telegram purported to be from President Warren Harding and promising an investigation of grievances and an elimination of the Baldwin-Felts guards. "To the miners encamped at or near Marmet with the avowed intention of marching on Logan and Mingo counties," she read from the paper. "I request that you abandon your purpose and return to your homes and I assure you that my good offices will be used to forever eliminate the gunman system from the state of West Virginia. Signed Warren G. Harding, President of this great republic."[30] (One march participant, however, remembered that Mother Jones, in reading the "signature," absentmindedly said "Warren A. Harding," thus alerting the more sophisticated of her audience that the message was spurious.)[31]

In any event, the miners demanded that Keeney verify the telegram. But Mother Jones retorted, "Go to hell," and insisted that the authenticity of the message was "none of your damn business." Mooney, however, made it back to Charleston where he wired Harding's office to seek confirmation. The answer came back from the president's staff: "President out of city. No such wire sent by him." Mooney returned and suggested that the telegram was spurious, but the miners did not listen. "They were total strangers to reason," he recalled.[32] A leaflet later was issued which called Mother Jones a traitor. District 17 leaders denied they published it or the fake telegram. Mother Jones left the West Virginia coal fields following the debacle.[33]

Despite the dispute over the telegram, many of the men began to turn back by August 26 or 27. In this they were encouraged by Keeney and Mooney, who had been told by Bandholtz that they would be held responsible for the marchers' acts. Many of the miners returned on two trains sent for them from Charleston.[34] Since most appeared to be dispersing, Bandholtz returned to Washington. Soon to follow him was

Brig. Gen. Billy Mitchell, commander of the infant Air Service. Mitchell had arrived in West Virginia shortly before with three planes and had offered this assessment: "All this could be left to the air service. If I get orders I can move in the necessary forces in three hours."

"We'd drop tear gas all over the place," he added. "If they refused to disperse then we'd open up with artillery preparations and everything."[35] Recently engaged in bombing exercises against warships to show aviation's practicality in battle, Mitchell welcomed the opportunity in southern West Virginia to exhibit the versatility of the airplane. Two days later, Don Chafin gave him the chance by rekindling the conflict. Chafin sent state police and deputies into union territory to arrest some union men. In the clash, several miners were killed. The news spread quickly, and many of the marchers regrouped in Madison. By the next morning, August 28, the miners had divided into two groups with Logan as their common objective.

Reportedly led by "General" Bill Blizzard, a district UMW official barely out of his teens, the marchers proceeded with military precision. Highways were patrolled. Passwords were required. Mess halls were set up in schoolhouses. Doctors and nurses were drafted; trains were commandeered; and stores were broken into and robbed of food, guns, and ammunition.[36] Governor Morgan later told the state legislature that "many were forced to join the armed force under penalty of death. This force of men patrolled the public roads, held up citizens in the vicinity of their rendezvous, confiscated stores of ammunition and supplies, commandeered automobiles and other conveyances and refused to disperse at the command of officers of the law who were impotent to enforce their command because of the numerical superiority of the armed mob."[37] The governor's hastily created national guard recruited two companies in Charleston, two in Huntington, one in Logan, and another in Bluefield, despite a protest by 3,000 union sympathizers at the state capitol. The governor also appealed again for federal troops.[38]

This time Harding did issue a proclamation ordering the miners home by September 1. General Bandholtz was sent to Charleston again, but the troops were not to be used unless the miners failed to obey the presidential decree. Within 36 hours after the fatal skirmish, Blizzard had his 6,000 troops at the headwaters of the Little Coal River, ready for the march across Blair Mountain and into Chafin's domain. The sheriff meanwhile was redoubling his defenses, even opening jail doors to prisoners who would fight the invaders. Chafin's 3,000 defenders reached the crest of the mountain first. Generally better armed than the attackers, they erected breastworks and waited.[39]

The "Battle of Blair Mountain" began September 2 and raged for two days with battle lines extended over ten miles. For more than 12 hours each day the miners and the Logan defenders maneuvered in military fashion. Aviators were even hired by the operators to make observations and drop bombs. Mitchell sent a squadron of 17 planes from Washington, and Bandholtz arrived with troops who split into two groups, each advancing to the rear of the combatants.

By September 4, most of the miners had been disarmed without resistance, and Bandholtz could report that night: "Troops control situation, 2000 of my men have taken up position with out any trouble." Logan remained untaken, and in fact, nonunion territory was not penetrated. Three deputies had been killed and 40 of the defenders wounded, but union casualities were never made known. In any event, the death toll was remarkably low in view of the numbers involved and the intensity of the fighting which several Spanish-American War veterans commented was heavier than they had encountered in the Philippines.[40] In a tragicomedy which did little to embellish the image of the air warriors, however, six of the Air Service planes crashed, killing at least four aviators. The remaining planes found fog, storms, and poor airfields more formidable than the miners' army.[41]

Without a shot being fired by the troops, the miners were put aboard trains again for departure from the area. Although a detachment from the Chemical War Service also had arrived from a Maryland arsenal, the only tear gas fired was in a demonstration for newsmen. Mitchell's planes, as it turned out, were used on a half dozen or so reconnaissance missions. Chafin's planes, however, dropped bombs on at least three occasions, one a dud dropping between two women who were washing clothes in a backyard. By September 5—Labor Day—all was quiet on the Logan Front, and by the 8th, the troops and the Air Service left for home. Later called the 436th Bombardment Squadron, the air group then known as the 88th Squadron claimed the distinction of being the only Air Corps unit to have participated in the quelling of a civil disturbance.[42]

The second march on Logan had been turned back. William Blizzard, Frank Keeney, Fred Mooney, and 325 other men were indicted that month by a Logan County grand jury on charges of treason and murder. The roll swelled to 500 defendents by the time of the trial. After a change of venue to Charles Town, more than 200 miles northeast, the trial began in the same courthouse where John Brown had been prosecuted for his Harpers Ferry raid. In legal battles lasting over the next two years, there were several other changes of venue, much conflicting testimony, charges of bribery, and even the murder of witnesses. Most of the charges were ultimately dismissed, or the defendents acquitted or paroled early.[43] By October 26, 1922, the strike was abandoned by the national UMW. The southern West Virginia miners remained isolated and unorganized, despite a struggle of rarely attained ferocity, a 28-month strike, at least 30 deaths, more than 50 woundings, property damage of more than $250,000, and one of Mother Jones's strangest acts.[44]

Conspicuously absent from her autobiography, written just three years later, is mention of the Logan March or her role in it. Theories about her rare restraint in West Virginia range from the deceitful to the prudent. Thomas L. Lewis, the former national UMW president who became executive secretary of West Virginia's New River Coal Operators Association, stated that Mother Jones often worked miners into a passion, then would take money from the operators and leave town. "The union knows all this but used her anyhow," he said.[45]

While she could have sold out on the Logan March, this seems even less in character than her brief advocacy of retreat. Perhaps the operators, rather than fearing a clash, were hoping for a major confrontation. Certainly, with extra guards, airplanes, and thousands of volunteers, they were not unprepared. Chafin's attack on the miners while they were generally in repose led to the Blair Mountain battle. With the law on their side, the operators had little to lose. Frank Keeney, for one, disputed the talk that Mother Jones had been paid off. Forty years later, he was quoted as saying that she "never took money from the operators. At that time she was ninety-one years old, and age had quenched much of the fighting spirit that characterized her earlier years."[46]

Perhaps she feared the "boys" in such numbers and so well armed would begin the revolution of which she so often talked abstractly. If they had taken over the towns, they would surely have invited even greater civil war. Or even more logically, given her estimation of the local leadership, she may have seen that nothing but defeat could develop from a mass encounter with the opposition. On this she was almost certainly correct. After hours of fierce fighting, the attackers never reached the top of the mountain. Though they outnumbered the defenders, the latter had built fortifications, and reinforcements were still coming. Continuation doubtlessly would have brought heavy casualities as well as defeat for the union miners.

Furthermore, the march was tragic enough in other respects. It and its legal backlash bankrupted local treasuries. A loss of confidence in local union officers ensued. The public was alienated, and credence was given to the operators' long-held contention that the UMW was intent on anarchy. Also, John L. Lewis had been national UMW president for not much longer than a year when the armed march occurred. Not consulted about the endeavor, he was resentful of the attempt at "trying to shoot the union into West Virginia." Although he aided in the legal defense, soon after the trials ended, he summarily dismissed Keeney, Mooney, and Blizzard and thus widened the schism.[47]

So Mother Jones's unusual peacemaking role—at no small cost to her hard-won respect from the rank-and-file—may have been the prudent, even courageous course. But it was also painful. In what may be a veiled, and jaundiced, mention of the incident in her autobiography, she wrote: "And once it was my duty to go before the rank and file and expose their leaders who would betray them. And when my boys understood, West Virginia's climate wasn't healthy for them." In truth, though, it was more nearly Mother Jones who found the climate onerous, although in 1923 she did return to win from Governor Morgan the release of a number of jailed Logan County miners.[48]

At any rate, she played her part. It may have lessened the bloodshed and even helped to save what remained of the union in West Virginia. For the Logan-Mingo area was not organized until the coming of the New Deal and its legislation protecting union members and prohibiting yellow-dog contracts and broad, antilabor injunctions. But after 1923 and before the New Deal, the UMW lost ground badly in West Virginia. In 1924, the state attorney general secured a court order restraining Chafin from appointing deputies for the operators, and this order was made permanent. But it still didn't make organizers welcome, and Logan County courts continued to serve them with injunctions.[49]

If the union had been successful either in the march or through more peaceful means, it might have been able to hold onto its gains in the remaining southern fields during the 1920s. But the competitive effects of the nonunion southern mines upon the northern coal operators, the unwillingness of the union to accept wage reductions in the northern field, a relative decline in the demand for coal, the beginnings of the Depression, and unemployment caused by all of these laid waste to the UMW in the state. Seventy percent of the coal there was mined under union contract in 1923. Ten years later, the figure was 20 percent.[50]

Employers renewed their open-shop drives. Big firms began abrogating their contracts and reopening mines on a nonunion basis. Dissension among the miners and resistance to Lewis's methods led to pluralism in the form of the National Miners' Union and the Progressive Mine Workers of America as well as the West Virginia Miners' Union, begun by Frank Keeney. Thus, the New Deal brought new life to the torturous struggle of more than 40 years. The National Industrial Recovery Act, section 7a, was known as the "Magna Charta" of the West Virginia coal industry. But it came too late for Mother Jones. "The story of coal is always the same. It is a dark story," she wrote. "For the privilege of seeing the color of their children's eyes by the light of the sun, fathers must fight as beasts in the jungle. That life may have something of decency, something of beauty—a picture, a new dress, a bit of cheap lace fluttering in the window—for this, men who work down in the mines must struggle and lose, struggle and win."[51] In 1929, just a year before Mother Jones's death, the UMW in West Virginia was said to have a paid-up membership of barely 600.[52]

SIXTEEN

I am not afraid of the press or the militia. I would
fight God Almighty himself if he didn't play square
with me.

—Mother Jones[1]

A flood of well-wishes and expressions of sympathy arrived at the
Washington, D.C., home of Terence V. Powderly in early September 1922. The messages, including one from West Virginia Governor E. F. Morgan, came soon after reports circulated that Mother Jones was critically ill. With the arduous Mexico trips and the tumult of West Virginia behind her, she was suffering from rheumatism and exhaustion and had come to Powderly's for a rest.[2] Two trained nurses and Emma Powderly helped get Mother Jones out of danger in about two weeks. It had been her second serious attack in ten months.[3] After the West Virginia episode she had been stricken with rheumatism while in Springfield, Illinois.

"I am suffering severely, and unable to do anything outside of moaning about my troubles," she then wrote Powderly in an uncharacteristic complaint.[4] Treated by a specialist, she recovered sufficiently to return to Washington, and once there and well, she soon was on the road again. Mother Jones stopped once more in Springfield to see her old comrade and fellow UMW-dissident John Walker, and she wrote Powderly in early March that she would speak to striking railroad shopmen in Fort Wayne on the 7th. "I am feeling better, but I won't hold many meetings for I won't take any chances, but those poor shopmen have been out since last July and I feel if I am able to crawl I owe them a duty to give them a word of encouragement. [*sic*] and let them know the sunshine of hope still throws out its rays."⁵

On March 5, 1923, the Very Reverend William R. Harris, a brother of Mother Jones, died. Younger than her by 17 years, he was an accomplished cleric, historian, and traveler who rose to become dean of the Archdiocese of Toronto. Educated in Canada and Rome, he served in a variety of United States and Canadian parishes. His first published volume, *The History of the Early Missions in Canada,* appeared in 1893, about the same time as his sister was doing her first notable work as a labor activist. He, too, was fond of Mexico, and wrote several books dealing with that country. In 1897 and 1916 he received honorary LL.D degrees from Ottawa University and Toronto University respectively, and in 1920, the Doctor of Letters from Laval.⁶ But his mode was the church and his sister's was labor, and there is no indication they met or even corresponded in adulthood. Both, although prolific writers, scrupulously avoided mention of their families. Save for a eulogy clipped from a Catholic magazine, Mother Jones's papers make no mention of Dean Harris, and his writings contain no known reference to her.

When she reached Chicago, Mother Jones began work on her autobiography. At least as early as 1916, she had been urged by free-lance writers to collaborate on such a project. "We would divide the profits and I believe each of us would have enough to DO THINGS WITH," one suggested.⁷ But helping Mother Jones now was Mary Field Parton, a forty-four-year-old former social worker and magazine writer. She was the wife of Lemuel F. Parton, a former Chicago newspaperman and later editor of papers in California and New York and a nationally syndicated columnist.

Mother Jones found the task trying. "I am getting so d—— tired writing this book," she wrote to a friend. "This work I am not used to."⁸ But she persevered, and in 1925, the 242-page volume was published by Charles H. Kerr and Company, the maverick Chicago publisher of *International Socialist Review.* The book in part reads like a stream-of-consciousness novel. The subject's passion for rhetoric and abhorrence of dates and place names is mirrored in each chapter. Whole eras are overlooked, and others are chronicled in detail, except for mention of Mother Jones. Events are shuffled in time. The Pullman Strike, a salient event in American labor history, is placed, for example in 1904, not 1894.

More important, Mother Jones dismissed the first 30 years of her life in the book's first two paragraphs. There is little about the strife within the UMW, except for her continuing rancor about John Mitchell. Mother Jones's part in the founding of the IWW is overlooked as is her role in the Farmer-Labor Party and the early roots of the Socialist Party. Omitted also are charges of prostitution, or their refutation. The Logan marches escape attention, and there is no examination of her political or economic philosophy or her relationship to violence or to her "boys." It would be interesting indeed to know of the editing process for the *Autobiography,* to know whether derogatory references to the Socialists or to the contemporary UMW leadership were excised. But such insights apparently are lost to history.

But what Mother Jones did do in her book was to etch, in fact and sometimes in hyperbole, a self-portrait of an ardent advocate. Much the same as the manner in which she stirred crowds of miners on state-house steps, she offered herself through anecdote and bombast as a simple, steadfast champion. The suffering of the workers, the callous corporations, the imperatives—and promises—of struggle are painted in a strident, often moving, style. Though often fragmented and chaotic, the autobiography caught something of the essence of her spirit and the germ of the past.

Many of the happenings and much of the dialogue in the book parallel her recitations before various Congressional inquiries or her remarks to newspapermen over a long period. She and Mary Parton may have drawn upon these sources heavily—and selectively—in writing the autobiography. Or just as likely, the utterances had become so learned by rote that Mother Jones disgorged them for Mrs. Parton much as she had for other interviewers decades earlier.

The book, despite Mother Jones's popularity, apparently did not meet with great success in its original edition. There was only one printing, believed to be of 10,000 copies. It proved to be a slow-moving item for Kerr, and although it got into many libraries, it was not much in demand as a trade edition.[9] Still, the book, with an introduction by Clarence Darrow, may have brought Mother Jones some money with which to live during her surprisingly long later years.

During those later years she found herself increasingly soured by the new generation of labor leaders. She found them self-indulgent, overly paid, and unmindful of the struggles which preceded them. To this melancholia, Powderly was an antidote, and his comfortable home and beautiful garden in Washington saw her often. Powderly, the mustachioed former Grand Master Workman of the Knights of Labor, and Mother Jones had been close friends for some 40 years, although they were very dissimilar. A lawyer, Powderly dabbled in politics and had been elected Labor Party mayor of Scranton, Pennsylvania, three times. After leaving the Knights, he stumped the Midwest for Republican William McKinley, much to the chagrin of Bryan-backing labor. But as a reward, Powderly was named United States commissioner general for immigration and served from 1897 to 1902. In 1906, Theodore Roosevelt appointed him special representative of the Department of Commerce and Labor to study the causes of emigration from Europe. Later, Powderly became chief of the division of information in the Bureau of Immigration.[10]

Powderly's ideas were the embodiment of the Knights' philosophy and were, as one historian put it, "idealistic, broadly humanitarian, and often contradictory in scope."[11] As much could be said for Mother Jones. Yet she was much more militant than mellow, even in old age. She spanned Powderly's era and the next. She had seen them all—the Knights, UMW, IWW, the American Railway Union, WFM, the steelworkers' committee, and other craft and industrial unions. But her fleeting attachments to them had kept her from being pulled into the backwater. She wanted union recognition and collective bargaining as immutable rights, a goal which no union, past or present, could quarrel with. Being ideologically uncommitted—or just unsure of herself— Mother Jones transcended organizations and endured where they failed.

In contrast to Powderly's timidity and vacillation, Mother Jones was forthright and generally steadfast. He was the old unionist. She was the eternal one. Furthermore, he was a teetotaler who admitted that nothing in the language "strikes more terror to my soul than the one word, 'rum!' " As the ranking labor official of the 1880s, he probably was the last and most influential of the utopian labor leaders. As such, he was infinitely more preoccupied with abstractions about the evils of the wage system and of private property than was Mother Jones. Like her, he was a spellbinding orator, although in a more florid style. But he also, quite unlike her, thought strikes were "a relic of barbarism."[12]

Powderly and Mother Jones were more friends than associates. He does not mention her in his autobiography nor she him. But when Powderly built his home in Washington, he put aside one room for "the man from over the hill," which was to say, for anyone seeking shelter. More often than not, it was the ever-mobile Mother Jones.[13] She always called him "Mr. Powderly" even though she was his senior by 19 years. But Mother Jones's less proper ways in other respects amused, and perhaps, irritated him. His house number, for example, was changed from 502 Quincy Street to 3700 Fifth Street NW. But Mother Jones never adapted and for years she wrote him and asked others to write her care of the Quincy Street address, causing some confusion.[14]

But their bond was history and fraternity. They shared memories of dimmer times, memories of labor's martyrs. Men like Martin Irons, who led a disastrous wildcat strike on Gould's southwest railways system in 1886, were revered by them both. In this first serious setback of the Knights of Labor, Irons came to be vilified by the press and by the public for what were considered to be the Knights' extravagant demands and violence. Mother Jones, in writing to Powderly of her visit to Irons's grave in Texas, noted that Powderly, too, received "long years of kicks and abuse. . . . I know of the many dark battles you had to fight. You were rocking the cradle of the movement, you made it possible for others to march on."[15]

Powderly, who was not a well man himself, bore much of Mother Jones's medical and other expenses. To a Chicago labor leader who asked if he could not help underwrite Mother Jones's medical care, Powderly replied: "Now don't talk about paying me anything for what I do for Mother Jones, that's a labor of love. My home is hers and as one of the family she don't count when it comes to expense. Her fidelity to the labor movement is her claim with me and my wife feels the same way about it."[16]

Powderly was soon to face death. When in one letter he wrote despairingly of the future, Mother Jones penned back something of her philosophy. "Don't be looking forward to the day you go away . . . look forward to the great grand work you have done in the past and the work there is to be done in the future," she stated. "Don't be dwelling on when we are going to take our final rest, we will have time enough to think of it."[17]

As if to personify that advice, Mother Jones while in Chicago had something of a final political fling. In fact, she may have taken what was her most radical stance. The scene was Carmen's Hall where about 800 delegates were gathered for the national Farmer-Labor Party convention. The party's founding three years earlier in 1920 had been cheered by Mother Jones as a significant breakthrough. "Too long has labor been subservient to the old betrayers, politicians and crooked labor leaders" was a common chant of hers in urging a third party.[18] But the movement had made a poor showing in the 1920 elections, and the Chicago conference was to be a regrouping of all factions opposed to the Republicans and Democrats.

On July 3, 1923, the first day of the meeting, Mother Jones and George S. Comings, Wisconsin's lieutenant governor, were the speakers. Mother Jones reiterated her plea about the increasingly vital struggle to keep labor honest and aggressive. "You must organize and use your head," she told the delegates. "You have been letting bosses override you too long. You must clear out the crooked labor leaders among yourselves.

"All you need to do is to unite politically and you can have a thorough clean-up. You will be able to clean out the gunmen in the coal fields, particularly in West Virginia. It is time to get back to the spirit of the Revolutionary fathers."[19]

But her rhetoric paled before the rest of the conference which heard directly or indirectly urged from the floor or from the speakers' platform the abolition of the United States courts; control of the government by the working classes; nationalization of the railroads; minimum wages; security against destitution, sickness, and high prices; and elaborate measures aimed at stabilization of agriculture, labor, and currency.[20] On the third day, a platform was written under the leadership of members of the Workers Party, which made no secret of its affiliation with the Third International in Moscow. The planks called for a maximum eight-hour day, no child labor under 18 years of age, social insurance, nationalization of all public utilities, and increasing the control of farmers and workers over industry. The Farmer-Labor Party leaders, headed by John Fitzpatrick, disagreed and sought to substitute a platform which would bar groups advocating violent overthrow of the government. But by a thunderous vote of 500 to 40, the conference roared its disapproval, causing a walkout by Fitzpatrick's group.[21]

Although a longtime friend, a comrade in the steel strike, and one who looked after her frequently, Fitzpatrick was not supported by Mother Jones, who voted to maintain the working relationship with the Communists. Despite her bond to Fitzpatrick, she, as well as Alex Howat and Duncan McDonald, could not see the logic of Fitzpatrick's inviting the Workers Party and then denouncing it.[22] The Red platform, under the leadership of William Z. Foster, was kept intact. Resolutions suggesting recognition of the Soviet Union and Mexico, elimination of "military propaganda," and enfranchisement of District of Columbia residents also were passed. It was all for naught, however.

The split mortally wounded both factions. The Federated Farmer-Labor Party, formed as a result of the conference, perished after a year, and Fitzpatrick's national Farmer-Labor Party also soon died. So Mother Jones's last hand at politics was not much different than her earlier tries. She at other times did not show a fondness for the Communists, and she sometimes excoriated them, along with the Socialists, in her interviews. Foster would charge that Samuel Gompers threatened Fitzpatrick's Chicago Federation of Labor with loss of funds if the Reds were not purged from the Farmer-Labor Party.[23] In any event, Mother Jones and Fitzpatrick remained good friends.

Actually, Mother Jones may have veered slightly to the right, politically, in her later years. Most often mentioned by her as a political idol was Senator William Borah of Idaho. He, strangely enough, had been cast in an unfriendly attitude toward labor back in the Coeur d'Alene troubles in the 1890s, and he had been a special prosecutor in the Haywood trial. But Mother Jones came to admire him greatly for his sympathy and tolerance for the workingman. A Chicago doctor at one point told her she had the stamina to live to be 115, and Mother Jones, taking him at his word, bragged about it to visitors. Later, she changed his goal: she wanted to live to see Senator Borah "in the White House and the Nation safe." Eight years as president and Borah "would see that every man and woman has employment," Mother Jones stated.[24] Further, in 1924, Mother Jones made a call on Calvin Coolidge and assured him that the majority of workers would vote for him for president. Coolidge's opponent was John W. Davis of West Virginia, who had been close to the business interests opposed to Mother Jones's agitations in the 1902 strike there.[25]

Early in 1924, Mother Jones also took part in a strike in the Chicago dressmaking industry. The dressmakers, the largest and least organized part of the city's women's clothing industry, struck February 27. But their walkout was paralyzed by sweeping injunctions and police interference. Mother Jones urged the women to fight until "all the bosses and their hired lawyers and other lackeys" will be forced to yield to the workers' collective strength. In a decisive defeat, the strike was lost by July after 1,500 arrests, 500 blacklisted workers, and some $300,000 in union funds had been expended.[26]

Mother Jones returned briefly to Washington where Powderly died in June. Then she left for Los Angeles where she had friends and yet another pardon to seek for a jailed comrade. She returned in August 1924 via Chicago where she visited Fitzpatrick and Ed Nockels, secretary of the Chicago Federation. She felt poorly, however, and by the first of the year, she was in California despite, or perhaps because of, another bout of inflammatory rheumatism. Returning to Washington in 1927, she became ill again, "hanging between life and death," she wrote, and spending four weeks in the hospital.[27] The years were taking their belated toll, and Mother Jones peripatetic nature was being dulled, though not with her assent.

"You know I have not given up hope to see my 100th anniversary and I will be in Chicago to feast with you," she told Fitzpatrick. "At least I hope so," she added.[28] Although Mother Jones spent much of her last two years in bed, she still spoke vigorously, sometimes profanely, to her visitors. That amazing voice leaping from her frail body to castigate the "tyrants" who were the "foes of labor" was chronicled by many a young reporter who came to interview her.

She did not cease pouring forth commentary on the issues, whatever they be. And it continually startled the pilgrims to her side, as it always had, that such an ardent warrior for liberalized labor laws would be so unpredictable on other matters, that she had had audiences with presidents and campaigned for senators and helped found political parties, for example, but sneered at women's suffrage. This seemed not in keeping with the tenets of a once much-feared socialist agitator. And, of course, it was not consistent. It was just Mother Jones's own tightly circumscribed view, borrowed from no one and resistant to all reason except her own.

For some time Mother Jones's doctor had prescribed a little whiskey for her. But one time when he apparently was out of town, she secured a similar prescription from another physician. Internal Revenue agents spotted the request and called Mother Jones to make sure someone else was not using her name.

"They were nice about it," she said of the agents, "and said it was all right. I don't like the stuff, but I have to take it. At my age, you know, I need it. And I told them what I thought about prohibition. Ugh! This country has never been bossed and won't be now." She described the Eighteenth Amendment as "stuffing a rag down the throats of the people."[29]

Regularly entertaining the press, Mother Jones was given to waxing on about the sorry state of the new generation of labor leaders. "We haven't got the great men we used to have—men who loved the people," she said. "Every fellow wants to get more: more money, more publicity. The greatest country in the world," she sighed "if handled right."[30] Mother Jones also read many daily newspapers and labor organs. She received old friends at her bedside and rekindled old memories. Her ire, too, was still flammable.

Most infuriating to her was the Massachusetts murder trial of Nicola Sacco and Bartolomeo Vanzetti. Mother Jones, too, knew something of the scales of justice being bent beneath the burden of enraged public opinion. "They'll never dare kill them!" she cried from her Garfield Hospital bed.[31] But she was wrong. On August 23, 1927, the two Italian immigrants, one a shoemaker and one a fish peddler, were electrocuted for what many thought was the crime of being foreign-born and radical. "If they did [execute them], it would stir up the whole world," Mother Jones had said.[32] And on that she was right. A worldwide controversy sprung up around the pair convicted of murdering a paymaster and a guard in a shoe-factory robbery.

But Mother Jones, now partially deaf and slowly losing her sight, never learned of the defendants' deaths. Callers to her hospital room were warned that she had been told the two men were given indefinite reprieves. She apparently never learned otherwise.[33] She did recover from her siege, at least enough to leave the hospital and to plan wistfully. "If I could get about on my legs, I would be out in the field organizing workers today instead of idling away my time here in Washington," she said on her ninety-ninth birthday.[34]

The chore of caring for her as well as for her finances and correspondence weighed heavily on Emma Powderly. In May 1929 Mother Jones visited the home of Mr. and Mrs. Walter E. Burgess. The retired miner and his wife lived in a farmhouse just outside Washington and from there Mother Jones would never leave alive. In her ninety-ninth year, she also was caught up in a strike of North Carolina textile workers, and she itched to be there. "The North Carolinians would have won their fight already," she said in December 1929, "if the Southern women had had experience in strikes and knew how to act in such a situation."[35]

Though her tenacity repeatedly was underestimated, Mother Jones's health was deteriorating. She planned her own funeral for Saint Gabriel's Roman Catholic Church in Washington and her burial in a little plot in the union-owned cemetery in Mt. Olive, Illinois. "So far as leaving anything behind us, I don't want as much as ten cents in my possession when I travel to the grave," she stated. "I want no fine coffin. There is too much heathenism about this display. They'll hammer us when we are alive and then march after us to the grave when we are dead. I want the tributes paid while we live."[36]

She told a reporter: "I'm not going to get up again. I'm just an old war-horse—ready to go into battle but too worn out to move."[37] Actually, her condition rose and fell repeatedly, although she did remain largely bedfast. She could be reported comatose one week and loquacious the next, in a sense not unlike her days at mill and mine.

On March 8, 1930, former President and Chief Justice William Howard Taft died at age seventy-two. He had always respected Mother Jones's courage and admired her wit. Mother Jones, still grateful to him for his intercession on behalf of the Mexican revolutionaries, was saddened deeply by his passing. Despite her cynical assessment of most politicians, she thought of the portly Taft as humane and approachable. One of her favorite stories, told in several variations, was her dialogue with the president just before he pardoned some of her Mexican cohorts. "Now, Mother, the trouble lies here: if I put the pardoning power in your hands there would be no one left in the jails," Taft warned her. "I'm not so sure of that, Mr. President," Mother Jones is said to have replied. "A lot of those who are in would be out, but a lot of those who are out would be in." The retort drew a chuckle from Taft, who a few days later granted her request.[38]

Two weeks after Taft's death, Mother Jones traded thoughts with Dan O'Brien, "King of the Hoboes." The two Irish iconoclasts complained of the growing unemployment in Depression America. In Washington to attend and testify at Senate labor hearings, the sixty-eight-year-old O'Brien was a veteran of Coxey's Army and the innovator of the first known bread line in Washington, D.C. O'Brien said he agreed with Mother Jones that the high joblessness seemed to be a permanent blemish on the capitalistic system.[39] Mother Jones's "once fierce eyes [are] now faded to a mild blue," but her voice was "miraculously strong and vibrant," the *New York Times* reported as Mother Jones approached the century point. Doctors said she was not ill but "just wearing out."[40]

The AFL set up celebrations in major cities in Mother Jones's honor, and she addressed the gatherings over the radio. She also warned Mrs. Burgess to have "plenty to eat" in case visitors came. On May 1, 1930, she was 100 years old. Hundreds of well-wishers, including a large contingent of the unemployed led by O'Brien, joined in the pilgrimage to the old, out-of-the-way Burgess farmhouse on Riggs Road, near Hyattsville, Maryland. Mother Jones's weakened condition prevented her from traveling to Chicago as she had hoped. But it did not preclude what must rank as one of the liveliest hundredth birthday parties.

She was carried from her sickbed for a few hours to gaze upon an enormous five-layer, 100-candle cake. She greeted friends and made her debut in motion pictures beneath the Burgesses's apple trees. Next to meeting old associates, Mother Jones was most excited about her appearance in the "talkies."[41] Mother Jones always had considered movie films a "lot of foolishnesss" and only once had she been to a theater, several years earlier. But she relished the chance, as ever, to express her opinion. As the Paramount News cameras rolled, Mother Jones urged workers to "stick together and be loyal to each other." She spoke fondly of what was to be Senator Borah's successful fight to have the Senate reject the United States Supreme Court nomination of Judge John J. Parker.[42] The North Carolina jurist had handed down a hated injunction in 1927 which upheld yellow-dog contracts, or antiunion agreements, in the West Virginia mines.

Mother Jones also took advantage of the forum to blast two of her favorite targets: prohibition and women's suffrage. When someone pinned a cluster of sweetpeas on her at the birthday party, she remonstrated, "Hell, I never have worn these and I don't want to now," although she soon acquiesced in the interest of festivity. Then she launched a tirade against the "old fools" who "forced prohibition on the country." She called it the "worst affliction" the nation suffers. Women, she continued, should make use, as she did, of their inherent power, instead of searching for fancy legal remedies of their own. "If the women of the country would only realize what they have in their hands there is no limit to what they could accomplish," she told the press. "The trouble is they let the capitalists make them believe they wouldn't be lady-like. Maybe it wouldn't but, hell, who wants to be a lady anyhow when women are what we want and they have a great mission to fulfill."[43]

Surrounded by banks of flowers and mounds of presents, Mother Jones read hundreds of telegrams of congratulations from all parts of the world, from labor leaders present and former, from public officials, from just plain people. She reminisced about some of her many close calls and told stories of outwitting a federal judge in West Virginia who sent her and other women to jail "for no other offense than trying to keep the scabs away." The women then, she said, sang all night and raised such a furor that they had to be released.[44]

One telegram she received had special significance:

PLEASE ACCEPT MY HEARTIEST CONGRATULATIONS ON YOUR 100TH BIRTHDAY ANNIVERSARY. YOUR LOYALTY TO YOUR IDEALS, YOUR FEARLESS ADHERENCE TO YOUR DUTY AS YOU HAVE SEEN IT IS AN INSPIRATION TO ALL WHO HAVE KNOWN YOU. MAY YOU HAVE CONTINUED HEALTH AND HAPPINESS AS LONG AS LIFE LASTS.

JOHN D. ROCKEFELLER, JR.[45]

Mother Jones had as recently as a few years earlier turned down a dinner invitation from the same man "because people would have said I sold out the workers." But she now was touched genuinely by his solicitude. "He's a damn good sport," she said. "I've licked him many times, but now we've made peace. . . . this telegram rather squares things."

The message also conjured up, of course, memories of Ludlow and the bitter Colorado strike, of indiscriminate killings, and of her being jailed for weeks. Her hatred for the Rockefeller family had remained intact despite the junior Rockefeller's dinner invitation. But this most recent peace overture triumphed.

"Like all rich men, fighting for their interests, they saw their duty differently," she said. "Mr. Rockefeller has a Christian heart, they always said that, and his message to me shows it is still beating.

"Now, I can't tell him that the past is buried and we are friends again, but I do want him to know I appreciate his message as much as any I received."[46]

To that end, Mother Jones on May 3, after the Burgess home became more serene, dictated a reply from her bed:

YOUR GOOD WISHES AND HOPES FOR CONTINUED LONG LIFE ON MY ONE HUNDREDTH BIRTHDAY WAS A HAPPY SURPRISE AND AMONG THOSE MESSAGES MOST APPRECIATED BY ME. KNOWING ALL THE RESPONSIBILITIES ON YOUR SHOULDERS, IT WAS A HUMAN ACT TO THINK KINDLY OF ME AT THIS TIME AND YOUR MESSAGE WAS AN EXPRESSION OF A CHRISTIAN HEART.[47]

Two months later, on the senior Rockefeller's ninety-first birthday, she reciprocated with a telegram: "Thank God we have some men in the world as good as you. We never needed them more than we do today. Most sincere wishes that you may be blessed with many more." After dictating the message, Mother Jones, in characteristic juxtaposition, said, "I wouldn't trade what I've done for what he's done. I've done the best I could to make the world a better place for poor, hardworking people."[48]

Following the exertion at the birthday party, Mother Jones suffered a relapse. Throughout the summer, friends who visited her wrote pessimistic appraisals of her condition. "She does not take solid nourishment but she is able to keep down the stimulant," one wrote in early July to Ed Nockels. "She looks pretty weak and it is very difficult for me to tell just how long she will last because the doctor himself does not know. He claims that her stomach is about gone, but judging from her color and her mind I would say that she might even recover from this attack."[49]

She did. Or at least long enough to get in one more lick against UMW President John L. Lewis. Declaring Lewis has "betrayed my boys," Mother Jones in early September 1930 gave $1,000 to John Walker as her contribution toward his campagin to oust Lewis. She had made her peace with the Rockefellers, but she never reached an understanding with Lewis. His heavy-handed dealing with intraunion dissent ran counter to her more democratic ideals, especially since the dissenters usually were among her friends.

Alexander Howat, Adolph Germer, and John Walker continued the fight against what they considered the union's totalitarianism. In 1929 they had formed the UMW Reorganized, a rump group, consisting largely of Illinois miners, which claimed to be heir to the UMW. In September 1930, Mother Jones called Walker, who was secretary-treasurer, to her bedside and placed a purse containing $1,000 in his hands. "I know of no better use for it," she told him. "It has broken my heart to see the United Mine Workers crushed. I only pray that I may live long enough to see John L. Lewis licked." The money had been given to Mother Jones years earlier by Walker when she needed it badly. Now she was returning it to a friend and to a cause in which she believed.[50] The UMW Reorganized, however, was to be struck down the following year by the courts.

In September Mother Jones's condition worsened in contrast to what it had been just a few weeks earlier. Normally a hearty eater even during her illness, Mother Jones was on a liquid diet and growing yet more emaciated. "I know I haven't long to live," she said on September 5. "But I'm not too old or too weak to give up fighting."[51] Soon, however, her body would refuse to retain any nourishment. Although she suffered from no organic ailment, she was, in effect, dying of starvation, doctors concluded. Nursing her became burdensome on Mrs. Burgess. At one point the strain became so great that Mrs. Burgess was said to be in a more serious condition than Mother Jones, and a nurse was brought in to care for them both.[52]

Until mid-September 1930 Mother Jones's mind and memory remained strong. After that there were times when she could not even remember her stock answers to reporters' predictable questions on well-worn subjects like the enfranchisement of women or the state of modern labor leadership. She began receiving brandy as her sole nourishment.[53] A month earlier, the Reverend William Sweeney, assistant pastor of Saint Gabriel's, had administered extreme unction and in mid-September he brought her the Blessed Sacrament. Mother Jones also reportedly tore up her will in September and decided the $10,000, later estimated at $6,000, that she had accumulated was not needed by the Burgesses as much as to fight unemployment. She said she would bequeath it to labor.[54]

Although her heart remained strong, chances of regaining any of her former vigor were lessening, said Dr. H. H. Howlett, her physician. She gradually lapsed into a coma. Throughout October, she alternated between a near-stupor and something of her old self, despite predictions of her imminent demise. Propped up on pillows, she delighted reporters with reminiscences about hearing Lincoln speak against slavery. "That is what we need, more men like Lincoln," she asserted, "but, alas, they are hard to find these days." The American people themselves are to blame for the Depression, she maintained. "They don't bother themselves, and don't make the ones they have elected bother to do the job."[55] But despite these flashes of her old spirit, the doctor soon reported that she remained alive largely due to her own will. In fact, she had grown so weak that she began falling asleep in the midst of conversations. Mother Jones was sinking rapidly, the doctor said, and death could come at any time.

AFL President William Green, Ed Nockels, John Walker, and others faithfully came to her side where she slept in a great four-poster bed, although she was practically blind and could not recognize them. But it was not until 11:55 P.M. on Sunday, November 30, 1930, that without a parting shot and thus contrary to character, Mother Jones simply and quietly ebbed into eternity.

Beneath a blanket of white carnations and white and purple chrysanthemums, a gray metal casket bearing the remains of Mary Harris Jones lay in Saint Gabriel's Roman Catholic Church in Washington on the morning of Wednesday, December 3, 1930. "Her interest in the cause of labor can never be forgotten," intoned Father Sweeney in a high requiem mass. "Her zeal and earnestness in behalf of the poor will be a pleasant memory long after her body is gone. We ask God to temper His justice with mercy and take her in His own good time."[56]

In the well-filled church were AFL President Green, Labor Secretary William Doak, AFL Secretary Frank Morrison, several international union presidents, the Burgesses, Fitzpatrick and Nockels, several Illinois miners, other friends, fond strangers, and many Washington area union business agents. There being no relatives, pallbearers were eight unionists, each representing a different organized trade. In the rear of the church was a group of men with tattered overcoats—the unemployed. But for the most part the visitors were working men and their families who sat through the services. From the church, the casket was taken to an undertaker's chapel where it remained until late that afternoon when it was put aboard a special Baltimore and Ohio railroad car.[57]

Accompanied by Nockels, Fitzpatrick, the Burgesses, Morrison, John Walker, and representatives of President Green and Labor Secretary Doak, the train departed for Illinois. Seven years earlier, Mother Jones had "made a thrilling speech" at the annual "Virden Day" celebration, October 12, in Mt. Olive. Soon afterwards, in a letter to "The Miners of Mt. Olive," she asked to be buried with their martyrs of the 1898 massacre. Those seven dead men, four of them buried in the Miner's Cemetery in Mt. Olive "are responsible for Illinois being the best organized labor state in America," she wrote. "I hope it will be my consolation when I pass away to feel I sleep under the clay with those brave boys."[58] She had not fought at Virden. But she felt she shared a common bond with those who to her epitomized righteous determination and sacrifice.

On the train which followed much the same route as that which bore Lincoln's body from Washington to Springfield, the remains of Mother Jones arrived at St. Louis's Union Station on December 4. There an escort of about 20 miners from Mt. Olive, Benld, Staunton, and Gillespie boarded. The car was switched from a Baltimore and Ohio to a Wabash train, and at 7:32 P.M. that night, it was sidetracked at the Mt. Olive depot, 40 miles northeast of St. Louis.[59]

"Nearer, My God, to Thee" was played by a band as onlookers bowed their heads and wept. Survivors of the Virden riot bore the casket to the Odd Fellows' Hall where it lay in state from the 5th through the 7th of December. The town of 3,500, with its strong and violent mining heritage, was thronged by thousands of coal diggers. They arrived by auto and by free buses from all over the state to pay final homage to "a unique and picturesque figure," as William Green put it, whose "services will never be surpassed or excelled."[60]

Thousands passed by to view the body in whose withered fingers a rosary was entwined. The casket was set amid banks of flowers, flickering candles, and bright red-blue-and-gold banners of the miners' unions. On the wall above the coffin were crepe-draped pictures of Mother Jones and the four Mt. Olive victims of Virden. Working people mostly, with wives in dark dresses and children strangely hushed by the occasion made up the procession which also included clerical workers, bank officers, storekeepers, and professional men.

One member of the honor guard, a miner far too young to have known Mother Jones at her peak, spoke for many when he commented to a reporter: "She was a sweet old lady. I remember when she came here seven years ago. I knew she was a scrapper and I expected to see a tough old person with a hard voice. Instead, I saw an old-fashioned woman, kind of like the old ladies in the movies that sit at home and do embroidery. You couldn't have helped loving her."[61]

More than 1,000 persons crowded into the hall for a memorial service on December 7. Another 1,000 massed on the sidewalks and into an overflow room upstairs where the service was heard over hastily arranged loudspeakers and also broadcast over WCFL, the Chicago Federation of Labor's radio station. The Reverend John W. F. Maguire, a labor activist and president of Saint Viator's College in Bourbonnais, Illinois, gave the memorial address and officiated the following day at the funeral in Mt. Olive's Roman Catholic Church of the Ascension.

"The eyes of the world are on Mt. Olive," one observer noted, and indeed, they were. Between 10,000 and 15,000 people swarmed around the church, which held only 200 to 300, for the funeral. Big-city reporters crowded into the office of the *Mt. Olive Herald* to file their stories. The streets were clogged with cars. Moving-picture cameras whirred in the little town which only once more would see such activity.

A choir of miners from nearby Glen Carbon sang part of the mass, and Father Maguire used a poem to catch the deceased's rapport with those who called her "Mother":

> And because I am of the people, I understand the people,
> I am sorrowful with their sorrow, I am hungry with their desire. . . .
>
> I speak to my people, and I speak in my people's name to the
>   masters of my people.
> I say to my people that they are holy, that they are august, despite
>   their chains,
> That they are greater than those who hold them, and stronger
>   and purer,
> That they have but need of courage and to call, on the name of
>   their God. . . .[62]

Of the frail, old woman whose withered body, sheathed in a lavender dress, they were about to bury, Father Maguire asked: "What weapons had she to fight the fight against oppression of working men?"

The answer: "Only a great and burning conviction that oppression must end. Only an eloquent and flaming tongue that won men to her cause. Only a mother's heart torn by the sufferings of the poor. Only a towering courage that made her carry on in the face of insuperable odds. Only a consuming love for the poor."

"Sometimes," he continued, "she used language that a polite family journal could not print. Sometimes she used methods that made the righteous grieve. . . . But let it be remembered that she was, after all, human. Her faults were the excesses of her courage, her love of justice, the love in her mother's heart."[63]

The conclusion of her hundred years, six months, and thirty days was met, the priest said, with an antithesis: "In their luxurious offices many a mine owner and capitalist breathes a sigh of relief while on the plains of Illinois, in the hills and valleys of West Virginia and Pennsylvania, in Colorado and California and British Columbia, horny-handed men and toil-worn women are in grief.

"The reasons for these contrasting emotions are identical. Mother Jones is dead."[64]

SEVENTEEN

Some day in the golden future, when our fight is
  past and won,
Man will make her deathless statues to mark the
  good that she has done,
So that all may know and love her as she loved
  her every son.
  —From "Mother Jones," by A Paint Creek Miner[1]

THE death of Mother Jones further fired the love of those whom she had helped or known or given strength by word or deed. Scores of poems and songs, often saccharine but deeply felt, were composed to her memory by rough hands unaccustomed to the task. The room in which she died became a shrine open on her birthdate, May 1, and other special occasions. Organizations, like the Illinois State Federation of Labor, observed a minute of silent prayer to her memory. A bust by sculptor Jo Davidson for a time would grace the foyer of the United States Department of Labor building in Washington. Radio station WCFL, the "Voice of Labor" in Chicago, broadcast a special program on her one-hundred-and-second birthday, and paraphrasing a poem to Lincoln, said:

> Her hands were used to break the iron chain—
> That held a race in bondage and despair.
> She lent a hand to those that tried to rend the bars in twain,
> That men might walk in freedom's blessed air.[2]

Aside, however, from such forgotten valedictories, no organization, no edifice, no movement remains to mark the effort of Mother Jones.

210

Nor, as Eugene Debs predicted, is her name "lovingly remembered" by the children of those she helped "and their children's children forever."[3] No streets or schools or even labor temples are named for her. She has never been on a postage stamp or in a school child's text. No one ever will be able to accurately gauge her contribution to the nation's social progress. This is as real and elusive as Mother Jones herself. Her forte was knowing how to arouse men to a fighting pitch, how to stir them to a realization of their plight and their power. Skill in starting a strike or in keeping one going is not the kind of aptitude that America ever has been quick to reward. Indeed, Mother Jones went unrewarded, save for the adulation of her "boys."

Her shortcomings were several and severe. She wrote no contracts, spawned no schools of thought, and was doggedly anti-institutional. Hers was a shallow, often contradictory, ideology. Doubtless she did incite violence, sometimes fruitlessly. Her mild profanity was more colorful than productive, and it has been said with truth that she was closer to the heart than to the brain of the labor movement. She was not as effective as her retouched recollections would have us believe. Only in a few disputes—notably West Virginia in 1912–13 and Colorado in 1913–14—did she really figure centrally in events. And then, it was largely because she made such a poignant picture imprisoned. This is a negative kind of greatness.

Her rhetoric could become inflamed and sometimes it backfired. More often, though, her listeners became inured. At the UMW conventions, for example, especially in Mother Jones's later career, she was a diversion. Her rambling speeches made her an irrelevant, if revered, cheerleader, replete with epithets and proletarian jargon but of slight consequence to the hard economic decisions at hand. In starkest terms, she was a spectacular supernumerary. She was not important in the sense, say, of a Gompers or a Mitchell or a Debs or even a Howat, whose protests stood for a particular principle. Thrust Mother Jones may have lent to the labor movement but not direction.

Yet it is as easy to dismiss her as it is to place her in a pantheon for which she is ill-suited. She was the human element, the spirit within the structure. Mother Jones was a necessary third dimension, a folk heroine whose inspiration reached down to those people who were unimportant in name or wealth or title but all-important in numbers. She lived as few Americans have, giving all for the unwanted and accepting in return only hardship and danger. In a sense, then, she may have personified some of the most noble strains in American history. Jettisoning her own ambitions, forsaking property, and discarding caution, she was true to her own homily: "The Lord loves a cheerful giver but is dead sore on hogs."[4]

If she was oft attuned more to the romantic than to the real, she nonetheless meant much to many people. She was so dramatic, so peripatetic, so passionate in her commitment to cause that she may have been among the nation's most beloved figures at the time of her death. Her importance was not in the magnitude of her acts but in the fabric of her personality. Mother Jones was colorful. But she cannot be dismissed as merely that. She was also extraordinarily effective in her limited field. Militiamen do not jail women for weeks because they are colorful, governors do not deport them on grounds of quaintness, and mayors do not forbid them to speak. More important, hard-bitten miners do not, at the risk of eviction, starvation, and death, throw down their tools at the call of an addled old woman. Rather, Mother Jones's involved personality provided the precise psychological support for those who, like her, yearned for both a preindustrial Arcadia and a restructured future.

On balance, she was neither a torch-waving revolutionary nor a diffident grandmother, although at times she pretended to be one or the other. She spurned both those who lashed out with no chance at victory and those unwilling to put themselves on the line for principle. Underlying all her inconsistencies, her sparse philosophy, her loose treatment of the truth, her dread of compromise, and what sometimes was her irascibility was the battle for bread. The economic fight was her fight and was foremost. Only because of this did she recoil from the feminist movement, did she wander all over the political landscape, did she persevere in the face of abject defeats.

Her socialism, vaguely defined as it was, had its roots in the sight of ill-housed, ill-paid workers and their families, not in Marxist tomes. Her unconcern with ideology, her wariness of factions, and her essentially moderate view of capitalism made her ill-fitted for the radical organizations of her time. The essence of her economic thought was that changes were due. From her younger days sprang her anger and her fervor and her unswerving faith in unionism as the remedy. In death as in life, though, Mother Jones was more than just a legend. Even in her grave, she was not far from controversy, and a fierce intraunion fight was waged almost literally over her dead body.

Quarreling between Illinois miners and the national UMW peaked in 1932 when John L. Lewis sought acceptance of a 30 percent wage cut proposed by the operators. Earlier he had pledged that the union would take "no backward step" by accepting wage reductions. But still being hurt by nonunion mines in West Virginia and Kentucky, Midwestern operators claimed they could not compete in the national market. Lewis feared that increased mechanization plus resistance to wage cuts could mean a disastrous loss of jobs in Illinois. But the Illinoisans recalled Lewis's earlier stance, and 50,000 miners struck April 1 for lack of a contract. In July they voted down a wage cut, and in August they again voted to reject a Lewis proposal to end the walkout. But the UMW president invoked his emergency powers after the voting tallies suddenly disappeared, and he imposed a $5.00-per-day contract, a drop from the previous $6.10 per day.

Protest meetings were held around the state, and pickets were set up to prevent the reopening of the mines. Some violence ensued. The strikers decided to concentrate their picketing on Franklin County mines, which produced about 20 percent of the state's coal. Massing in a car and truck caravan, they formed at Gillespie in Macoupin County and streamed southeasterly more than 100 miles. Just short of the county line, highway patrolmen directed them to Mulkeytown where the would-be pickets were repulsed August 24 in a gun battle with the sheriff and his special deputies, who, the strikers claimed, were financed by Lewis.[5] Returning to Gillespie, the insurgents held a September 1 convention and voted to break from the UMW and form the Progressive Miners of America. A vicious fight between the two unions followed for the next five years. Houses and autos were bombed, union halls dynamited, trains blown off the tracks, and shootings were common. Carrying arms became such a standard practice that at least one company put up a "gun board" where miners could check their weapons before going underground to work.[6]

It was in such a milieu that the most lasting remembrance to Mother Jones was conceived. Progressive Miners Local 35 elected a ten-member Mother Jones Memorial Committee and began soliciting funds in the fall of 1934 for a monument in the miners' cemetery at Mt. Olive. The effort met strong opposition, including a restraining order, from the

UMW. But by the fall of 1936, the monument—80 tons of Minnesota pink granite, 22 feet high on a 28-by-18-foot base—was largely complete. It consisted of a bas-relief of Mother Jones on an obelisk flanked by life-size statues of two miners in their working gear. The monument was dedicated October 11, 1936, in commemoration of the Virden Massacre.[7] As a testament to the times, ten Progressive Miners armed with rifles and shotguns had hidden in the shrubbery of the cemetery from dusk until dawn for ten days previous to protect the monument from suspected enemies. At least once the guardians came perilously close to marking Mother Jones's grave with blood when an unsuspecting but well-intentioned miner came to meditate at the site.[8]

On the appointed day, five special trains and 25 buses brought miners and their families to the quiet little town just off United States Route 66. Two hour-long parades involved some 32,000 participants, and a total of 50,000 reportedly attended the dedication which was covered by Pathé News and broadcast over radio station KMOX in St. Louis. Refreshment stands lined the streeets, and striking miners and their families received a ton and a half of meat and huge amounts of bread and coffee paid for by the sale of pictures of the monument. Ringed by 40 American flags, the monument was unveiled to pay homage to Mother Jones, the Virden martyrs, and to members of the Progressive Miners who lost their lives in the recent secessionist battle. Among those dedicating the $30,000 monument were Mrs. Burgess; former District 12 official, Duncan McDonald; Rush Holt, the young United States senator from West Virginia; C. Wayland Brooks, Republican gubernatorial nominee in Illinois; and William Lemke, a North Dakota Congressman and a presidential candidate of the Union Party.[9]

Reading from Mother Jones's autobiography, Holt found passages which he said "proved the silver tongued, white-haired woman who toured the country from east to west and north to south, wherever there was trouble brewing, would have been against John Lewis." Lemke said the crowd could "vote for the principles of Mother Jones" by voting for him, and Brooks called her "the aristocrat of America's fighting woman."[10] Despite the evoking of her memory, the fight to expand the Progressive Miners beyond Illinois proved largely futile. Organizing campaigns in West Virginia, Kentucky, Kansas, and Pennsylvania failed. Adverse rulings from the National Labor Relations Board, heavy court costs in criminal cases, and the inability to negotiate substantially better contracts than the UMW meant that in the long run the Progressive Miners—later called the Progressive Mine Workers under the AFL— became little more than a "paper" organization. The cemetery in Mt. Olive, the only union-owned plot in the nation, remains among the few assets of the group whose early efforts drew so heavily upon Mother Jones for inspiration.[11]

The final speaker on the day of the monument dedication was Mrs. Burgess. She told of Mother Jones's declining years and how the old agitator "did express the wish that she could live another hundred years in order to fight to the end that there would be no more machine guns and no more sobbing little children."[12] But perhaps the simplest and most profound epitaph ever offered came years earlier from Mother Jones herself. "Die when I may," she said to a friend, "I want it said of me by those who know me best, that I always plucked a thistle and planted a flower when I thought a flower would grow."[13]

References and Notes

Index

REFERENCES AND NOTES

Books

Adams, Graham, Jr. *Age of Industrial Violence 1910–15: Activities and Findings of the U.S. Commission on Industrial Relations.* New York: Columbia University Press, 1966.

Ambler, Charles H., and Summers, Festus P. *West Virginia: The Mountain State.* Englewood Cliffs, N.J.: Prentice Hall, 1958.

Ashby, LeRoy. *The Spearless Leader: Senator Borah and the Progressive Movement in the 1920s.* Urbana: University of Illinois Press, 1972.

Aurand, Harold W. *From the Molly Maguires to the United Mine Workers.* Philadelphia: Temple University Press, 1971.

Benedict, C. Harry. *Red Metal: The Calumet & Hecla Story.* Ann Arbor: University of Michigan Press, 1952.

Bernstein, Irving. *The Lean Years: A History of the American Worker 1920–1933.* Boston: Houghton Mifflin Co., 1960.

Beshoar, Barron B. *Out of the Depths: The Story of John R. Lawson A Labor Leader.* Denver: Golden Bell Press, 1958.

Blaisdell, Lowell L. *The Desert Revolution.* Madison: University of Wisconsin Press, 1964.

Brody, David. *Labor in Crisis: The Steel Strike of 1919.* Philadelphia: J. B. Lippincott Co., 1965.

Brooks, Thomas R. *Toil and Trouble: A History of American Labor.* New York: Delacorte Press, 1964.

Brophy, John. *A Miner's Life.* Madison: University of Wisconsin Press, 1964.

Busch, Francis X. "The Haymarket Riot and the Trial of the Anarchists." In *An Illinois Reader,* edited by Clyde C. Walton. DeKalb: Northern Illinois University Press, 1970.

Capers, Gerald M., Jr. *The Biography of a River Town. Memphis: Its Heroic Age.* Chapel Hill: University of North Carolina Press, 1939.

Carsel, Wilfred. *A History of the Chicago Ladies' Garment Workers Union.* Chicago: Normandie House, 1940.

Chaplin, Ralph. *Wobbly: The Rough-and-Tumble Story of an American Radical.* Chicago: University of Chicago Press, 1948.

219

Coleman, McAlister. *Men and Coal*. New York: Farrar and Rinehart, 1943.

Cometti, Elizabeth, and Summers, Festus P., eds. *The Thirty-Fifth State*. Morgantown: West Virginia University, 1966.

Conlin, Joseph R. *Big Bill Haywood and the Radical Union Movement*. Syracuse: Syracuse University Press, 1969.

——. *Bread and Roses Too: Studies of the Wobblies*. Westport, Conn.: Greenwood Publishing Corp., 1969.

Corbin, David. *The Socialist & Labor Star*. Huntington, W.Va.: Appalachian Movement Press, 1971.

Cornell, Robert J. *The Anthracite Coal Strike of 1902*. Washington, D.C.: Catholic University of America Press, 1957.

Cornwell, John J. *A Mountain Trail*. Philadelphia: Dorrance and Co., 1939.

Cromie, Robert. *The Great Chicago Fire*. New York: McGraw-Hill, 1958.

Davis, James D. *The History of the City of Memphis*. Memphis: Hite, Crumpton, and Kelly, 1873.

Debs, Eugene V. *Debs: His Life, Writings and Speeches*. St. Louis: Phil Wagner, 1908.

Dixon, George T. *The Archdiocese of Toronto and Bishop Walsh*. Jubilee Volume. Toronto, 1892.

Dulles, Foster Rhea. *Labor in America*. New York: Thomas Y. Crowell Co., 1960.

Encyclopaedia Britannica, 1971 ed.

Foner, Philip S. *History of the Labor Movement in the United States*. Vols 1–3. New York: International Publishers, 1947.

Foster, William Z. *From Bryan to Stalin*. New York: International Publishers, 1937.

——. *The Great Steel Strike and Its Lessons*. New York: B. W. Huebsch, 1920.

Founding Convention of the Industrial Workers of the World, The. New York: Merit Publishers, 1969.

Frost, Richard H. *The Mooney Case*. Stanford: Stanford University Press, 1968.

Ginger, Ray. *The Bending Cross: A Biography of Eugene Victor Debs*. New Brunswick: Rutgers University Press, 1949.

Gluck, Elsie. *John Mitchell, Miner*. New York: John Day Co., 1929.

Great Chicago Fire, The. Chicago: Chicago Historical Society, 1946.

Harriman, Florence. *From Pinafores to Politics*. New York: Henry Holt, 1923.

Harris, Evelyn L. K., and Krebs, Frank J. *From Humble Beginnings: West Virginia State Federation of Labor 1903–1957*. Charleston, W.Va.: Labor History Publishing Fund, 1960.

Harris, Herbert. *American Labor*. New Haven: Yale University Press, 1938.

Harvey, Katherine A. *The Best-Dressed Miners: Life and Labor in the*

Maryland Coal Region, 1835–1910. Ithaca: Cornell University Press, 1969.

Hinds, William A. *American Communities and Cooperative Colonies.* Chicago: Charles H. Kerr & Co., 1908.

Hoes, Rose G. *The Dresses of the Mistresses of the White House.* Washington, D.C.: 1931.

Jones, Mary Harris. *Autobiography of Mother Jones.* Edited by Mary Field Parton. Chicago: Charles H. Kerr & Co., 1925.

Keating, Edward. *The Story of "Labor".* Washington: Darby Printing Co., 1953.

Keating, J. M. *A History of the Yellow Fever.* Memphis: The Howard Association, 1879.

Keiser, John H. "John H. Walker: Labor Leader from Illinois." In *Essays in Illinois History,* edited by Donald F. Tingley. Carbondale: Southern Illinois University Press, 1968.

Lahne, Herbert J. *The Cotton Mill Worker.* New York: Farrar and Rinehart, 1944.

Langdon, Emma F. *The Cripple Creek Strike.* Denver: Great Western Publishing Co., 1905.

Lantz, Herman R. *People of Coal Town.* New York: Columbia University Press, 1958.

Laslett, John H. *Labor and the Left: A Study of Socialist and Radical Influences in the American Labor Movement, 1881–1924.* New York: Basic Books, 1970.

Lee, Howard B. *Bloodletting in Appalachia.* Morgantown: West Virginia University, 1969.

Lindsey, Almont. *The Pullman Strike.* Chicago: University of Chicago Press, 1942.

McDonald, David J., and Lynch, Edward A. *Coal and Unionism: A History of the American Coal Miners' Union.* Silver Spring, Md.: Lynald Books, 1939.

McIlwaine, Shields. *Memphis Down in Dixie.* New York: E. P. Dutton, 1948.

Madison, Charles A. *American Labor Leaders.* New York: Harper and Brothers, 1950.

Moody, T. W., and Martin, F. X. *The Course of Irish History.* New York: Weybright and Talley, 1967.

Mooney, Fred. *Struggle in the Coal Fields.* Edited by James W. Hess. Morgantown: West Virginia University Library, 1967.

Morgan, John G. *West Virginia Governors.* Charleston, W.Va.: Agency Corp., 1960.

Morris, Homer. *The Plight of the Bituminous Coal Miner.* Philadelphia: University of Pennsylvania Press, 1934.

Patterson, Charles. *Paint Creek Miner: Famous Labor Songs from Appalachia.* Huntington, W.Va.: Appalachian Movement Press, 1971.

Perlman, Selig, and Taft, Philip. *Labor Movements. History of Labor in the United States 1896–1932,* vol. 4. New York: Augustus Kelley, 1966.

Powderly, Terence V. *The Path I Trod.* New York: Columbia University Press, 1940.

Quint, Howard H. *The Forging of American Socialism.* Columbia: University of South Carolina Press, 1953.

Roosevelt, Theodore. *An Autobiography.* New York: Macmillan Co., 1913.

Rosalita, Sister M. *No Greater Service: The History of the Congregation of the Sisters, Servants of the Immaculate Heart of Mary.* Detroit, 1948.

Ross, Malcolm. *Machine Age in the Hills.* New York: Macmillan Co., 1933.

Sandburg, Carl. *Complete Poems.* New York: Harcourt Brace, 1950.

Selvin, David F. *The Thundering Voice of John L. Lewis.* New York: Lothrop, Lee & Shepard, 1969.

Sinclair, Upton. *The Brass Check: A Study of American Journalism.* Pasadena, Calif., 1918.

Smith, G. Wayne. *Nathan Goff, Jr.: A Biography.* Charleston, W.Va.: Education Foundation, Inc., 1959.

Snow, Sinclair. *The Pan-American Federation of Labor.* Durham: Duke University Press, 1964.

Spargo, John. *The Bitter Cry of the Children.* New York: Grosset & Dunlap, 1906.

Spivak, John L. *A Man in His Time.* New York: Horizon Press, 1967.

Stimson, Grace. *Rise of the Labor Movement in Los Angeles.* Berkeley: University of California Press, 1955.

Suffern, Arthur E. *Conciliation and Arbitration in the Coal Industry of America.* Boston: Houghton Mifflin, 1915.

Turner, John Kenneth. *Barbarous Mexico.* Austin: University of Texas Press, 1969.

Vorse, Mary Heaton. *A Footnote to Folly.* New York: Farrar and Rinehart, 1935.

———. *Men and Steel.* New York: Boni and Liveright, 1920.

Ward, Robert D., and Rogers, William W. *Labor Revolt in Alabama, 1894.* University: University of Alabama Press, 1965.

Warne, Frank Julian. *The Coal-Mine Workers.* London: Longmans, Green and Co., 1905.

Weinstein, James. *The Decline of Socialism in America 1912–1925.* New York: Monthly Review Press, 1967.

Wilson, Edmund. *The American Jitters: A Year of the Slump.* New York: Charles Scribner's Sons, 1932.

Wish, Harvey. "The Pullman Strike: A Study in Industrial Warfare." In *An Illinois Reader,* edited by Clyde C. Walton. DeKalb: Northern Illinois University Press, 1970.

Government Documents

Andrews, John B., and Bliss, W. D. P. *History of Women in Trade Unions.* Vol. 10 of *Report on Conditions of Women and Child Wage-Earners in the United States.* Senate Doc. 645, 61st Congress, 2nd Session, 1911.

Colorado Adjutant General's Office. *The Military Occupation of the Coal Strike Zone of Colorado by the Colorado National Guard.* Denver, 1914.

Congressional Record. Vols. 50–51. Washington, D.C., 1913, 1914.

Report of the U.S. Coal Commission. Part 3. Washington, D.C., 1925.

U.S. Commission on Industrial Relations. *Final Report and Testimony.* Vol. 11. Senate Doc. 415, 64th Congress, 1st Session, 1916.

U.S., Congress, House. Subcommittee of the Committee on Mines and Mining. *Conditions in the Coal Mines of Colorado.* 2 vols. 63d Cogress, 2nd Session, 1914.

———. Rules Committee. *Hearings for a Joint Committee to Investigate Alleged Persecutions of Mexican Citizens by the Government of Mexico.* 61st Congress, 2nd Session, 1910.

———. Subcommittee of the Committee on Mines and Mining. *Report on the Colorado Strike Investigation.* House Doc. 1630, 63d Congress, 3d Session, 1915.

U.S., Congress, Senate. Committee on Education and Labor. *Investigation of Strike in Steel Industries.* 66th Congress, 1st Session, 1919.

———. Subcommittee of the Committee on Education and Labor. *Conditions in the Paint Creek District, West Virginia.* 63d Congress, 1st Session, 1914.

———. *Insurrection and Martial Law.* Senate Doc. 43, 63d Congress, 1st Session, 1913.

———. *Investigation of Paint Creek Coal Fields of West Virginia.* Senate report 321, 63d Congress, 2nd Session, 1913–14.

———. *Report of Labor Disturbances in the State of Colorado, from 1880 to 1904.* Senate Doc. 122, 58th Congress, 3d Session, 1905.

U.S., Department of Labor. *Michigan Copper District Strike.* Washington, D.C.: Bureau of Labor Statistics, Bulletin 139, 1914.

———. *Report on the Bisbee Deportations.* Washington, D.C.: President's Mediation Commission, 1918.

West, George P. *Report on the Colorado Strike.* Washington, D.C.: U.S. Commission on Industrial Relations, 1915.

Newspapers

American Miner. Springfield, Ill., 1930.

Appeal to Reason. Girard, Kans., 1895–1922.

Arizona Daily Star. Tucson, 1916.

Boston Herald. 1904.
Calumet (Mich.) *News.* 1905, 1913.
Capital Times. Madison, Wis., 1962.
Charleston (W.Va.) *Daily Mail.* 1919.
Charleston (W.Va.) *Gazette.* 1913, 1919.
Chicago Tribune. 1905.
Copper Country Evening News. Calumet, Mich., 1905.
Copper Times. Lake Linden, Mich., 1905.
Daily Mining Gazette. Houghton, Mich., 1905.
Daily State Journal. Parkersburg, W.Va., 1902.
Denver Post. 1903.
Federation News. Chicago: Federation of Labor, 1930–32.
Labor. 1930.
Milwaukee Journal. 1936.
Miner's Magazine. Denver, 1900–1903, 1910–21.
New York Tribune. 1902–3.
New York Times. 1895–1906, 1913–30.
New York World. 1903.
Polly Pry. Denver, 1903–5.
Pittsburgh Post. 1919.
Pittsburgh Press. 1919.
Rocky Mountain News. Denver, 1938.
St. Louis Post-Dispatch. 1930, 1936.
Sunset News and Observer. Princeton-Bluefield, W.Va., 1957.
Tucson Citizen. 1916.
United Mine Workers Journal. Indianapolis, 1899–1930.
Washington Daily News. 1927, 1930.
Washington Evening Star. 1928–30.
Washington Herald. 1930.
Washington Post. 1902, 1930.
Wheeling Register. 1897.
Wilkes-Barre (Pa.) *Record.* 1901.

Periodicals

Baker, Ray Stannard. "The Reign of Lawlessness: Anarchy and Despotism in Colorado." *McClure's Magazine,* May 1904, pp. 43–57.

Betten, Neil. "Strike on the Mesabi—1907." *Minnesota History,* fall 1967, pp. 340–47.

Brissenden, Paul F. "The Launching of the Industrial Workers of the World." *University of California Publications in Economics,* November 25, 1913, pp. 1–82.

Chay, Marie. "The Day They Struck the School." *Empire Magazine* of the *Denver Post,* June 25, 1972, pp. 30–33.

Fitch, John A. "Law and Order: The Issue in Colorado." *Survey,* December 5, 1914, pp. 242–47.

"Garment Workers Strike." *International Socialist Review,* November 1915, pp. 260–64.

Green, Archie. "The Death of Mother Jones." *Labor History,* winter 1960, pp. 68–80.

Harris, Sheldon H. "Letters from West Virginia: Management's Version of the 1902 Coal Strike." *Labor History,* spring 1969, pp. 228–40.

Hudson, Harriet D. "The Progressive Mine Workers of America: A Study in Rival Unionism." *University of Illinois Bureau of Economics and Business Research Bulletin Nr. 73,* 1952.

Hunt, G. W. P. "The Autobiography of George Wiley Paul Hunt." *Arizona Historical Review,* January 1933, pp. 253–63.

"Indomitable Spirit of Mother Jones." *Current Opinion,* July 1913, pp. 19–20.

Iron Molders International Journal, October 1867.

Karr, Carolyn. "A Political Biography of Henry Hatfield." *West Virginia History,* October 1966, pp. 10–12.

Jones, Mother Mary. "A Picture of American Freedom in West Virginia." *International Socialist Review,* September 1902, pp. 177–79.

———. "Civilization in Southern Mills." *International Socialist Review,* March 1901, pp. 539–41.

———. "The Coal Miners of the Old Dominion." *International Socialist Review,* January 1902, pp. 575–78.

Keiser, John H. "The Union Miners Cemetery at Mt. Olive, Illinois." *Journal of the Illinois State Historical Society,* autumn 1969, pp. 229–66.

Lindquist, John H. "The Jerome Deportation of 1917." *Arizona and the West,* autumn 1969, pp. 233–46.

Lynch, Lawrence R. "The West Virginia Coal Strike." *Political Science Quarterly,* December 1914, pp. 626–63.

McCormick, Kyle. "The National Guard of West Virginia During the Strike Period of 1912–13." *West Virginia History,* October 1960, pp. 34–35.

Mailly, William. "The Anthracite Coal Strike." *International Socialist Review,* August 1902, pp. 79–85.

Marcy, L. H. "On the Strike Field." *International Socialist Review,* March 1913, pp. 647–54.

Maurer, Maurer, and Senning, Calvin F. "Billy Mitchell, the Air Service, and the Mingo War." *West Virginia History,* October 1968, pp. 339–50.

Michelson, M. "Sweet Land of Liberty." *Everybody's Magazine,* May 1913, pp. 615–28.

Michelson, Peter C. "Mother Jones." *Delineator,* May 1915, p. 8.

"Mother Jones and Mr. Rockefeller." *Outlook,* February 10, 1915, p. 302.

"New York Street Car Strike, The." *International Socialist Review,* October 1916, pp. 213–14.

"1919: The First Great Steel Strike." *Steel Labor,* November 1969, p. 11.

Older, Cora. "Answering a Question." *Collier's,* April 19, 1913, pp. 26–27.
———. "The Last Day of the Paint Creek Court Martial." *Independent,* May 15, 1913, pp. 1084–89.
Pew, Marlen. "Shop Talk at Thirty." *Editor and Publisher,* December 6, 1930, p. 56.
Rastall, Benjamin M. "The Labor History of the Cripple Creek District: A Study in Industrial Evolution." *Bulletin of the University of Wisconsin,* February 1908, pp. 1–166.
Smith, Russell E. "The March of the Mill Children." *Social Science Review,* September 1967, pp. 298–303.
"Some Gems of Thought by Mother Jones," *Arizona, The State Magazine,* August 1916, back cover.
Steel, Edward. "Mother Jones in the Fairmont Field, 1902." *Journal of American History,* September 1970, pp. 290–307.
Time, 1923.
Wiebe, Robert H. "The Anthracite Strike of 1902: A Record of Confusion." *Mississippi Valley Historical Review,* September 1961, pp. 229–51.

Archival Collections

Collins, Justus. Papers. West Virginia University, Morgantown.
Debs, Eugene V. Papers. Indiana State University, Terre Haute.
Fitzpatrick, John. Papers. Chicago Historical Society.
Germer, Adolph. Papers. Wisconsin State Historical Society, Madison.
Haldeman Papers. University of Indiana, Bloomington.
Jones, Mother. Papers. Catholic University of America, Washington.
———. Speeches, August–September, 1912. West Virginia University, Morgantown.
Mitchell, John. Papers. Catholic University of America. Washington.
"Old St. Mary's Church" file. Chicago Historical Society.
Powderly, Terence V. Papers. Catholic University of America. Washington.

Theses and Dissertations

Anson, Charles P. "A History of the Labor Movement in West Virginia." Ph.D. University of North Carolina, 1940.
Barb, John M. "Strikes in the Southern West Virginia Coal Fields, 1912–1922." Master's. West Virginia University, 1949.
Camp, Helen Collier. "Mother Jones and the Children's Crusade." Master's. Columbia University, 1970.
Crawford, Charles B. "The Mine War on Cabin Creek and Paint Creek, West Virginia, in 1912–13." Master's. University of Kentucky. 1939.

Gowaskie, Joseph M. "John Mitchell: A Study in Leadership." Ph.D. Catholic University of America, Washington, 1968.

Johnson, Alan V. "Governor G. W. P. Hunt and Organized Labor." Master's. University of Arizona, 1964.

McGovern, George S. "The Colorado Mine War, 1913–14." Ph.D. Northwestern University, 1954.

Mikeal, Judith Elaine. "Mother Mary Jones: The Labor Movement's Impious Joan of Arc." Master's. University of North Carolina, 1965.

Posey, Thomas Edward. "The Labor Movement in West Virginia, 1900–1948." Ph.D. University of Wisconsin, 1948.

Raffaele, John Francis. "Mary Harris Jones and the United Mine Workers of America." Master's. Catholic University of America, 1964.

Synder, Betty Hall. "The Role of Rhetoric in the Northern West Virginia Activities of the United Mine Workers 1897–1927." Master's. West Virginia University, 1955.

Trail, William R. "The History of the United Mine Workers in West Virginia, 1920–1945." Master's. New York University, 1950.

Walsh, William J. "The United Mine Workers of America as an Economic and Social Force in the Anthracite Territory." Ph.D. Catholic University of America, 1957.

Willis, Edmund P. "Colorado Industrial Disturbances, 1903–1904." Master's. University of Wisconsin, 1955.

Pamphlets and Labor Union Proceedings

American Federation of Labor. *Proceedings.* 1914.

Committee of Coal Mine Managers. *The Activities in Colorado of "Mother" Jones.* Facts Concerning the Struggle in Colorado for Industrial Freedom, series 1, pamphlet no. 13, Denver, 1914.

Fink, Walter H. *The Ludlow Massacre.* Denver: United Mine Workers, District 15, 1914.

Life and History of Mother Jones. Welch, W.Va.: *McDowell Recorder,* 1915.

Pan-American Federation of Labor. *Report of the Proceedings of the Third Congress of the Pan-American Federation of Labor,* 1921.

St. John, Vincent. *The I.W.W.: Its History, Structure and Methods.* Chicago: Industrial Workers of the World, 1919.

Statement to the U.S. Coal Commission by Non-Union Operators of Southern West Virginia. Bluefield, W.Va., 1923.

Swain, George T. *The Incomparable Don Chafin.* Charleston, W.Va.: Ace Enterprises, 1962.

United Mine Workers of America. *Minutes of the Special Convention.* Indianapolis, July 17–19, 1902.

———. *Proceedings of the Convention of the United Mine Workers of America,* 1905–24.

NOTES

Chapter 1

1. P. Michelson, p. 8.
2. Cromie, pp. 8–25.
3. *The Great Chicago Fire,* p. 11; "Chicago," *Encyclopaedia Britannica,* 1971; Cromie, pp. 242–45.
4. Jones, *Autobiography,* p. 12; "Old St. Mary's Church" file, Chicago Historical Society. Although Mother Jones places her shop on Washington, the Chicago city directory for 1871 lists a Mrs. Mary Jones at 174 Jackson.
5. According to Mother Jones's own dating, which was used with some consistency throughout her career. A few otherwise accurate accounts—for example, a UMW *Journal* profile of April 25, 1901, and a biographical article in the *Wilkes-Barre Record* for March 30, 1901— give her birthdate as 1843. If true, this would be at odds with Mother Jones's statements and the preponderance of information, but it might help explain other inconsistencies. See Ch. 16, n. 6. However, Irish genealogical records are not conclusive.
6. *Federation News,* Dec. 20, 1930, p. 3.
7. T. W. Moody and F. X. Martin, pp. 248–50; several sources recount the bayonet episode, including the *Milwaukee Journal* of Dec. 23, 1936, and an International News Service dispatch of Dec. 25, 1929, as included in the Mother Jones Papers.
8. *Washington Post,* April 25, 1930; INS dispatch, Dec. 25, 1929, Jones Papers.
9. Mikeal, pp. 1–3.
10. Ibid.
11. Sister M. Rosalita, p. 240; *New York Times,* June 1, 1913.
12. Jones, *Autobiography,* p. 11.
13. P. Michelson, p. 8; however, Rose G. Hoes, appears to dispel this; Jones, *Autobiography,* pp. 11–12; Mikeal, p. 2 and other sources report various names for the husband. But the preponderance of usage is "George," and union records bear this out. See n. 21 to this chapter.
14. *Boston Herald,* Sept. 11, 1904.

15. Capers, p. 188.
16. Ibid., pp. 182, 188.
17. Jones, *Autobiography*, p. 12.
18. McIlwaine, pp. 167–69.
19. J. Keating, pp. 91, 134–35; the gender of the children is in doubt, and mortality records for the epidemic are incomplete.
20. Jones, *Autobiography*, p. 12.
21. *Iron Molders International Journal*, Oct. 1867; Jones, *Autobiography*, p. 12; Capers, p. 188.
22. Jones, *Autobiography*, p.13.
23. Ibid.
24. Mother Jones apparently compressed the order of events since it is doubtful that the Knights had spread to Chicago by the time of the fire. Dulles, p. 130, indicates that the group's initial growth was slow and not until 1874 did the Knights spread beyond the Philadelphia area.
25. Dulles, pp. 138–42; Andrews and Bliss, pp. 113–14; Brooks, pp. 59–60.
26. Jones, *Autobiography*, p. 14.
27. *Conditions in the Coal Mines*, p. 2917.
28. Writing in "Introduction" to Jones, *Autobiography*, p. 5.
29. *Federation News*, Dec. 13, 1930, p. 3.

Chapter 2

1. Jones, *Autobiography*, p. 17.
2. Brophy, p. 74.
3. Chay, p. 30.
4. UMW *Proceedings*, 1916, p. 967.
5. An earlier anecdote recounted in the *Washington Evening Star*, Dec. 1, 1930.
6. P. Michelson, p. 8; the possibility that Mother Jones traveled to Europe is suggested in the *Wilkes-Barre Record*, March 30, 1901, the *Boston Herald*, Sept. 11, 1904, and the Pan-American Federation of Labor, p. 75.
7. Raffaele, p. 3; Mikeal, p. 5. Powderly did not join the Knights until 1874, according to Dulles, p. 130.
8. Foner, vol. 1, p. 439.
9. Foner, vol. 2, p. 50.
10. Brooks, p. 50.
11. Ibid.
12. Foner, vol. 1, p. 464.
13. Ibid.
14. Ibid., pp. 466–67; Jones, *Autobiography*, p. 14.
15. Brooks, p. 52.
16. Dulles, pp. 119–20; Brooks, p. 52.

17. Foner, vol. 1, p. 473; Dulles, pp. 119–22.
18. Jones, *Autobiography,* pp. 15–16.
19. H. Harris, pp. 80–81.
20. Jones, *Autobiography,* pp. 19–20; H. Harris, p. 84.
21. H. Harris, pp. 85–86; *Dulles,* p. 124.
22. Busch, pp. 290–91.
23. Dulles, pp. 124–25.
24. Jones, *Autobiography,* pp. 21–23.
25. H. Harris, p. 91.
26. Ibid.
27. Brooks, p. 84; Dulles, p. 146.
28. Suffern, pp. 47–48; Keiser, "The Union Miners Cemetery," pp. 249–50.
29. Suffern, pp. 47–48; Gluck, p. 46.
30. Keiser, "The Union Miners Cemetery," p. 256; "Mother Jones and Mt. Olive Miners," *Capital Times,* Dec. 28, 1962. The latter is a recollection by Mother Jones's friend and associate, Adolph Germer.
31. Jones, *Autobiography,* pp. 24–27.
32. Suffern, pp. 33–34.
33. Foner, vol. 2, p. 255.
34. Harvey Wish, p. 353; Foner, vol. 2, pp. 261–62; Ginger, pp. 92, 106–9.
35. Foner, vol. 2, pp. 262–64.
36. Jones, *Autobiography,* p. 115; Ward and Rogers, pp. 13–106; Lindsey, p. 261.
37. Jones, *Autobiography,* pp. 115–16.
38. Ward and Rogers, pp. 13, 134; Foner, vol. 2, pp. 268–75; Wish, pp. 366–77.
39. Jones, *Autobiography,* pp. 116–17.
40. Foner, vol. 2, p. 276.
41. Jones, *Autobiography,* p. 118.
42. Jones, "Civilization in Southern Mills," p. 541.
43. Lahne, pp. 105–12.
44. Jones, *Autobiography,* p. 119.
45. Jones, "Civilization in Southern Mills," p. 539.
46. Jones, *Autobiography,* pp. 120–21.
47. Jones, "Civilization in Southern Mills," p. 540.
48. Ibid.
49. *New York Times,* June 1, 1913; Jones, *Autobiography,* p. 122.
50. *New York Times,* June 1, 1913.
51. Jones, *Autobiography,* pp. 125–26.
52. Ibid., p. 29; Mikeal, p. 9.
53. Jones, "Civilization in Southern Mills," p. 541.
54. Ginger, p. 200; Perlman and Taft, p. 224; Hinds, p. 488; Jones, *Autobiography,* p. 28.
55. Hinds, pp. 496–98; *Appeal to Reason,* Sept. 7, 1895.
56. Perlman and Taft, p. 225.

57. Ginger, p. 201; Jones, *Autobiography,* p. 29; Mikeal, p. 10.
58. *Appeal to Reason,* Mar. 17, 1900.

Chapter 3

1. Jones, *Autobiography,* p. 235.
2. Lynch, p. 626; Harris and Krebs, p. xvii.
3. Ambler and Summers, pp. 445–46; Posey, pp. 24, 203; Harris and Krebs, p. xv. Estimates of the number of West Virginia miners vary greatly.
4. *Wheeling Register,* July 28, 1897.
5. Barb, p. 38.
6. Ambler and Summers, pp. 445–46; Harris and Krebs, pp. xix, xxii.
7. Wiebe, pp. 230–31.
8. Anson, p. 202.
9. H. Harris, pp. 114–15.
10. *Washington Post,* Feb. 17, 1903.
11. Wiebe, p. 231.
12. Mikeal, pp. 48–50.
13. UMW *Journal,* Dec. 27, 1900, p. 1.
14. *Boston Herald,* Sept. 11, 1904. This is a long feature article on Mother Jones and her methods, etc.
15. *Washington Post,* Feb. 17, 1903.
16. *American Miner,* Dec. 13, 1930, p. 2.
17. Jones, "A Picture of American Freedom in West Virginia," pp. 177–78.
18. Ibid., p. 178.
19. UMW *Journal,* May 1, 1902, p. 1; Mother Jones to John Mitchell, Mar. 14, 1902, and Feb. 7, 1902, in Mitchell Papers.
20. Steel, pp. 291–93.
21. Ibid., p. 294.
22. Ibid., p. 295; Jones, *Autobiography,* pp. 43–44.
23. *Washington Post,* Feb. 17, 1903.
24. Steel, p. 296; Snyder, p. 87.
25. *Daily State Journal,* June 21, 1902; Snyder, pp. 87–88.
26. Jones, *Autobiography,* p. 49.
27. Steel, p. 297.
28. Gowaskie, p. 141.
29. UMW *Minutes of the Special Convention,* p. 46; Wiebe, pp. 231–40; Steel, pp. 298–99.
30. *New York Tribune,* July 25, 1902; Steel, pp. 300–301.
31. Steel, p. 301.
32. Mikeal, p. 55; Jones, *Autobiography,* p. 53; Steel, p. 301.
33. *New York Tribune,* July 25, 1902.
34. Steel, p. 302.
35. Mikeal, pp. 52–54.

36. Jones, *Autobiography,* pp. 63, 65.
37. M. Michelson, p. 616; Jones, *Autobiography,* p. 68.
38. Jones, *Autobiography,* p. 69; M. Michelson, p. 617. Mother Jones later would cite as one of the most heartbreaking scenes in her career the time just after the Mt. Stanaford violence when she saw a little girl dig at the grave of her murdered father. See Commission on Industrial Relations, p. 10623.
39. S. Harris, pp. 234–38.
40. Ibid., pp. 238, 240.
41. Lynch, p. 628; Ambler and Summers, p. 446.
42. Steel, pp. 305–6.
43. Harris and Krebs, p. xxv.
44. Steel, p. 307.

Chapter 4

1. *Calumet News,* Apr. 20, 1905.
2. *Appeal to Reason,* March 17, 1900; Mikeal, p. 13, quotes William B. Wilson, UMW secretary-treasurer.
3. Aurand, pp. 21–47; Walsh, pp. 77–94.
4. Walsh, pp. 95–98. See also Perlman and Taft, p. 33.
5. Mikeal, p. 12.
6. Jones, *Autobiography,* pp. 36–37.
7. Brophy, p. 74.
8. Harvey, p. 315; Mikeal, p. 14.
9. Walsh, pp. 98–101; Cornell, pp. 46–47, indicates 125,000 men were off the job by the end of the first week, and 136,000 of the anthracite area's 142,500 miners were not working by September 28.
10. Raffaele, pp. 19–21.
11. Ibid., pp. 22–24; *New York Times,* Sept. 21, 1900; Cornell, pp. 51–52.
12. Jones, *Autobiography,* pp. 89–90; Raffaele, p. 24; *New York Times,* Sept. 23, 1900; Cornell, p. 52.
13. *New York Times,* Sept. 27, 1900.
14. Jones, *Autobiography,* p. 90.
15. UMW *Journal,* Sept. 27, 1900, p. 8; Jones, *Autobiography,* p. 90.
16. Commission on Industrial Relations, p. 10619; UMW *Journal,* Sept. 27, 1900, reported that the group was met by the sheriff and "a large force of deputies" who accompanied the marchers to a meeting ground.
17. Warne, pp. 173–75.
18. UMW *Journal,* Sept. 27, 1900, p. 8; Mikeal, p. 17; Raffaele, pp. 27–29.
19. *New York Times,* Sept. 23, 1900.
20. Ibid., Oct. 11, 1900; Raffaele, p. 30.
21. Jones, *Autobiography,* p. 91; Cornell, pp. 47–48.
22. Cornell, p. 52.
23. *Appeal to Reason,* Nov. 17, 1900.

24. Walsh, p. 107; Wiebe, p. 236; Raffaele, p. 32; UMW *Journal*, Oct. 4, 1900, p. 8.
25. Mitchell quoted in McDonald and Lynch, p. 54; Cornell, pp. 59–61; Walsh, p. 104.
26. Mother Jones to John Mitchell, Nov. 30, 1900, as cited in Mikeal, pp. 18–19.
27. UMW *Journal*, Apr. 25, 1901.
28. Walsh, p. 109.
29. Wiebe, pp. 239–42; Walsh, p. 116; McDonald and Lynch, p. 57.
30. Walsh, p. 115.
31. UMW *Journal*, Aug. 21, 1902, p. 1.
32. Raffaele, p. 34.
33. Roosevelt, pp. 505, 514; Walsh, pp. 119–20; Wiebe, p. 247; Cornell, pp. 173–89.
34. Brooks, p. 100; Cornell, pp. 216–17, 235, 252.
35. Walsh, p. 123; Jones, *Autobiography*, p. 62.
36. Gluck, p. 132; Mikeal, p. 22.
37. Brooks, p. 100; Wiebe, pp. 249–50.
38. Jones, *Autobiography*, p. 58.
39. Ibid., pp. 59–60.

Chapter 5

1. Camp, p. 21.
2. Ibid, pp. 1–2.
3. Jones, *Autobiography*, p. 71; Camp, p. 8.
4. Jones, *Autobiography*, pp. 71–72.
5. Spargo, pp. 148–51.
6. Camp, p. 7; Spargo, p. 142.
7. Spargo, p. 151.
8. Camp, pp. 11–14.
9. Ibid.
10. R. Smith, p. 301; Jones, *Autobiography*, p. 74.
11. *New York Tribune*, July 11, 1903; *New York World*, July 11, 1903.
12. *New York Tribune*, July 11, 1903.
13. Camp, p. 15; *New York Times*, July 11, 1903.
14. *New York Times*, July 12, 1903.
15. Jones, *Autobiography*, pp. 76–77.
16. Camp, pp. 16–17; *New York Times*, July 14, 1903.
17. *New York Times*, July 14, 1903.
18. Camp, p. 19.
19. Mikeal, p. 27.
20. Camp, p. 21.
21. Ibid., pp. 21–24.
22. *New York Times*, July 20, 1903.

23. Ibid.
24. Pew, p. 56.
25. Camp, p. 25.
26. Jones, *Autobiography*, pp. 77–78; *New York Times,* July 24, 1903; Camp, pp. 26–27.
27. *New York Times,* July 24, 1903.
28. *New York Tribune,* July 24, 1903; *New York Times,* July 24, 1903.
29. *New York Tribune,* July 24, 1903.
30. Camp, pp. 28–30.
31. *New York Times,* July 27, 1903; Camp, p. 30.
32. *New York Times,* July 27, 1903.
33. Ibid. See also Jones, *Autobiography*, pp. 80–81, for a slightly different version of the meeting.
34. Camp, p. 32; UMW *Journal,* Aug. 6, 1903, p. 1.
35. Camp, pp. 33–34.
36. UMW *Journal,* Aug. 6, 1903, p. 1; Camp, p. 34.
37. Camp, p. 35; R. Smith, p. 303.
38. UMW *Proceedings,* 1916, p. 965. In addressing West Virginia miners on the Charleston levee in August, 1912, Mother Jones would note that Roosevelt was running again for president. "May God Almighty grant that he die before election comes," she said. "He sent two thousand guns in to blow my brains out in Colorado and I have got it in for him." Jones Speeches, Charleston levee speech, Aug. 1, 1912, p. 7.
39. UMW *Journal,* Aug. 6, 1903, p. 1; UMW *Journal,* Aug. 27, 1903, p. 5.
40. UMW *Journal,* Aug. 6, 1903, p. 1; Camp, p. 38.
41. R. Smith, p. 303; Camp, pp. 36–37.

Chapter 6

1. Jones, *Autobiography*, p. 94.
2. UMW *Journal,* Sept. 3, 1903, p. 1; Jones, *Autobiography*, p. 95.
3. Gluck, p. 167.
4. Rastall, p. 87; *Report of Labor Disturbances,* pp. 51–65.
5. Baker, p. 52.
6. *Report of Labor Disturbances,* pp. 31, 330.
7. Willis, pp. 49–52; Rastall, p. 67; Gluck, p. 167.
8. Rastall, p. 88; Willis, pp. 56–77.
9. UMW *Journal,* Oct. 29, 1903, p. 1; ibid., Nov. 9, 1903, p. 1; Jones, *Autobiography*, pp. 95–96.
10. McDonald and Lynch, p. 65.
11. *Report of Labor Disturbances,* pp. 332–34; Willis, pp. 86–87.
12. *Report of Labor Disturbances,* p. 335.
13. *Denver Post,* Nov. 22, 1903; Willis, pp. 91–92; Gluck, pp. 168–70.

14. *Denver Post,* Nov. 22, 1903.
15. Ibid. See also Jones, *Autobiography,* pp. 99–100.
16. *Denver Post,* Nov. 22, 1903.
17. *Report of Labor Disturbances,* pp. 335–36.
18. Ibid.
19. Jones, *Autobiography,* pp. 100–101. Not long after the announcement of withdrawal of national UMW support for the southern strike, Mitchell and another UMW delegate left for Paris and the International Mining Congress. They also viewed mining operations in Great Britain, France, Germany, and Belgium, and Mitchell wrote a series of articles on the experience. See UMW *Proceedings,* 1905, pp. 105 ff.
20. Pew, p. 56.
21. Jones, *Autobiography,* pp. 87–88. See also Gluck, p. 86.
22. Dulles, p. 190; Raffaele, p. 97.
23. Gluck, p. 168.
24. W. P. Gillen to John Mitchell, Aug. 27, 1905. Mitchell Papers.
25. Mother Jones to John Walker, Jan. 4, 1905. Mitchell Papers.
26. Jones, *Autobiography,* pp. 100–101.
27. *Report of Labor Disturbances,* p. 330; Gluck, pp. 170–71.
28. *Appeal to Reason,* Jan. 30, 1904.
29. *Report of Labor Disturbances,* p. 350.
30. Jones, *Autobiography,* p. 103.
31. Mother Jones to John Mitchell, Apr. 16, 1904. Mitchell Papers.
32. Commission on Industrial Relations, p. 10624.
33. Jones, *Autobiography,* pp. 104–6.
34. *Miner's Magazine,* Dec. 7, 1911; Jones, *Autobiography,* p. 107.
35. Jones, *Autobiography,* pp. 107–8; Mikeal, pp. 98–99. Local newspapers for the period, see especially *Eastern Utah Advocate,* seem to suggest Mother Jones was in the Helper area only for a week or so, although she wrote Mitchell from there on April 16. In a later Colorado strike, Mother Jones was imprisoned for 26 days, and she may have confused the two incidents.
36. Gluck, p. 173; Langdon, p. 271.
37. Willis, p. 101; Gluck, p. 173.
38. Willis, p. 65; cost figure cited in UMW *Proceedings,* 1905, p. 204.
39. Rastall, pp. 119, 125, 131–38; Willis, pp. 110–20.
40. *New York Times,* Aug. 8, 1904.
41. Langdon, p. 272, includes a contribution written by Mother Jones.
42. Mother Jones to John Walker, Jan. 4, 1905. Mitchell Papers.
43. UMW *Proceedings,* 1905, pp. 177–78, 184–85. In many works, the name of Mitchell's antagonist is spelled "Randall."
44. Ibid., pp. 179–80.
45. Ibid., pp. 193–225, 227–28; Gowaskie, pp. 272–75.
46. UMW *Proceedings,* 1905, pp. 193, 229.
47. Ibid., pp. 231–32.

Chapter 7

1. Commission on Industrial Relations, p. 10620.
2. Brissenden, pp. 4–5.
3. *Chicago Tribune,* June 27, 1905; Perlman and Taft, pp. 230–31.
4. Conlin, *Big Bill Haywood,* pp. 49–50; Ginger, pp. 237–38.
5. Brissenden, p. 14.
6. Dulles, p. 211; *Chicago Tribune,* June 28, 1905.
7. *Chicago Tribune,* June 30, 1905.
8. St. John, p. 5.
9. *Founding Convention of the Industrial Workers of the World,* p. 509.
10. Brooks, p. 118; Conlin, *Bread and Roses Too,* pp. 3–6.
11. Conlin, *Big Bill Haywood,* p. 127. See also Perlman and Taft, pp. 232–36.
12. "Indomitable Spirit of Mother Jones," p. 20.
13. Conlin, *Big Bill Haywood,* pp. 29–31; Perlman and Taft, pp. 185–87.
14. Perlman and Taft, pp. 209–10; Conlin, *Big Bill Haywood,* p. 54.
15. Mikeal, p. 36.
16. Ginger, p. 247; Perlman and Taft, p. 210.
17. Mother Jones to Terence Powderly, May 24, 1907. Jones Papers; Perlman and Taft, p. 211.
18. Mikeal, pp. 35–36.
19. Conlin, *Big Bill Haywood,* pp. 55–58.
20. Quint, pp. 293–94.
21. Perlman and Taft, pp. 228–29.
22. Debs, pp. 269–70; Weinstein, p. 59, indicates that Mother Jones worked as a Socialist Party organizer in some years after 1910. See Mailly, p. 83, for a testimonial to Mother Jones's diligence in distributing Socialist literature.
32. "Indomitable Spirit of Mother Jones," p. 20.
24. Jones, *Autobiography,* p. 114; Mother Jones to Walter Wayland, Nov. 15, 1918. Haldeman Papers.
25. Jones, *Autobiography,* p. 114.
26. Ibid., p. 136.
27. *Daily Mining Gazette,* April 21, 1905; Perlman and Taft, p. 248.
28. *Daily Mining Gazette,* April 18, 1905; *Copper Country Evening News,* April 20, 1905.
29. *Copper Country Evening News,* April 20, 1905.
30. Perlman and Taft, p. 248.
31. Mother Jones to Terence Powderly, May 24, 1907. Jones Papers.
32. Turner, p. 238; Jones, *Autobiography,* pp. 136–37.
33. Turner, p. 239.
34. *Hearings for a Joint Committee,* p. 91.
35. UMW *Proceedings,* p. 376.
36. Jones, *Autobiography,* p. 139.

37. *Hearings for a Joint Committee,* p. 93; UMW *Proceedings,* 1909, p. 377.
38. Blaisdell, pp. 5–9.
39. Turner, pp. 246, 249.
40. Stimson, p. 321.
41. *Hearings for a Joint Committee,* p. 92.
42. Ibid.
43. Turner, p. 253.
44. Magon, Villarreal, and Rivera to Mother Jones, Nov. 31 [*sic*], 1909. Jones Papers.
45. UMW *Proceedings,* 1909, pp. 378–79; *Proceedings,* 1911, p. 264.
46. Jones, *Autobiography,* pp. 141–42, 144.
47. Turner, p. xxiii.
48. UMW *Proceedings,* 1912, p. 78.
49. Cited in Mikeal, p. 40.
50. *New York Times,* May 23, 1915.
51. Betten, pp. 340, 345.
52. Ibid., pp. 344–46; Perlman and Taft, p. 389.
53. Mikeal, p. 41.
54. *Miner's Magazine,* Dec. 7, 1911.
55. Perlman and Taft, p. 323.
56. Gluck, pp. 85, 225; Dulles, pp. 186–87.
57. UMW *Proceedings,* 1911, pp. 266–67.
58. Gluck, pp. 235–37, 240 ff; UMW *Proceedings,* 1911, pp. 748–49.
59. UMW *Proceedings,* 1911, pp. 264–65; Mikeal, p. 44. See also Jones, *Autobiography,* pp. 145–47.

Chapter 8

1. P. Michelson, p. 8.
2. Lynch, pp. 630–31.
3. *Miner's Magazine,* Apr. 4, 1912 and June 6, 1912; Mikeal, p. 59; Jones, *Autobiography,* p. 148.
4. Jones, *Autobiography,* p. 148.
5. Cometti and Summers, p. 522; *Investigation of Paint Creek Coal Fields,* p. 23.
6. Lynch, pp. 632–33; Lee, pp. 18, 20–24.
7. UMW *Journal,* July 4, 1912, p. 8.
8. Lee, pp. 27–29.
9. Crawford, pp. 37, 39. Crawford was a justice of the peace in the strike area.
10. *Conditions in the Paint Creek District,* p. 2257.
11. Chaplin, p. 120.
12. *Conditions in the Paint Creek District,* p. 2258.
13. Ibid.

14. Ibid., p. 2261.
15. Mikeal, p. 62; Jones, *Autobiography*, pp. 154–55.
16. Mooney, p. 26.
17. Ibid.
18. *Conditions in the Paint Creek District,* pp. 1443, 1450–52.
19. Mooney, p. 28.
20. Ibid. An even more melodramatic account is recorded in Jones, *Auto-biography*, pp. 157–59.
21. *Conditions in the Paint Creek District,* p. 1619.
22. Ibid. pp. 1447–48.
23. Lynch, p. 635.
24. *Conditions in the Paint Creek District,* pp. 2264, 2267, 2272–73, 2275.
25. Ibid., p. 2275.
26. Lynch, p. 645.
27. Mooney, p. 20.
28. Commission on Industrial Relations, p. 10643.
29. Jones, *Autobiography*, p. 171; Commission on Industrial Relations, p. 10643.
30. Lynch, p. 637; Lee, pp. 30–31.
31. Lee, p. 31; Crawford, p. 42.
32. *Conditions in the Paint Creek District,* p. 2281.
33. Lee, p. 33; UMW *Journal*, Sept. 26, 1912, p. 1.
34. *Miner's Magazine,* Sept. 26, 1912.
35. Lee, p. 33; Mikeal, p. 69.
36. Lee, p. 34.
37. Harris and Krebs, p. 76; Lee, p. 34.
38. *Conditions in the Paint Creek District,* pp. 379–80.
39. *Miner's Magazine,* Oct. 31, 1912; Raffaele, p. 51.
40. Lee, p. 37; Mikeal, p. 71; Raffaele, p. 51; Jones, *Autobiography*, p. 160.
41. Jones, *Autobiography*, p. 161; Raffaele, p. 52.
42. Lynch, p. 639; Lee, pp. 38–39; Harris and Krebs, p. 75.
43. Mooney, p. 21.
44. *Insurrection and Martial Law,* p. 35; Older, "The Last Day of the Paint Creek Court Martial," p. 1084.
45. Lee, p. 40.
46. *Charleston Gazette,* Feb. 14, 1913.
47. Older, "Answering a Question," p. 26.
48. *New York Times,* Mar. 11, 1913.
49. *Insurrection and Martial Law,* pp. 36, 65–66.
50. Commission on Industrial Relations, p. 10630.
51. *Insurrection and Martial Law,* pp. 38 ff, 60.
52. Ibid., pp. 61, 65–67.
53. Mother Jones to Powderly, Mar. 3, 1913. Powderly Papers.
54. Karr, pp. 145–46; Lee, p. 45.

55. Karr, p. 146.
56. *New York Times,* Mar. 13, 1913.
57. *Appeal to Reason,* Mar. 29, 1913, p. 1.
58. Ibid., Apr. 26, 1913, p. 1.
59. Ibid. Apr. 5, 1913; Mother Jones to Terence Powderly, May 1, 1913. Powderly Papers.
60. Jones to Powderly, May 1, 1913. Jones Papers. During this period, however, Mother Jones appears to calculate her age at two years less than her usual reckoning.
61. *Congressional Record,* vol. 50, pt. 2, May 9, 1913, p. 1403.
62. Ibid., May 14, 1913, pp. 1526, 1535; May 19, p. 1642.
63. Ibid., May 15, 1913, p. 1551.
64. G. Smith, p. 284; *Congressional Record,* vol. 50, pt. 2, May 14, 1913, p. 1535.
65. Commission on Industrial Relations, p. 10630; *Congressional Record,* vol. 50 pt. 2, May 19, 1913, p. 1643.
66. *Congressional Record,* vol. 50, pt. 2, May 9, 1913, p. 1403.
67. Karr, p. 146; lynch, p. 641.
68. Lee, p. 46; Karr, p. 146. Mother Jones later would refer to her five-year sentence by the tribunal; see Mother Jones to Margaret Prevey, Oct. 31, 1916. Jones Papers.
69. *Congressional Record,* vol. 50, pt. 2, May 9, 1913, p. 1403.
70. Commission on Industrial Relations, p. 10630; Mikeal, p. 80.
71. Raffaele, p. 59; *New York Times,* May 9, 1914.
72. *New York Times,* May 28, 1913.
73. *Congressional Record,* vol. 50, pt. 2, May 27, 1913, pp. 1778–79; Raffaele, p. 61; *Investigation of Paint Creek Coal Fields,* p. 2.
74. Debs to Germer, June 19, 1913, and Germer to Debs, July 18, 1913. Germer Papers. Although Mother Jones did not give testimony, stenographic reports of some of her West Virginia speeches are appended to the record of hearing.
75. See Corbin, pp. 11–14, 40–49.
76. *Investigation of Paint Creek Coal Fields,* pp. 18–19.
77. McCormick, pp. 34–35.
78 Jones, *Autobiography,* p. 156.
79. *Insurrection and Martial Law,* p. 36.
80. Harris and Krebs, pp. 78, 88; Lynch, p. 641.

Chapter 9

1. "Some Gems of Thought by Mother Jones."
2. P. Michelson, p. 8.
3. *New York Times,* June 1, 1913.
4. Commission on Industrial Relations, p. 10621.

5. Mother Jones to Tom Mooney, Dec. 15, 1916. Jones Papers.
6. Ibid.
7. *New York Times,* June 1, 1913.
8. UMW *Proceedings,* 1919, p. 537.
9. Commission on Industrial Relations, p. 10644.
10. Pan-American Federation of Labor, pp. 74–75.
11. *New York Times,* June 1, 1913.
12. Jones, "Civilization in Southern Mills," p. 539.
13. Jones, "Coal Miners of the Old Dominion," p. 576.
14. Rev. John W. F. Maguire in *Federation News,* Dec. 20, 1930, p. 2.
15. Jones, *Autobiography,* p. 41.
16. *Conditions in the Paint Creek District,* p. 2264.
17. Ibid., p. 2272.

Chapter 10

1. Adams, p. 162.
2. McGovern, pp. 37–57.
3. Ibid, pp. 16, 23; West, p. 76.
4. West, p. 56; See also *Colorado Strike Investigation,* p. 38.
5. McGovern, pp. 2, 81.
6. Beshoar, pp. 3, 7; McGovern, p. 6.
7. West, pp. 74, 76.
8. Adams, p. 149; West, p. 15.
9. Beshoar, pp. 9, 17.
10. Ibid, ppp. 17, 26; McGovern, pp. 128–29; *Colorado Strike Investigation,* p. 6.
11. Beshoar, pp. 27, 31. See also UMW *Proceedings,* 1911, p. 261.
12. Beshoar, pp. 27, 31.
13. UMW *Proceedings,* 1911, pp. 259–60.
14. Beshoar, pp. 39, 43.
15. McGovern, pp. 129–31.
16. *Colorado Strike Investigation,* p. 6; West, pp. 29–30.
17. "Indomitable Spirit of Mother Jones," p. 20.
18. McGovern, p. 141.
19. Ibid., p. 143.
20. Beshoar, p. 57.
21. Ibid., pp. 60–61; *Colorado Strike Investigation,* p. 18; West, p. 31.
22. *Colorado Strike Investigation,* p. 5; McGovern, pp. 147, 165; West, p. 62.
23. Colorado Adjutant General's Office, p. 10; Adams, p. 153; McGovern, p. 186.
24. Adams, p. 153.
25. *Conditions in the Coal Mines,* p. 2917; Mother Jones to Terence Powderly, Sept. 20, 1913. Powderly Papers.

26. Beshoar, p. 65.
27. Ibid.
28. Colorado Adjutant General's Office, pp. 70–71; West, p. 115.
29. Adams, p. 154.
30. Beshoar, p. 89; *Colorado Strike Investigation,* p. 16.
31. Frank J. Hayes to Mother Jones, Nov. 28, 1913. Jones Papers.
32. Beshoar, p. 89; Adams, p. 160.
33. Beshoar, pp. 105, 115; McGovern, p. 245.
34. Beshoar, p. 115; McGovern, p. 247; Mikeal, p. 109.
35. McGovern, pp. 247–48; Beshoar, p. 115.
36. *Conditions in the Coal Mines,* p. 2923; Jones, *Autobiography* p. 187.
37. Beshoar, p. 128.
38. *Conditions in the Coal Mines,* p. 2924; Beshoar, p. 128.
39. McGovern, p. 257; *Conditions in the Coal Mines,* p. 2924; West, p. 122.
40. Beshoar, pp. 129–30; *Conditions in the Coal Mines,* p. 2924.
41. Commission on Industrial Relations, p. 10632; Beshoar, p. 130.
42. *Conditions in the Coal Mines,* p. 2924.
43. Beshoar, p. 130; McGovern, pp. 257, 260.
44. Beshoar, pp. 130–31.
45. Colorado Adjutant General's Office, p. 47; McGovern, p. 256.
46. Beshoar, p. 132.
47. Colorado Adjutant General's Office, p. 28; Beshoar, pp. 132–35.
48. UMW *Proceedings,* 1914, pp. 411–12.
49. Colorado Adjutant General's Office, p. 28.
50. Mother Jones to Terence Powderly, Mar. 22, 1914, as cited in Mikeal, p. 112; *Conditions in the Coal Mines,* p. 2924.
51. Beshoar, pp. 140–42, 153; McGovern, p. 258.
52. Jones, *Autobiography,* p. 183.
53. Ibid., pp. 183–84; *Conditions in the Coal Mines.* p. 2925; Colorado Adjutant General's Office, p. 48.
54. McGovern, p. 258; *New York Times,* Mar. 23, 1914, and Mar. 24, 1914.
55. Commission on Industrial Relations, p. 10636.
56. Mikeal, pp. 115–16.
57. *Miner's Magazine,* Mar. 26, 1914.
58. Colorado Adjutant General's Office, p. 46.
59. Jones, *Autobiography,* pp. 185–86.
60. *Appeal to Reason,* Mar. 21, 1914; Mother Jones to Terence Powderly, Mar. 22, 1914, as cited in Mikeal, p. 114.
61. Adams, p. 156.
62. *Conditions in the Coal Mines,* p. 2874.
63. Ibid, p. 2850; Colorado Strike Investigation, pp. 42–43.
64. *Conditions in the Coal Mines,* pp. 2929–35.
65. Ibid., pp. 2928, 2939.

66. West, pp. 123–24; Beshoar, p. 230.

67. Beshoar, p. 164; McGovern, pp. 274, 280.

68. McDonald and Lynch, p. 115; McGovern, pp. 285–87; West, p. 127.

69. McDonald and Lynch, p. 115; McGovern, p. 287. See also Adams, pp. 159–60.

70. Adams, p. 160; Beshoar, p. 207.

71. Fink, p. 19; Adams, p. 147.

72. Beshoar, p. 220.

73. Ibid., pp. 209–10.

74. McGovern, pp. 340, 343; *Colorado Strike Investigation,* pp. 40–41.

75. *New York Times,* May 14, 1914, and July 18, 1914.

76. McGovern, p. 343.

77. *New York Times,* Oct. 20, 1914.

78. Ibid.

79. AFL *Proceedings,* 1914, p. 310.

80. John MacLennan, District 15 president, quoted by Colorado Adjutant General's Office, p. 46, and *New York Times,* Oct. 24, 1914.

81. Committee of Coal Mine Managers, p. 62; Colorado Adjutant General's Office, p. 46.

82. McGovern, p. 355.

83. Beshoar, p. 246.

84. McGovern, pp. 355, 358–60.

85. Jones, *Autobiography,* p. 202.

86. *Colorado Strike Investigation,* pp. 16, 40.

87. *New York Times,* Jan. 27, 1915.

88. Adams, pp. 162–63.

89. Ibid., p. 164.

90. "Mother Jones and Mr. Rockefeller," p. 302.

91. *New York Times,* Jan. 29, 1915.

92. Brooks, p. 130; McGovern, pp. 430–37.

93. Adams, p. 172; *New York Times,* Jan. 29, 1915.

94. *New York Times,* May 14, 1915.

95. Commission on Industrial Relations, p. 10645.

96. West, pp. 21–23.

97. Jones, *Autobiography,* pp. 195–99; Beshoar, p. 315; McGovern, p. 430.

98. *Conditions in the Coal Mines,* p. 2927.

Chapter 11

1. UMW *Proceedings,* 1909, p. 377.

2. Spivak, p. 72.

3. *Polly Pry,* Sept. 5, 1903, p. 4. See also the *Rocky Mountain News,* July 17, 1938, for obituary and biographical information on the *Polly Pry* publisher.

4. *Polly Pry,* Jan. 2, 1904, pp. 4–5.

5. Ibid., Jan. 9, 1904, p. 5.
6. *Congressional Record,* vol. 51, pt. 17 appendix, June 13, 1914, p. 638.
7. Powderly to Kindel, about June 20, 1914. Powderly Papers.
8. Mitchell to Mrs. Mary E. Breckson, Mar. 17, 1904. Mitchell Papers.
9. Gowaskie, p. 275*n.*
10. Cited ibid.
11. Sinclair, pp. 180–81.
12. *Life and History of Mother Jones,* p. 2.
13. Fitch, pp. 244–45.
14. UMW *Proceedings,* 1916, p. 967.
15. "Wendell Phillips," *Encyclopaedia Britannica,* 1971.
16. "Louise Michel," *Encyclopaedia Britannica,* 1971.
17. *Conditions in the Paint Creek District,* p. 2273.
18. UMW *Proceedings,* 1916, p. 965.
19. *New York Times,* June 1, 1913.
20. Perlman and Taft, p. 249.
21. Ibid., p. 248.
22. *Michigan Copper District Strike,* p. 8.
23. *Calumet News,* Aug. 5, 1913.
24. Benedict, pp. 228–31; Perlman and Taft, p. 251.
25. Perlman and Taft, p. 252; Benedict, p. 228.
26. Perlman and Taft, p. 252.
27. *New York Times,* Jan. 22, 1915.
28. Ibid., May 22, 1915.
29. Ibid., Feb. 7, 1915.
30. Carsel, pp. 89–91.
31. "Garment Workers Strike," pp. 260–64.
32. Johnson, pp. 5–17.
33. Ibid., pp. 56–64; Jones, *Autobiography,* p. 172.
34. *Arizona Gazette* as cited in Johnson, p. 67.
35. Unidentified newspaper clipping dated June 16, 1916 in Jones Papers.
36. *Arizona Daily Star,* Tucson, Sept. 9, 1916; *Tucson Citizen,* Aug. 11, 1916.
37. Johnson, p. 69.
38. *Arizona Daily Star,* Nov. 15, 1916, as cited in Johnson, p. 70.
39. Johnson, pp. 69, 76–85.
40. Linquist, p. 245; Johnson, p. 91.
41. Mooney, p. 132.
42. Frost, p. 41.
43. Ibid., p. 85.
44. Ibid., p. 108.
45. Ibid., p. 41.
46. Tom Mooney to Mother Jones, Nov. 25, 1916; Jones to Tom Mooney, Dec. 15, 1916. Jones Papers.

47. Mikeal, p. 127.
48. Frost, pp. 277, 282.
49. Mother Jones to Mrs. Sara J. Dorr, WCTU president, Dec. 16, 1918. Jones Papers.
50. Mother Jones to John Fitzpatrick, Dec. 14, 1927. Fitzpatrick Papers.
51. *Federation News,* May 7, 1932.
52. "The New York Street Car Strike," pp. 213–14.
53. *New York Times,* Oct. 6, 1916.
54. Ibid.
55. *Federation News,* Dec. 20, 1930.
56. *New York Times,* Oct. 7, 1916.
57. Ibid.
58. Ibid.
59. Lee, p. 198.
60. *Statement to the U.S. Coal Commission by Non-Union Operators of Southern West Virginia,* p. 10; Lee, p. 199.

Chapter 12

1. *Calumet News,* Aug. 5, 1913; *New York Times,* June 1, 1913.
2. E. Keating, p. 131.
3. UMW *Proceedings,* 1916, p. 962.
4. *Miner's Magazine,* Mar. 23, 1911.
5. Ibid., Mar. 30, 1911.
6. Quoted in L. H. Marcy, "On the Strike Field," p. 648.
7. *Conditions in the Paint Creek District,* p. 2270.
8. "Indomitable Spirit of Mother Jones," p. 20.
9. *New York Times,* June 1, 1913.
10. Weinstein, pp. 164–65.
11. Ibid., p. 56.
12. Harriman, p. 143.
13. Mother Jones to Eugene Debs, July 5, 1913. Debs Papers; Ginger, pp. 321–22.
14. Ginger, pp. 334–37.
15. An account of an Evansville, Ind., speech, 1916, in an unidentified newspaper clipping. Jones Papers.
16. Mother Jones to Margaret Prevy [*sic*], Oct. 31, 1916. Jones Papers.
17. Mother Jones to Mrs. [Ryan] Walker, Apr. 27, 1913. Haldeman Papers; *Appeal to Reason,* May 10, 1913.

Chapter 13

1. Jones, *Autobiography,* p. 215.
2. Jones to Powderly, June 19, 1919. Jones Papers.

3. Jones, *Autobiography*, p. 214.
4. Brody, p. 15.
5. Ibid., pp. 16–18; Dulles, pp. 166–68.
6. Jones, *Autobiography*, p. 214.
7. *Pittsburgh Post*, Aug. 15, 1919.
8. Brody, pp. 93–94.
9. *Pittsburgh Press*, Aug. 21, 1919.
10. Jones, *Autobiography*, pp. 212–13; *Pittsburgh Press*, Aug. 27, 1919. For a different version, see UMW *Proceedings*, 1919, pp. 539–40.
11. Vorse, *Men and Steel*, pp. 77–78.
12. Vorse, *A Footnote to Folly*, p. 281; Jones, *Autobiography*, p. 218.
13. Brody, p. 94; Jones, *Autobiography*, p. 218.
14. *Pittsburgh Post*, Sept. 24, 1919; Jones, *Autobiography*, pp. 218–19. Mother Jones gives a different account in UMW *Proceedings*, 1919, p. 539.
15. *Investigation of Strike in Steel Industries*, p. 20.
16. Vorse, *Men and Steel*, p. 69.
17. Brody, pp. 95–104; UMW *Proceedings*, 1919, pp. 538, 540.
18. "1919: The First Great Steel Strike," p. 11; Brody, pp. 112–13; Vorse, *Men and Steel*, p. 57.
19. Brody, p. 114; "1919: The First Great Steel Strike," p. 11.
20. *Investigation of Strike in Steel Industries*, p. 387; Brody, pp. 135, 144.
21. Dulles, p. 234; "1919: The First Great Steel Strike," p. 11.
22. Jones, *Autobiography*, p. 216.
23. Vorse, *A Footnote to Folly*, p. 288.
24. Ibid.
25. Jones, *Autobiography*, p. 210.
26. Foster, *The Great Steel Strike*, p. 53.
27. *New York Times*, Oct. 24, 1919.
28. Brody, pp. 162–63; "1919: The First Great Steel Strike," p. 11.
29. "1919: The First Great Steel Strike," p. 11.
30. Brody, p. 174.
31. Ibid., pp. 175, 178; Dulles, p. 233; "1919: The First Great Steel Strike," p. 11.
32. Jones, *Autobiography*, pp. 224–25.

Chapter 14

1. Jones *Autobiography*, p. 203.
2. "Indomitable Spirit of Mother Jones," p. 20.
3. R. Smith, p. 298.
4. "Indomitable Spirit of Mother Jones," p. 20.
5. *Conditions in the Paint Creek District*, p. 2272.
6. Jones, *Autobiography*, pp. 203–4.

7. UMW *Proceedings,* 1916, pp. 960–61.
8. UMW *Proceedings,* 1909, p. 378.
9. P. Michelson, p. 8.
10. UMW *Proceedings,* 1911, pp. 258–59.
11. *New York Times,* May 2, 1930.
12. *Copper Country Evening News,* Apr. 20, 1905.
13. UMW *Proceedings,* 1916, pp. 230–34, 311, 314–15.
14. Ibid., p. 318.
15. Ibid., p. 960. See also Jones, *Autobiography,* p. 127.
16. Selvin, p. 24.
17. Lantz, pp. 150–56.
18. *Federation News,* Dec. 20, 1930.
19. Quoted with permission of Harcourt Brace Jovanovich, Inc., from *Complete Poems* (1950), pp. 103–4.
20. Ross, p. 148.
21. Jones Papers.
22. *Milwaukee Journal,* Dec. 23, 1936; *American Miner* Dec. 6, 1930, p. 2.
23. *Milwaukee Journal,* Dec. 23, 1936.
24. *Washington Post,* Feb. 17, 1903.
25. Perlman and Taft, p. 473.
26. Bernstein, pp. 132–33; Keiser, "John H. Walker: Labor Leader from Illinois," pp. 84–85.
27. Laslett, p. 224.
28. Ibid.
29. Perlman and Taft, pp. 475–76.
30. Unidentified newspaper article by Tom Tippett, Federated Press correspondent, in Jones Papers; Jones, *Autobiography,* pp. 228–29.
31. *New York Times,* Feb. 19, 1922. See also Jones *Autobiography,* pp. 228–30.
32. Mother Jones to Terence Powderly[?], undated, Jones Papers; Bernstein, p. 369.
33. Snow, pp. 43–51, 53–62.
34. Ibid., pp. 105–9, 112.
35. Mooney, p. 79.
36. *New York Times,* Jan. 10, 1921; Jones, *Autobiography,* p. 239.
37. Jones, *Autobiography,* p. 239.
38. Mooney, p. 81; Jones, *Autobiography,* p. 239.
39. Mooney, pp. 84–85.
40. Snow, p. 112.
41. Pan-American Federation of Labor, p. 72.
42. Ibid., pp. 73, 75–76.
43. Ibid., p. 76.
44. Ibid.
45. Mooney, p. 85.

46. Snow, pp. 147–50.
47. Powderly to Mother Jones, April 9, 1921. Jones Papers.
48. Haberman to Mother Jones, April[?] 1921. Jones Papers. The Haberman letter, though undated, refers to Good Friday as the day it was written. "I know that soon you will be with us again," he wrote. That and the date and content of the above citation lead to the conclusion that Mother Jones left Mexico after the January conference, probably went to California, then returned.
49. Mother Jones to John Fitzpatrick, May 16, 1921. Fitzpatrick Papers.
50. Ibid.
51. Ibid.

Chapter 15

1. Jones, *Autobiography,* pp. 234–35.
2. Mooney, p. 58.
3. Ibid.
4. Jones, *Autobiography,* p. 206; *Charleston Daily Mail,* July 3, 14, and 15, 1919.
5. Jones, *Autobiography,* p. 207; *Charleston Gazette,* July 4, 1919.
6. George Wolfe, manager of Winding Gulf Colliery, to Justus Collins, president of Winding Gulf Coal Co., Apr. 30, 1917. Collins Papers.
7. Mooney, p. 58.
8. Anson, p. 125.
9. *Statement to the U.S. Coal Commission by Non-Union Operators of Southern West Virginia,* pp. 2–3.
10. *Report of the U.S. Coal Commission,* p. 1431.
11. Ibid., pp. 1457, 1466.
12. Barb, pp. 20–22.
13. Swain, pp. 6–12; Spivak, p. 51; Lee, p. 89.
14. Swain, p. 12.
15. Barb, p. 30; Lee, p. 91.
16. Barb, p. 31.
17. Anson, pp. 227–30; Harris and Krebs, p. 152.
18. *Charleston Gazette,* Aug. 5, 1919; Mooney, p. 68.
19. Lee, p. 94; Spivak, p. 67.
20. Barb, p. 51; Cornwell, pp. 57–59.
21. Cornwell, pp. 59–60.
22. Ibid.
24. Harris and Krebs, pp. 152–53; Lee, pp. 52–69.
24. Mooney, p. 89.
25. Lee, p. 96. However, Mooney, p. 89, said Mother Jones and the others spoke in a conciliatory manner. Keeney later denied the "high-power rifle" statement, although it was widely attributed to him. See Trail, p. 22.

26. Mooney, p. 89.
27. Lee, p. 96.
28. Maurer and Senning, pp. 34–35; Barb, p. 106.
29. Barb, p. 105.
30. Mooney, p. 90.
31. Recollection of Charles G. Holstein, Chesapeake, W.Va., and relayed to author by Dr. Fred Barkey, Morris Harvey College, June 23, 1971.
32. Mooney, pp. 90–91.
33. Barb, p. 105.
34. Ibid., pp. 102, 105.
35. Maurer and Senning, p. 343.
36. Anson, p. 233; Lee, pp. 98–99; Coleman, p. 104.
37. Morgan, p. 53.
38. Barb, pp. 106–7; Lee, p. 98.
39. Lee, pp. 99–100.
40. Anson, pp. 232–35; Lee, pp. 100–101.
41. Maurer and Senning, pp. 347–48.
42. Ibid., pp. 348–50.
43. Barb, pp. 110–12.
44. Ibid., p. 113.
45. Quoted in *Sunset News and Observer*, March 23, 1957.
46. Lee, p. 97.
47. Ibid., p. 115.
48. Jones, *Autobiography*, p. 233–35; Mother Jones to Terence Powderly, May 3, 1923. Jones Papers.
49. Anson, p. 235.
50. Posey, pp. 203–4.
51. Jones, *Autobiography*, p. 231.
52. Morris, p. 126.

Chapter 16

1. "Some Gems of Thought by Mother Jones."
2. Mikeal, pp. 133–34.
3. Powderly to Edward Nockels, Sept. 20, 1922. Powderly Papers.
4. Mother Jones to Terence Powderly, Nov. 23, 1921. Jones Papers.
5. Mother Jones to Powderly, March 1, 1923. Jones Papers.
6. "Dean Harris: Historian and Archaeologist," an unidentified clipping by Dr. Thomas O'Hagan in the Mother Jones Papers. The Washington Evening Star, Dec. 1, 1930, includes a statement that Harris was Mother Jones's brother, and other newspapers at the time of her death make similar reference. Dixon, p. 326, further cites Harris's background and accomplishments, though not mentioning Mother Jones. Both brother and sister appear to have had a penchant for obscuring their early years. Harris's birthdate of March 3, 1847, in Cork, however, does

not seem to fit with what is known of the Harris family's emigration to America. Unless, of course, they returned to Ireland at some point, or if perhaps he was a half-brother to Mother Jones. Records of the Genealogical Office at Dublin Castle appear to yield little of substance in tracing the Harris parentage in Cork. Furthermore, queries to Canadian ecclesiastics do not throw light on this inconsistency.

7. Emma T. Martin to Mother Jones, Dec. 27, 1916. Jones Papers.
8. Mother Jones to Emma Powderly, June 11, 1923, as cited by Mikeal, p. 135.
9. Letter of Virgil J. Vogel to author, Oct. 7, 1972. Vogel is president of Charles H. Kerr & Co. The *Autobiography* was reprinted in 1969 by Arno Press and in 1972 by Kerr. The latter includes a 13-page introduction and bibliography by Fred Thompson.
10. Madison, pp. 49, 67.
11. Dulles, p. 136.
12. Madison, pp. 51, 54.
13. E. Keating, p. 130.
14. Terence Powderly to Edward Nockels, Sept. 20, 1922. Powderly Papers.
15. Mother Jones to Terence Powderly, May 24, 1907. Jones Papers; UMW *Proceedings,* 1916, p. 967. See also Dulles, p. 143, and Powderly, p. 118.
16. Terence Powderly to Edward Nockels, Sept. 20, 1922. Powderly Papers.
17. Mother Jones to Terence Powderly, May 3, 1923. Jones Papers.
18. Jones, *Autobiography,* p. 238.
19. *Time,* July 16, 1923.
20. *New York Times,* July 4, 1923.
21. Ibid., July 6, 1923, and July 7, 1923.
22. Foster, *From Bryan to Stalin,* p. 179.
23. Ibid.
24. Ashby, p. 90; *Washington Post,* Dec. 1, 1930; *Washington Star,* May 4, 1930.
25. *New York Times,* Sept. 27, 1924; Steel, p. 302.
26. Carsel, pp. 168–70.
27. Mother Jones to John Fitzpatrick and Edward Nockels, Nov. 14, 1927. Fitzpatrick Papers.
28. Mother Jones to John Fitzpatrick, Jan. 11, 1928. Fitzpatrick Papers.
29. *Washington Evening Star,* April 25, 1929.
30. Ibid.
31. *Washington Daily News,* Aug. 23, 1927.
32. Ibid.
33. *Washington Post,* Aug. 24, 1927.
34. *Labor,* May 14, 1929.
35. *Washington Post,* Dec. 27, 1929.
36. Mother Jones to Terence Powderly, May 3, 1923. Jones Papers.
37. *Labor,* Dec. 9, 1930.

38. *Washington Daily News,* Dec. 2, 1930.
39. *Washington Herald,* Mar. 21, 1930; Wilson, pp. 8–9.
40. *New York Times,* Apr. 20, 1930.
41. *Washington Herald,* May 1, 1930.
42. Ibid.; *Federation News,* May 7, 1932; Bernstein, pp. 406–9.
43. *Washington Herald,* May 2, 1930.
44. Ibid. See also Jones, *Autobiography,* pp. 145–47, for what appears to be a recounting by Mother Jones of a similar incident in a different setting.
45. *Washington Evening Star,* May 4, 1930; *New York Times,* May 4, 1930.
46. *Washington Evening Star,* May 4, 1930; *Washington Daily News,* Dec. 1, 1930.
47. *New York Times,* May 4, 1930.
48. Ibid., July 9, 1930.
49. John M. Baer to Edward Nockels, July 8, 1930. Fitzpatrick Papers.
50. *Washington Evening Star,* Sept. 5, 1930; *New York Times,* Sept. 6, 1930.
51. *Washington Evening Star,* Sept. 5, 1930.
52. Ibid., Sept. 14, 1930 and Oct. 13, 1930; *Washington Post,* Oct. 7, 1930.
53. *Washington Evening Star,* Sept. 14, 1930.
54. *Washington Daily News,* Dec. 1, 1930.
55. *Washington Post,* Oct. 3, 1930.
56. *Washington Post,* Dec. 4, 1930.
57. *Federation News,* Dec. 20, 1930.
58. Keiser, "The Union Miners Cemetery," p. 256.
59. *St. Louis Post-Dispatch,* Dec. 5, 1930.
60. UMW *Journal,* Dec. 15, 1930, p. 5.
61. *St. Louis Post-Dispatch,* Dec. 6, 1930.
62. Keiser, "The Union Miners Cemetery," p. 258.
63. *St. Louis Post-Dispatch,* Dec. 8, 1930.
64. Ibid.; *Federation News,* Dec. 20, 1930.

Chapter 17

1. Patterson.
2. *Federation News,* May 7, 1932.
3. Debs, p. 270.
4. *Federation News,* Dec. 20, 1930.
5. Hudson, pp. 13–19; Keiser, "The Union Miners Cemetery," p. 260; Bernstein, pp. 373–76.
6. Hudson, pp. 43–44.
7. Keiser, "The Union Miners Cemetery," p. 261; *St. Louis Post-Dispatch,* Oct. 11, 1936.

8. Interview with Joseph Ozanic, Mt. Olive, Ill., on Sept. 2, 1970. Ozanic was chairman of the monument committee and of the dedication ceremony.
9. *St. Louis Post-Dispatch,* Oct. 12, 1936; Keiser, "The Union Miners Cemetery," pp. 263–64.
10. *St. Louis Post-Dispatch,* Oct. 12, 1936.
11. Hudson, pp. 65–68; Keiser, "The Union Miners Cemetery," p. 233.
12. Keiser, "The Union Miners Cemetery," p. 263.
13. *Federation News,* Dec. 20, 1930.

INDEX

ment, 100: releases Mother Jones, 100–101

Hatfield, Sid, 184

Hatfield Contract, The, 100, 102, 103

Hayes, Frank: accompanies Mother Jones to Mexico, 82; sent to Colorado, 112; optimistic about Colorado strike, 114; praises Mother Jones's lobbying effort, 116; opposes Rockefeller plan, 131; mentioned, 94, 113, 130, 167

Hayes, Rutherford, 12

Haymarket Square riot: affected Mother Jones's early career, 13–14; hurt Knights of Labor, 15; mentioned, 71, 76, 145, 170, 177

Haywood, William ("Big Bill"): leads IWW founders, 71–72; "kidnapping" and trial, 74–76; mentioned, 73, 79, 101, 141, 152, 198

Heizer, J. L., 182

Hill, James J., 17

Holt, Rush, Sen., 214

Howat, Alex: fought compulsory arbitration and Lewis, 171–73; mentioned, 198, 205, 211

Howells, William, 61

Howlett, H. H., Dr., 205

Hunt, G. W. P., Gov.: handling of labor wins Mother Jones's plaudits, 142–43; proclaims Mother Jones's greatness, 144

Illinois coal miners. *See* United Mine Workers District 12

Illinois State Federation of Labor, 210

Industrial Workers of the World (IWW): founding, 70–72; Mother Jones's aloofness toward, 72, 73; impact, 72–73; mentioned, 67, 78, 87, 144, 194, 195

International Socialist Review: published early Mother Jones articles, 22, 77; mentioned, 71, 193

International Workers Defense League: Mother Jones urged to help, 144; raised questions about Mother Jones's jailings, 144

Ireland: conditions at time of Mother Jones's birth, 2–3

Irons, Martin: revered by Mother Jones, 196

Iroquois Theater fire, 137

Jackson, John J., Judge: enjoins demonstrations and meetings, 31–32; courtroom dialogue with Mother Jones, 33–34; suspends sentence on Mother Jones, 34; mentioned, 45, 99

Jones, George E. (husband of Mother Jones): marriage, 3; death, 5; mentioned, 228n13

Jones, Mary, Mother: Irish birth and heritage, 2–3; made homeless by Chicago fire, 2, 5; parents emigrate to America, 3; schooling, 3; marriage to George Jones, 3–4; family stricken in yellow fever epidemic, 4–5; husband and children die, 5; longevity during tumultuous era, 6–7, 170; encounters Knights of Labor in Chicago, 6, 10, 229n24; generally unorthodox and inconsistent, 7–8, 9; appearance and voice, 9–10, 28, 160; possible foreign travels, 10; abhorred self-indulgence, 62–63, 179; ambivalent toward Socialists, 76, 77–78, 150–52, 153–54; hypocritical on use of violence, 104–6, 147–48; allegedly a former prostitute, 123, 134–37, 194; object of other accusations, 137–38; compared to other iconoclasts, 138–39; masked her educative inclinations, 139–40; inexact in money matters, 149; opposed women's suffrage, 163–65, 170, 199, 202–3; opposed Prohibition, 165–66, 170, 174, 200; acted as diversion at UMW conventions, 166–67, 172, 211; meshed into coal miners' culture, 167–70; becomes ill, 192–93, 199; brother dies, 193; writes autobiography, 193–94, ideologically ambivalent, 195, 211; personality contrasted to Powderly's, 195–96; guest of Powderly's, 196; takes radical stand at Farmer-Labor convention, 197–98; celebrates hundredth birthday, 202–3; opposes Lewis's methods, 204–5; health worsens, 205–6; dies, 206; mass celebrated in Washington, 206; taken by train to Mt. Olive, Ill., 207; eulogized and buried, 207–9; few lasting tributes to her memory, 210–11; career assessed, 210–13; memorial erected amid intra-union dispute, 213–15; provides own "epitaph," 215; esti-